THE POLITICAL ECONOMY OF ISRAEL'S OCCUPATION

The Political Economy of Israel's Occupation

Repression Beyond Exploitation

Shir Hever

First published 2010 by Pluto Press
345 Archway Road, London N6 5AA

www.plutobooks.com

British Library Cataloguing in Publication Data
A catalogue record for this book is available from the British Library

ISBN 978 0 7453 2795 2 Hardback
ISBN 978 0 7453 2794 5 Paperback
ISBN 978 1 8496 4544 7 PDF eBook
ISBN 978 1 7837 1418 6 EPUB eBook
ISBN 978 1 7837 1419 3 Kindle eBook

Library of Congress Cataloging in Publication Data applied for

This book is printed on paper suitable for recycling and made from fully managed and sustained forest sources. Logging, pulping and manufacturing processes are expected to conform to the environmental standards of the country of origin.

10 9 8 7 6 5 4 3 2 1

Designed and produced for Pluto Press by
Curran Publishing Services, Norwich

CONTENTS

FIGURES, TABLES, AND MAPS

FIGURES

TABLES

MAPS

ABBREVIATIONS

ACRI	Association for Civil Rights in Israel
CBI	Central Bank of Israel
CEO	chief executive officer
COGAT	Coordinator of Government Activities in the Occupied Territories
CPI	Consumer Price Index
GDP	gross domestic product
GNI	gross national income
GNP	gross national product
GSS	General Security Service ("Shabak")
ICBS	Israeli Central Bureau of Statistics
IMFA	Israeli Ministry of Foreign Affairs
ISM	International Solidarity Movement
IWA	Inside Wall Area
PMoP	Palestinian Ministry of Planning
NGO	non-governmental organization
NII	National Insurance Institute
NIS	New Israeli Shekel
OECD	Organization for Economic Cooperation and Development
OPT	Occupied Palestinian Territories
OWA	Outside Wall Area
PA	Palestinian Authority
PCBS	Palestinian Central Bureau of Statistics
PLO	Palestinian Liberation Organization
TIM	Temporary International Mechanism
UN	United Nations
UN OCHA	United Nations Office of Coordinating Humanitarian Affairs (UN)
UNRWA	United Nations Relief and Works Agency
UNSCO	United Nations Special Coordinator for the Middle East Peace Process
VAT	Value Added Tax
WFP	World Food Programs
WZO	World Zionist Organization

PREFACE

The 1990s were a decade of change in Israel/Palestine, and a decade of change for me personally as well. My dual interests in economic theory and in political analysis were both deeply affected by the Oslo Process. At the time, these negotiations filled me with hope. I must confess that I was taken in by Israeli politicians who promised peace, and by economists who said that peace coupled with a "free market" would lead to prosperity for both sides.

As the decade passed, reality gave me a hard slap in the face, and my twofold belief in the free market and the peace process was shattered. I was a student of economics at Tel-Aviv University, where I became aware of the profound shortcomings of mainstream economic theory, and was intrigued to explore alternative economic theories. It was also a time when a global social movement began emerging to protest against the growing economic gaps around the world and the impoverishment of millions in the name of "free trade."

At the time, prime minister Ehud Barak (for whom I regrettably voted) made his "generous offer" to the Palestinians, ignoring international law and proposing a fragmented, cantonized state, declaring that it was the "best offer" that Israel would ever make. Meanwhile, the World Health Organization published a report that the drinking water in the Gaza Strip was no longer fit for human beings (Gray, 2007). Only the illegal Israeli settlers in Gaza continued to receive fresh and clean water from Israel. Then opposition leader Ariel Sharon entered the Al-Aqsa Mosque with armed guards in tow. These provocations led to the outbreak of the second intifada. They also betrayed the fact that Israel's leadership had chosen occupation over peace.

I followed the events with horror, took every opportunity to hear eyewitness reports of Palestinians, attended demonstrations and other political events. These demonstrations were an opportunity to observe the occupation first hand, and after finding myself staring down the barrel of a gun and being beaten by Israeli soldiers, I felt the need to take more effective action to change the reality in my country.

I was given a rare opportunity to express my twofold interest in politics and economic analysis at the Alternative Information Center, where I founded a project to publish economic reports on the occupation. Some of these reports have been compiled into this book. In the course of my work, I discovered that although there were plenty of studies and reports on both the Israeli and Palestinian economies, and many studies about the prospects of peace and the effects of peace on the economy, contemporary studies on the economic elements of the occupation itself were few and far between.

The "economy of the occupation" does not refer to the study of the Palestinian or Israeli economic realities, but to the study of the economic aspects of the relations between the Israeli authorities and the occupied Palestinians. It is the study of the economic exploitation, repression, and resistance that define the relations between the Palestinians and their occupiers.

Going into a relatively desolate field of study is a mixed blessing. Finding an audience for my reports and lectures was easy, because very few others were competing over this niche. However, research ideally should be conducted in a community, in which it is possible to exchange ideas. Conflicting thinkers help to hone the arguments, yet the field of study of the economy of the occupation does not offer many opportunities for any such debate between informed scholars. Although filling that void is beyond my abilities, I have made the greatest effort to map the economic interests that keep the occupation in perpetual existence and block any advance in negotiations. I have strived to identify those who profit from the occupation and those who suffer from it. I am glad to say that interest in the economic aspects of the occupation has grown, and the literature on the subject today is many times greater than it was when I first delved into the topic.

This book is a compilation of work from five years of research on the economy of the occupation, which has been selected to highlight the main findings from my research. The book contains materials that have been published before by the Alternative Information Center, updated and adapted, as well as some new materials.

Shir Hever

ACKNOWLEDGMENTS

Writing this book has taught me a lesson in humility; it has shown me that writing a book is not the task of an individual, but the project of a community. Without the many comments, pieces of invaluable advice and encouragement along the way, this book would never have been brought to completion.

My first thanks go to the staff of the Alternative Information Center (AIC), who gave me a place where I could combine political action with research and make a living in the process. The collective experiences and knowledge of the AIC staff were invaluable to me in providing an education on the occupation and its history, and I always found a welcoming yet critical ear for my half-formulated ideas. The research that I have conducted as a member of the AIC has been the foundation of this book. I would like to acknowledge the help of Connie Hackbrath, Sergio Yahni, Nassar Ibrahim, Avital Mozes, Michael Warchawski, Ahmad Jaradat, and also many others, some who wish to remain anonymous, and many interns and volunteers who are too numerous to list here. One intern, Uri Yaakobi, deserves special mention, as he spent many hours helping me sift through materials, in addition to which he read through the book's early stages and offered very useful advice. His help in locating data and sources has also been essential to the research process.

I want to give special thanks to Shimshon Bichler and Jonathan Nitzan, who have not only inspired me to critically examine economic methodologies which I was taught at university and set on my own path, but have also accompanied me along that path with frequent advice and guidance, without expectation of anything in return. They have also given me permission to use some of their materials in this book.

My work on this book has also benefited greatly from the support of Adi Ophir, my thesis advisor, and of Yuval Yonai, my co-advisor. Ophir has been using his university position to create a space for trailblazing research into Israel's occupation of the Occupied Palestinian Territories (OPT), and has devoted more than was required to help educate me about various aspects of the occupation. Yonai has helped greatly in sorting through the numerous and often-conflicting economic theories that have been mentioned in this book.

Yehouda Shenhav has also spent a great deal of time offering priceless advice and supporting me in the course of my research.

I owe many thanks to the group at the Van Leer Institute: "Humanitarian Action in Catastrophe." The group's members, Tal Arbel, Sari Hanafi, Ariel Handel, Michal Givoni, Ruthie Ginsburg, Adi Ophir, and others, have each shared their own insights and findings about the occupation from different perspectives, and were happy to listen to my own perspectives and respond critically.

During the writing of this book, I received very useful advice from Sara Roy, Fanny-Michaela Reisin, and Grietje Baars.

I would like to give special thanks to Uri Yaakobi, Rami Adut, and Yael Berda for their comments, insights, and contributions to the book, and Ruvik Danieli for his dedicated work on the language of the book.

The Israeli Committee Against House Demolitions, and particularly Jimmy Johnson and Jeff Halper, have been invaluable in providing information and advice, and in inviting me and including me in inspiring and enlightening discussions that contributed to my research.

For their unflinching support during my work, my heartfelt gratitude goes to my family, who have often had to endure my frustration and even social pressure because of their association with me and with my political views: Hadas, Hannan, Orly, Tal, Yaar, and Yael, I am deeply grateful to all of them.

Hadas deserves special mention here, for I cannot imagine how the book would have been completed without her taking precious time off of her work to spend countless hours helping me go through the book and making invaluable comments.

However, the mistakes in this book are all my own.

INTRODUCTION

Conflict situations encourage us to think in terms of a zero-sum game. Prolonged conflicts intensify this problem, and the conflict between Jews and Palestinians is over a century old. The zero-sum approach has infected both sides of the conflict. Israeli authorities have prevented the Palestinian economy from developing, out of fear that any gain for the Palestinians would be turned against Israel (B'tselem, 2007a: 10–11). Many pro-Palestinian thinkers have often argued that the occupation is profitable to Israel: that Israel uses its military to control the Palestinian areas and population in order to exploit the Palestinian economy, labor, and resources, and has been stealing the property of Palestinians to enrich the Jewish population.

Both views have become increasingly less popular in recent years among critical and mainstream thinkers alike. Israel's frustration of Palestinian development has only intensified the conflict, saddling Israel with a great moral debt which is likely to become a financial debt as well – and which could mean the end of the Jewish state. The Palestinians and their supporters who view the occupation as a chicken that lays golden eggs are also wrong; they fail to realize that the occupation has taken a heavy toll on the Israeli economy, that in the 40 years since 1967 Israeli social gaps have widened, poverty has increased, and Israel can no longer be considered a Western, developed country.

An analysis of why the occupation persists, despite its heavy costs to the Israeli side and the continual damage it causes the Palestinians, requires going beyond the zero-sum approach. The occupation can be considered as a phenomenon that has a very strong economic element to it, and yet profit alone cannot explain the actions of the many actors perpetuating or resisting the occupation.

But before delving into the analysis itself, some of the concepts that will be used in this book need to be clarified. The book refers mostly to the economic aftermath of the war of 1967, in which Israeli occupied the Gaza Strip, Golan Heights, Sinai Peninsula (which Israel evacuated in 1982 following a peace treaty with Egypt), and the West Bank, including East Jerusalem. The word "occupation" will be used hereafter to refer to this 1967 occupation, although this is not an attempt to ignore the other military invasions and occupations in Israel's history. Israel annexed large tracts of land in 1948 and invaded Lebanon in 1982, occupying the south of the country for 18 years.

The term "Occupied Palestinian Territories" (OPT) is used extensively throughout the book to designate two areas that Israel occupied in 1967 and which are mostly populated by Palestinians – the Gaza Strip and the West Bank. These two areas have a distinct quality that makes their occupation especially interesting – they have remained densely populated even after the occupation. Following the occupation, Israel implemented a complex apparatus of control to subjugate the local population, and the latter's resistance to Israeli rule has been a decisive factor in the historical development of the Israeli control of these two areas.

But in fact, the word "occupation" itself can be misleading. The term has become entrenched in the critical discourse on Israel's control over the OPT, but the term lends an air of temporariness to this control. Perhaps a better perspective, and one that has become increasingly more prevalent among critical thinkers, is to think of Israel/Palestine as a single state, one that stretches over the entire area controlled by the Israeli army – including the Gaza Strip, the Golan Heights, and the West Bank, as well as the internationally recognized borders of Israel. This state has a single sovereign government, a single dominant army, and a single population registry (controlled by Israel's Ministry of the Interior), but it has several groups of subjects, layered by their rights (Benvenisti, 1988: 11–55). These groups begin with the full Jewish citizens of Israel and end with the residents of the Gaza Strip, who are devoid of rights and held in prison-like conditions. In-between these two extremes are groups such as the Jews of Arab descent ("Mizrahim"), Palestinian citizens of Israel, and Bedouins (Yftachel, 2000).

Looked at in this framework, the spatial economic distinctions between the OPT and Israel become largely artificial. There is no area in Israel/Palestine that is free from Israeli control, no area where a different set of economic laws apply. Even though most Palestinian cities are far poorer than most Israeli cities, drawing a clear geographic distinction between two economic units is impossible. The homogeneity of the economic units is interrupted by illegal settlements[1] in the West Bank and by the impoverished communities

1 The term "settlements" or "illegal settlements" to refer to Israel's civilian communities constructed on occupied Palestinian land has recently

within Israel (such as the unrecognized Bedouin villages in the south of Israel).

However, there is a distinction regarding people, not territory. Non-citizen Palestinians living in the OPT fall under a special set of rules and regulations, suffer from extreme levels of poverty and unemployment, and receive a different bundle of services and welfare benefits than Israeli citizens. We can talk about two economies coexisting under Israeli control. For the sake of simplicity and clarity, I will talk about the "Israeli economy" as referring to the economic practices, property, jobs, and economic policies relevant to Israeli citizens (both living inside Israel and in the settlements in the West Bank), and about the "Palestinian economy" as referring to the economic practices, property, jobs, and economic policies relevant to the non-citizen Palestinians subject to Israeli control in the West Bank and the Gaza Strip.

It is important to remember that these categories are neither mutually exclusive, nor do they together form a comprehensive picture of the economy of Israel/Palestine. There are many economic actors that are neither Israeli citizens nor Palestinians living in Israel and the OPT, and there are non-citizen Palestinians in Israel. Also, both economies (especially the Israeli economy) contain internal inequalities, and therefore certain Palestinian businesspeople and politicians are much better-off than certain Israelis of the lower socioeconomic classes.

Nevertheless, the "occupation" remains the topic of the book, being understood here as the complex system of means of control, subjugation, and exploitation that was put in place by the Israeli authorities in the OPT, targeting the indigenous population and its property, starting with the war of 1967. This system of control has informed the economic reality that has evolved in Israel/Palestine, and thus must be understood in order to analyze and understand the existing economic relations in Israel/Palestine.

In order to re-examine the intricate economic system that has evolved in Israel/Palestine, the book's chapters deal with a series of seemingly unrelated topics, yet the unifying theme is that these are all modes of economic relations that have shaped the lives of Israelis and Palestinians alike. From the shaping of the terms of the occupation through massive international funding, to the shaping of

---

been challenged, and scholars have begun to use the term "colonies" instead. This is in fact more accurate, since it indeed reflects the process of colonizing an occupied territory with citizens of the occupying country. However, since the term "settlements" is still more widely used and better known, I will continue to use it throughout the book.

daily life in Israel/Palestine with the Wall of Separation, economic endeavors have had no less effect on the nature of the conflict than military maneuvers. Only through an understanding of these modes of economic relations can the conflict ever be unraveled.

The book is divided into two parts and an introduction. The Introduction, including Chapter 1, provides a brief background on the Palestinian economy. There is no background on the Israeli economy, although specific points are taken up throughout the book. The Introduction is meant merely to put the remainder of the book in perspective, so an overall historical overview of the events described in this chapter would be better sought elsewhere. Part I, comprising the bulk of the book, is a series of case studies on various aspects of the economy of the occupation, including aid, the Wall of Separation, inflation, and the effects of the occupation on Israel's economy. Chapter 2 focusses on international aid to the region; Chapter 3 deals briefly with inflation as a political-economic phenomenon shaping the relations between the Israeli and Palestinian economies; Chapter 4 describes the economic cost of the occupation to Israel; and Chapter 5 describes the impact of the occupation on Israel's economy. Chapter 6 describes the case study of the Wall of Separation in East Jerusalem, a story that combines many of the features described in Chapters 2 through 5. Through these case studies and the economic effects that spill over from one aspect to the others, a partial picture of the economic situation in Israel/Palestine is drawn, preparing the ground for the third and final section.

Part II is an attempt to take a broader perspective on the economy of the occupation, to understand the forces shaping the economic realities of the region, and the possibilities that exist for ending the occupation. Set at a different pace, this section deals more with theoretical concerns and analysis than with the empirical data. Chapter 7 is highly theoretical and can safely be skipped by readers who wish to focus more on the facts and less on the academic disagreements regarding their interpretation. Chapter 8 concludes the book in a more informal manner, and it is where I have allowed myself broader generalizations and a greater emphasis on my own opinions and recommendations.

Covering every aspect of the economic relations between Israel and the occupied Palestinians is far beyond the scope of this book. Therefore, the five chapters comprising Part I are devoted to specific topics, which are intended to outline a rough picture of the complex economic reality underlying the Israeli occupation of the Palestinian territories, and to highlight the main aspects of the economy of the occupation. These points have not been selected in order to highlight the suffering caused by the occupation (reports by the United Nations do a very good job portraying that suffering already), but for their value in bringing about an understanding of the future of the occupation: is it sustainable? Are the Palestinians on the verge of mass famine? Can Israel profit from maintaining the occupation, or might peace dividends[2] be more worthwhile to the Israeli economy?

First on this list of topics is the international aid to the Palestinians and to Israel.

The centrality of the Israeli–Palestinian conflict in global politics is staggering, considering the small size of the area and the relatively small number of people involved. A territory of only about 29,000 sq. km (about the size of Massachusetts) and a total population of a little over 10 million (about 0.2 percent of the world's population) is the object of a very much greater proportion of international media coverage and interest by global political and economic actors.

The reason for this focus is discussed later (see Chapter 8), but it is important to note that this international interest has led to massive international expenditures in this area. The Middle East has become one of the central arenas of battle between conflicting economic interests. Political victories in the Middle East have acquired significance beyond mere economic gain, concerning matters of national pride and diplomatic scorekeeping.

Years of bloody conflict have weakened both the Palestinian and Israeli economies (although the Palestinian economy has suffered the brunt of this economic decline), further emphasizing the importance of international aid in comparison with the size of the local sources of income. In the current stage of Israel's domination of the OPT, foreign aid, in the form of humanitarian assistance and development aid, is a defining feature of the economy.

REALITY IN CONSTANT FLUX

As I sat down to write this book, I was keenly aware that it needed to be written swiftly. The events of recent years have proved that

---

2 "Peace dividends" is a term that saw widespread use regarding the Israeli–Palestinian peace process in the 1990s. The term hints at the potential economic prosperity that peace can bring by freeing funds currently spent on military matters and security, and by encouraging tourism and trade (Bichler and Nitzan, 2001).

reality in the Israeli–Palestinian context changes very rapidly, and any day a piece of news may shatter preconceptions and require updated analysis. The facts and figures in this book began to lose some of their relevance as soon as they were written down. Nevertheless, I have tried to use the most recent data whenever possible, and to give a historical perspective that helps to take in new developments in their proper context. I hope some of the insights in this book will remain relevant in the future.

As I was about to finish writing the book, my worst fears were realized as the ceasefire between Israel and Hamas collapsed, and Israel launched an unprecedented attack on the Gaza Strip in December 2008. The Israeli army broke its own record for the number of innocent lives taken in a single day, and the Israeli media and general public expressed uncritical support for the attack. The significance of this attack and its aftermath will only be understood with the benefit of hindsight. However, it is already apparent that, by proving that Israel will not respect any Palestinian leadership that it itself did not choose, the attack puts at risk the Israeli policies of separation of the populations. It has also made it harder for Israel to keep pursuing the policy of pressuring Palestinians to accept a new economic structure built on foreign investments and restricted movement, because such investments could be destroyed at any time by Israeli forces. The attack also increases the possibility that Palestinians will rally around a new leadership, perhaps even more belligerent and uncompromising.

Furthermore, the Israeli policy towards the Gaza Strip – namely to keep it constantly on the verge of a humanitarian catastrophe (Azoulay and Ophir, 2008: 289–328) – seems to have changed, and the Israeli leadership appeared willing to risk going beyond the threshold of catastrophe, doubtless thinking about the February 2009 elections in Israel.

The Israeli–Palestinian conflict and the occupation defy reductionist arguments. As this book will attempt to show, Israel has undertaken contradictory policies, and the Israeli political leadership has consistently failed, in over four decades of occupation, to formulate a coherent and long-term strategy for dealing with the OPT (Gordon, 2008b: 15–17). These many contradictions include, among other things, the construction of illegal settlements in areas from which Israel intended to withdraw, the annexation of areas without concomitant bestowal of citizenship on the annexed population, investing effort to improve the standard of living of occupied Palestinians to make them more docile, followed by the launch of brutal attacks which destroy the infrastructure necessary for the survival of the Palestinian population (Gordon, 2008b: 15–17). Perhaps one of the most important contradictions in the context of this book is Israel's welcoming of international aid to the occupied Palestinians, in order to relieve Israel of the need to take responsibility for the Palestinians' living conditions, while at the same time Israel erects obstacles to aid, harasses aid agencies, puts certain Palestinian areas under blockade, and thus prevents the aid from reaching its target.

This is not to say there are no contradictions on the Palestinian side as well. The Palestinians' representatives in the Oslo negotiations agreed to relinquish their demand for immediate and full sovereignty in exchange for participation in a process allowing them gradually to attain sovereignty. However, when the process failed the strategies remained the same, and the Palestinian leadership failed to take the initiative and propose long-term plans for ending the occupation.

The Palestinian political sphere has fallen into a state of crisis since early 2006, and it would seem (as many Palestinians feel) that the Palestinian representatives, elected or not, are more concerned with internal bickering than with ending the Israeli occupation. The Fatah party, once a dedicated guerrilla force which fought for Palestinian independence, has turned its guns on fellow Palestinians and even accepted help from Israeli military forces to fight against opposing factions, thus eroding much of its popular legitimacy in the public eye. The Hamas party, which refused to cooperate with the Israeli occupation forces and has embraced a more violent course of action, has failed to offer any coherent strategy for ending the Israeli occupation, and seems unable and unprepared to find allies, supporters, or even sympathizers from the international community in the fight against the occupation.

The current political impasse does not seem likely to be overcome soon, and thus it is all the more important to investigate the evolving economic reality in Israel/Palestine. The economic changes which will be described in this book are reshaping and redefining the terms of the occupation in profound ways, and often in ways that do not line up with the political aspirations of either the Israeli or the Palestinian leaderships.

1

BACKGROUND ON THE PALESTINIAN ECONOMY

DEPENDENCY

The Palestinian economy under occupation has undergone many changes, but its defining characteristic is still that it has been under the control of a hostile foreign power for over 42 years. Today, every aspect of the Palestinian economy is affected by Israel.

From an economic perspective, the early years of the occupation brought an unexpected wave of prosperity to the Palestinian population. Taking their lesson from the wave of decolonization and the mid-century fall of empires, Israeli forces used light-handed methods to control the Palestinians, relying on the cooperation of the occupied population, and took steps to ensure the continued functioning of the Palestinian economy (Gazit, 1985: 73–4, 251). There are five main reasons that the Palestinian economy experienced a boom shortly after the Israeli occupation.

First, in order to minimize cheap exports to the Israeli market (Yahav, 2004: 72–4), Israel followed an "open bridges" policy, which enabled the Palestinians to continue to trade with Jordan and to some extent with Egypt, countries with which Israel did not have diplomatic relations at the time (Gazit, 1985: 206–15). Second, Israeli professionals were sent to the occupied territories to "modernize" the Palestinian economy – implementing innovations in irrigation, vaccination of livestock and land reclamation (Gordon, 2008b; Kanovski, 1970: 61–2).[1] Third, Israelis began to tour the

1 The development efforts of the Israeli government in the Occupied Palestinian Territories (OPT) were a point of pride to Israeli institutions, but outside researches found that these efforts were limited in nature and did little to alleviate the damage caused during the 1967 war, or the severe

Palestinian territories, marveling at the cheap prices and buying local products (Segev, 2005: 457, 476). Fourth, and most importantly, Israeli employers began to employ Palestinian workers, paying them only a fraction of what Israeli workers would normally get. These salaries were nonetheless considerably higher than the wages for jobs within the West Bank and Gaza, resulting in a surge of the Palestinian population's income in the OPT. The Israeli government even created special projects to employ Palestinians in order to secure employment for the occupied population (Gordon, 2008b: 62–9, 78; Kanovski, 1970: 61–2). Fifth and last, after the rise of oil prices in 1973, the Gulf states began to encourage Palestinian migrant laborers to perform skilled work in these newly wealthy countries. Remittances from these workers were sent back to the OPT and promoted growth in the Palestinian economy (Awartani, 1988).

However, although this period of relative prosperity was shaped by Israeli economic interests, it was not an accidental result of the situation that emerged after the occupation, but the outcome of a premeditated and well-planned policy of the Israeli Ministry of Defense and the military leadership. High-ranking Israeli officials have attested that they made conscious efforts to improve the standard of living of Palestinians and increase employment and productivity, in order to improve their control over the occupied population and stifle resistance (Gordon, 2008b: 62–9).

These policies were largely successful in suppressing Palestinian resistance for the first two decades of occupation. They made it more difficult for the Palestine Liberation Organization (PLO) to recruit members, and hid the true extent of the subjugation of the Palestinian economy to Israel. Israel's authorities put in place a complex system forcing Palestinians to obtain permits for nearly any economic activity, from going to work inside Israel to setting up a shop in the OPT. These permits had to be renewed repeatedly, and were revoked in the case of any Palestinian accused by the General Security Service (GSS)[2] of dissenting political activity (Gordon, 2008b: 62–9).

Between 1968 and 1972, the West Bank saw an average annual growth rate of 15 percent, and the Gaza Strip of 11 percent (Arnon, 2007). Although rapid growth was expected, as the Palestinian

limitations on economic development in the OPT (Azoulay and Ophir, 2008).

2 The GSS is Israel's secret police, and one of the most prominent organizations used by the Israeli authorities to control the Palestinian population, as well as to suppress political activity within Israel that it deems potentially disloyal (Gordon, 2008b: 31–2).

economy was still recovering towards its pre-war economic levels, the Central Bank of Israel published a report stressing how the occupation benefited the Palestinian population (Bergman, 1974: 1–3).

However, in parallel with these measures benefiting the Palestinian population, severe restrictions were imposed as well. Israel prevented the Palestinians from developing any local industries that could possibly compete with Israeli industries (including most types of heavy manufacturing, as well as many forms of light manufacturing), augmenting and perpetuating the Palestinian economy's dependency on Israeli imports. Industry's share of the Palestinian GDP fell from 9 percent in 1968 to 7 percent in 1987. Israel also prevented the Palestinians from operating financial institutions in the OPT (Arnon et al., 1997: 80; Gordon, 2008b: 71–6).

The Palestinian economy has grown in overall size, as measured in total income and in average household consumption, but it has also become increasingly dependent on the Israeli economy. As local sources of income were suppressed by Israeli authorities, the main source of income to the Palestinians became remittances from Palestinian workers working in Israel, in the Jewish settlements in the OPT, and in the Gulf states. By 1974, a third of the Palestinian workforce was already employed in Israel, comprising nearly 70,000 workers. Many Palestinian farmers abandoned their farmlands in order to work in Israel, and Israeli authorities often took advantage of this and confiscated land that remained uncultivated for a certain period of time (Gordon, 2008b: 128–31).[3]

The changes in the Palestinian economy also had a profound impact on Palestinian society. They have affected the authority structure within the household and the status of women in society. Since only Palestinians who avoided political activity were able to receive work permits from the Israeli authorities, the class divide also began to signify a political division within Palestinian society (Gordon,

3 Neve Gordon lists seven strategies for taking control over Palestinian land that have been used to varying degrees to redistribute land in the OPT: declaring land to be absentee property, declaring land to be the property of a hostile state or body, confiscating land for public needs, declaring land to be part of a natural reserve, confiscating land for military needs, declaring land to be state property, and helping Jewish citizens purchase land from Palestinian owners. Gordon adds that in addition to these methods, land was officially and unofficially confiscated for the purpose of constructing settlements, bypass roads and the Wall of Separation (Gordon, 2008b: 119–22).

2008b: 119–22). The Palestinians who worked in Israel, however, also became keenly aware of the great disparity in freedom of speech and political action between Israeli citizens and Palestinian subjects in the OPT (Azoulay and Ophir, 2008: 140–3).

After ten years of occupation, disillusionment came quickly. The 1980s marked the end of the trend of economic prosperity under occupation, and the Palestinian economy suffered a series of blows, unmitigated by the proceeds from its new contact with the Israeli economy. Declining oil prices during the 1980s (US Department of Energy, 2008) significantly reduced the demand for Palestinian migrant workers in the Gulf states, thus depleting a major source of income to the Palestinian families back in the West Bank and the Gaza strip – remittances from migrant labor. Second, Israel itself was undergoing economic upheavals, with extremely high inflation followed by a massive collapse in the stock market. This led to a rapid deterioration in the real income generated by Palestinian workers in Israel, and to the tightening of work opportunities for Palestinians in Israel. Palestinian workers in Israel reported abuses, humiliation, and discrimination. Accumulated frustration and resentment, together with the sudden drop in income, formed an explosive combination (Angrist, 1996; Gordon, 2008b: 150–4). Third, the rapidly growing population of Jewish settlers expanded into the OPT by building on confiscated Palestinian land, with more land being confiscated or fenced off to serve the settlers' security demands. This continuing loss of land has had a cumulative negative impact on the Palestinian economy (Yahav, 2004: 73–5). And finally, the Israeli government ceased its efforts to support the Palestinian economy, and stopped trying to create employment for Palestinians, or ease the burden of the occupation (Gordon, 2008b: 78–9).

There were many causes for the first intifada, the rebellion against Israel's occupation which erupted in 1987. The economic deterioration in the occupied territories described above was one of the most important reasons, though not the only one (Schiff, Yaari, and Friedman, 1990: 92). Even if the occupation had been economically gainful to the Palestinians, it was naïve to think that the Palestinians would simply give up their personal and collective freedom, their national aspirations, and their dignity for money.

THE OSLO PROCESS

The escalation of the conflict between Israel and the Palestinians has taken a heavy toll on the Palestinian economy, and the estimated decline in the standard of living is 30–40 per cent (Gordon, 2008b: 166–8). Many saw the Oslo Process (1993–2000) as offering hope for a recovery of the Palestinian economy, as well as a chance for Palestinian sovereignty, independence, and freedom from occupation (Gross, 2000). However, because of the closure regime that was implemented by Israel in parallel with the negotiations – preventing Palestinians from entering Israel to work or do business, and even from moving freely within the OPT – the standard of living of the Palestinians actually fell during the Oslo years. The hope that prosperity and peace would reinforce each other in a reciprocal way has persisted in Israel, which enjoyed a high growth rate, but has dwindled rapidly in the occupied territories, where the Oslo years brought only poverty and unemployment (Arnon and Weinblatt, 2001).

When the Oslo negotiations began, they were managed mostly by Shimon Peres, who filled the negotiating team with representatives of Israeli business interests. Israeli company owners were hoping to transform the occupation from a colonial into a neocolonial project, to allow the Palestinians their own autonomy (in order to keep the population docile), but to ensure continued economic dependency (Selby, 2003: 76–9, 95–7).

The main achievement of the negotiating team during those years was the signing of the Oslo Accords. The 1994 Protocol on Economic Relations, signed by representatives of Israel and the PLO on April 29 in Paris, was meant to resolve the economic issues raised by the Oslo Accords. The **accords themselves** offered a trade-off: until a final status agreement was reached, Israel would control customs and trade, while Palestinians would be allowed to enter Israel and work there. However, the latter part of the agreement fell apart with the closures that Israel imposed on the OPT, and only the customs union remained in effect (Arnon et. al., 1997: 36–7, 62, 83–4, 225–7, 236–8). The limitations imposed on Palestinian workers entering Israel, in violation of the agreements, caused a serious decline in the Palestinian economy because of the loss of this central income source (Farsakh, 2002).

This economic arrangement has effectively extended the system that has existed in the OPT since 1967 of a single customs envelope controlled by Israel. It has been estimated that the loss of revenue to the Palestinian economy during the years from 1970 to 1987 as a result of the one-sided customs envelope totaled US $6–11 billion, or about 13 percent of the Palestinians' GDP. It could thus be argued that until 1995, when Israel began to transfer the customs revenue to the Palestinian Authority (PA), the lost revenue accumulated even more. The agreements did not mention returning this money to the Palestinians (Gordon, 2008b: 186).

Yitzhak Rabin, Israel's prime minister during the first years of the Oslo negotiations, rejected Peres's move towards an economic neocolonial model. Rabin, a former general, pursued a policy aimed at ensuring that peace would free the Israeli army to focus on military operations and cease to act as a policing force in the OPT. He also tried to impose a strict separation between the Israeli and Palestinian populations, and seal Israel's borders. Thus, in 1995 Rabin replaced members of the negotiating team with like-minded military men. Although the economic agreements were not renounced, the policy of separation was used to prevent Palestinian workers from entering Israel, thus effectively breaking the agreements (Selby, 2003: 135).

During the Oslo years, from 1994 to 2000, Israel enjoyed an economic boom, fueled by immigration from the former Soviet Union, by loan guarantees from the United States, and by massive international investment in the Israeli economy. Israel was then seen as a country on the path to peace. Also, the Arab boycott against Israel was largely dismantled. During the same years the Palestinian economy contracted, with poverty and unemployment increasing. In the Oslo years, Israel's per-capita GDP increased by 14.2 percent, while Palestinian per-capita GDP fell by 3.8 percent (Gordon, 2008b: 183). For the first time since the 1967 occupation, the Israeli and Palestinian economies were moving in opposite directions.

In September 2000, the second intifada broke out after Ariel Sharon entered the Al-Aqsa Mosque (Honig-Parnass, 2001), the drinking-water crisis in the Gaza Strip (Gray, 2007), and the collapse of the negotiations between the Palestinian Authority and Israel (Philo and Berry, 2004: 83–7). Most importantly, the intifada expressed the disillusionment of the general Palestinian public with the peace process, after seven years in which Israel had made almost no concessions or withdrawals, and the economic situation in the occupied territories had kept on deteriorating (Arnon and Weinblatt, 2001).

Following the collapse of negotiations and the outbreak of the second intifada, a quick escalation in the level of violence provoked a crisis in both the Israeli and Palestinian economies. The effect on the Israeli economy was to rapidly widen social gaps between rich and poor, since some parts of the population were able to weather the recession and even profit from the escalating conflict. For the Palestinians, poverty and unemployment spiked, income fell, and the Palestinian economy became dependent on international aid to stave off a massive humanitarian catastrophe (Brauman, Hilal and Ophir,

2005). The years since the outbreak of the second intifada have been years of economic standstill for the Palestinians. The opportunities to work in Israel have dwindled, international donors have been reluctant to restart development efforts after the first wave of efforts was foiled by Israel, and military conflict has kept investments low and poverty high (PCBS, PMA, and MAS, 2007).

During these years it became increasingly apparent that the Palestinian Authority is not the forerunner of a future independent state, but rather a kind of rentier state, built on favoritism, international support, and Israeli manipulation. The Palestinian Authority's reliance on income collected on its behalf by Israel, and on the economic power of certain monopolies owned by people close to the PA leadership, has made it very vulnerable to pressure from Israeli economic interests (Selby, 2005). In fact, Rabin once said that he believed the Palestinian Authority would control the Palestinian population for Israel without the limitations on the use of power that the Israeli legal system imposes on the Israeli forces, a policy which Neve Gordon calls "outsourcing the occupation" (Gordon, 2008b: 169–96). The Palestinian Authority has failed to improve the living conditions of Palestinians under occupation, and the practicalities of its own survival have often pushed it to act in collusion with Israel's occupation policies. This has become especially apparent following the appointment of Salam Fayyad as prime minister of the Palestinian Authority despite the results of the January 2006 elections. PA police officers have turned their guns against Palestinian protestors, and failed to defend the civilians under their charge from Israeli settlers and military attacks (Warschawski, 2008a; Reuters, 2008).

CORRUPTION IN THE PALESTINIAN AUTHORITY

In order to shift the blame for the lack of economic development away from Israel, Israeli officials and their supporters have frequently argued that the Palestinian Authority is a corrupt institution, which has been wasting its funds paying bribes and amassing wealth for the leadership, while neglecting the needs of the Palestinian people. Many Palestinians have also joined this criticism, as they also felt they have a right to expect more from their leadership, and were not satisfied with the Palestinian Authority's public services. In 2001 only 17 percent of Palestinian households received assistance from the Palestinian Authority, compared to 18 percent from religious organizations, 45 percent from the UN Relief and Works

Agency (UNRWA), and 20 percent from other sources (JMCC, 2001, fig. 14).

These accusations have overlooked the role played by Israel and the international community in shaping the economic structure of the Palestinian Authority. The Palestinian Authority has been excluded from providing many public services because these were being disbursed, often with greater efficiency, by the United Nations or by non-governmental organizations (NGOs), and because one of its main sources of budget is Israel – that is, customs and value-added tax (VAT) collected on the Palestinian Authority's behalf by Israel. During the early PA years, Israel transferred many of these funds directly to a bank account belonging to Yasser Arafat, then chairman of the Palestinian Authority (Selby, 2005). Israel did this because Israeli officials were hoping that Arafat would use these funds to cement his leadership and purchase the political support that he needed in order to make significant concessions in the negotiations.

The first audit which the Palestinian Authority's comptroller conducted in 1997 was very critical of the Authority. Following that audit, the pressure to increase transparency in the Palestinian Authority grew among the Palestinian public as well as from international donors. Former finance minister Salam Fayyad was one of the prominent figures who fought corruption within the Authority. This helped pave the way for him to be appointed prime minister of the Palestinian Authority in 2007, although he was not democratically elected (AIC, 2008).

After the second intifada, several international actors, most notably the International Monetary Fund (IMF),[4] also accused the Palestinian Authority of corruption. These accusations, and especially the 2003 IMF report, had a profound negative impact on the image of the Palestinian Authority, weakening it in the negotiations with Israel. Ironically, the Israeli Ministry of Foreign Affairs joined the allegations and argued that unaccounted-for PA funds were being funneled to "finance terrorism," not mentioning Israel's role in the clandestine

4 The IMF report of 2003 revealed that taxes worth US$591 million were processed outside the Palestinian Ministry of Finance in the years 1995–2000. A large part of that sum did in fact consist of funds coming from Israel, transferred directly to Arafat's bank account. The IMF official who compiled the chapter on PA corruption was Karim Nashashibi, himself a Palestinian. The IMF noted that the problem had been resolved by April 2000, but that part of the IMF's report was ignored by the IMFA (IMF, 2003: 84–122).

money transfers. The Israeli Ministry of Foreign Affairs did not offer any evidence or examples of this funding (IMFA, 2002).

One indication that the accusations of corruption were exaggerated for political reasons was the World Bank survey in 2001, which revealed that corruption statistics in the OPT were not particularly high. The survey reported that corruption did not affect the business environment, nepotism and influence were not a problem in the private sector, and bribes were not required of businesspeople. The frequency of informal payments was comparable to that of certain OECD countries, and much lower than the rate of informal payments in developing countries (Sewell, 2001). Yet despite these findings that show relatively low levels of corruption and a strong internal drive toward reform, according to Palestinian opinion polls 82 percent of Palestinians think that nepotism is very common in the public sector, and the corruption perception put the Palestinian Authority in 107th place out of 158 countries (first place being the least corrupt) in Transparency International's 2005 Corruption Perception Index (Transparency International, 2006).

These polls indicate that Palestinians have high expectations of their public officials and hold them to a high standard. The internal political discourse in the Palestinian Authority has been very critical of corruption. The chairs of the Palestinian Legislative Council's Monitoring Committee, as well as parties in the opposition, in the leftist elements of the coalition, and even within the ruling Fatah party itself, have all demanded explanations from the executive branch for the appointment of previously exiled PLO members, and for mismanagement of donor funding (AIC, 2008).

Corruption, when used in the context of a political discourse, carries a deeper meaning than the technical violation of the law. It also implies a failure of morality, and the betrayal of the public's trust by its official representatives. Many Palestinians saw these accusations of corruption as proof that the Palestinian Authority does not truly represent them, and that it is not the right institution to carry the Palestinians to independence. Indeed the issue of corruption was one of the main reasons for the victory of the Hamas party in the 2006 elections. Hamas was perceived as representing more of a "clean hands" approach to government, and it was thought that the religious piety of its leaders would serve as a bulwark against the temptation to abuse power for personal enrichment. In the Palestinian internal discourse, corruption does not include just mismanagement of funds or authority, but also poor negotiations with Israel, leading to concessions and the delay of Palestinian independence. Negotiators who misrepresented the Palestinian interest have been criticized from within, but received acclaim and preferential treatment from the international community.

The internal campaign to fight corruption and promote transparency was subdued during the second intifada (2001–04), because the thousands of deaths and the constant struggle for survival of millions of Palestinians pushed other matters aside. Yet when the Hamas truce signaled the end of the second intifada, efforts were immediately resumed to reform the Palestinian Authority. In 2004, a group of Palestinian intellectuals and parliamentarians signed a document accusing the Palestinian Authority of nepotism in appointments and of embezzlement, with concerns voiced over the personal enrichment of some politicians in Arafat's circle. Some of the critics were arrested by the Palestinian police, yet the demands for accountability could not be silenced (AIC, 2008).

Eventually the PA leadership had to commit to open elections in January 2006, which were won by Hamas under the slogan "Change and Reform." Once again, the voices calling for transparency in the Palestinian Authority were undermined by outside forces, when Israel, the United States and the European Union united to reject the results of the Palestinian elections and used illegal means to bring down the elected government and prevent it from governing the Palestinian Authority. Furthermore, donors began to resume the very same practices that the critics had warned of – sending funds directly to the President's Office and sending payments only to political allies. As services and resources became hard to come by because of the international boycott, the old system of services in exchange for favors was restored in many places. Because of the severe limitations on sending funds to the Palestinian Authority, unofficial and non-transparent measures were implemented, such as carrying suitcases full of cash through the Rafah border crossing. Finally, as funding of public services was transferred from the Palestinian Authority to NGOs, the accountability of the Palestinian Authority to the public was greatly diminished – many public services became the responsibility of unelected NGO workers (AIC, 2008).

The conclusion to be drawn from all the above is that corruption is another force that undermines the chances of Palestinian independence, and that although the general Palestinian public is adamant in fighting corruption, the outside forces applied by the Israeli authorities and by international donors have made the struggle against it an uphill battle.

PART I

SELECTED TOPICS IN THE ECONOMY OF THE OCCUPATION

2

INTERNATIONAL AID

> Throughout the entire evolution of conspicuous expenditure ... of goods or of services or human life, runs the obvious implication that in order to effectually mend the consumer's good fame it must be an expenditure of superfluities. In order to be reputable it must be wasteful. No merit would accrue from the consumption of the bare necessaries of life, except by comparison with the abjectly poor who fall short even of the subsistence minimum.
>
> Thorstein Veblen (1994: 60)

AID EFFORTS TO THE PALESTINIAN TERRITORIES: HISTORICAL OVERVIEW

The main source of aid to the Palestinians until the 1990s was the UN Relief and Works Agency (UNRWA), the UN agency for refugees. UNRWA maintained refugee camps for Palestinian refugees who had been forcefully expelled from their homes in the war of 1948 (the Israeli war of independence), providing them with shelter, food, and education. Some of these camps were located in the West Bank, many more in the Gaza Strip. When Israel occupied these areas in 1967, UNRWA stayed behind and continued to manage the refugee camps. UNRWA has been the target of criticism that it was effectively helping the Israelis manage the occupied Palestinian population, or that the camps should be dismantled and Israel left responsible for the well-being of the refugees. Legally, Israel is still obligated to allow the refugees to return to the lands from which they were evicted in 1948 (Schiff, 1989).

This exemplifies the problems that donors faced prior to the Oslo negotiations. Providing aid under occupation would have been (correctly) perceived as indirect aid to the occupying power, Israel, since Israel was responsible for the Palestinian economy. Any donors taking on a part of that burden would be helping Israel maintain the minimum living standards of the Palestinians under occupation

(Hoseini, 2006: 26). Meanwhile, Israel neglected its own responsibility towards the Palestinian population, relying on the Palestinians' own local enterprises and international aid to keep the Palestinian economy afloat, a policy that has proved ineffective in the long run, since the Palestinian economy has deteriorated rapidly in the past three decades (Gazit, 2003: 312–33). The peace negotiations, officially aimed at achieving eventual independence and sovereignty for the Palestinians, made it politically possible for donors to begin sending development aid, since now the aid was officially intended for the future Palestinian state (Le More, 2005).

Indeed, following the Oslo Accords, a significant flow of foreign money and commodities came into the Occupied Palestinian Territories (OPT), intended to help the Palestinians develop an independent economy. This aid has left a widespread imprint on the Palestinian and Israeli economies, and is one of the central factors influencing the economy of the occupation since Oslo. Foreign aid to the OPT was designed to promote an independent Palestinian economy, and therefore funneled into development and the creation of jobs. Thus, until 2000 development projects received five times as much funding as humanitarian aid and crisis management (Morli, 2004: 49–50). Aid was offered as a boon to the Palestinians and to Israel for their willingness to make peace. Donors assumed that Israel's eventual withdrawal from the OPT would leave the Palestinians unprepared to sustain themselves economically after decades of occupation. The financial aid was meant to smooth the transition from complete Israeli control to Palestinian autonomy and statehood.

But has the Palestinian economy really achieved any more independence?

First, the aid money has circumvented a central question: should Israel not compensate the Palestinians for decades of neglecting their infrastructure and limiting their opportunities to develop their own economy? Second, the donors did not take into account the critical influence of the Protocol on Economic Relations, signed by Israel and the Palestinian Liberation Organization (PLO) in 1994, on the effects of aid. Described in Chapter 1, the protocol, nicknamed the Paris Protocol, stipulated that all aid to the Palestinians would pass through Israeli customs, making it possible for the Israeli government to exact tariffs from the aid goods.

Following the outbreak of the second intifada in September 2000, the Israeli army escalated its measures against the Palestinians. In addition to a steep rise in the killings of Palestinians, measures such as house demolitions, closures, curfews, and the uprooting of trees had profound economic consequences. The Palestinian economy was devastated. In the two years between September 2000 and late 2002, the per capita GDP (the annual domestic production per Palestinian) dropped by over 40 percent. This rate of decline is almost unprecedented, and surpasses the rate of decline during the Great Depression of 1929 in the United States, or during the 2001 financial collapse in Argentina (Shearer, 2004).

As the scale of the calamity unfolded, it became clear that the billions of US dollars invested in development projects funded by the international community were actually wasted. The projects were unable to improve the Palestinian economy, as they were too dependent on the goodwill of the Israeli authorities to allow the free movement of workers and raw materials, goodwill which was lacking. The international donors that saw their projects destroyed chose not to sue Israel for the destruction (Le More, 2008).

To help the Palestinians survive this onslaught, the amount of foreign aid funneled to the OPT was almost doubled in 2001. Simultaneously, the ratio of the funds was reversed from 5:1 in favor of development to 7:1 in favor of crisis management (Morli, 2004: 49–50). As humanitarian aid grew, the Palestinians' own means of producing income diminished.

The clearest indication of this loss of productivity was the sharp increase in unemployment. Jobs were lost when Israel's closure policy prevented Palestinians from entering Israel to work. Between 2000 and 2003, the number of West Bank Palestinians permitted to enter Israel fell by 53.45 percent, and the number of Gaza Palestinians permitted to enter Israel fell by 86.66 percent (World Bank, 2004b). Jobs inside the OPT were lost because of the internal closures and checkpoints, as well as the widespread destruction of Palestinian infrastructure necessary for production, transportation, and communication. The reliability of unemployment figures regarding the OPT is low, because of the transient and temporary nature of many Palestinians' jobs. There are, however, strong indicators that the second intifada (2000–03) and the Israeli attacks on Palestinians during that time, the financial embargo of the Hamas government in 2006–07, and the siege of the Gaza Strip in 2007–09 have all restricted access to employment opportunities, with only a brief respite in 2004–05.

FOREIGN AID AND HUMANITARIAN AID

Differentiating between general foreign aid and humanitarian aid is theoretically important, but very difficult to do in practice. Officially and legally, foreign aid and humanitarian aid are distinct from each other. Foreign aid is usually granted to governments, while humanitarian aid is often disbursed to the population through the mediation of non-governmental organizations (NGOs). Foreign aid is normally considered a political act. Financial aid to a particular government implies endorsement of its activities and agenda. Humanitarian aid often attempts to appear apolitical, a direct support to people in need.

It is almost self-evident that foreign aid (if it comes in the form of money) can be used for humanitarian purposes, but humanitarian aid is not as easily converted into other uses. However, this separation is often artificial. First, governments are obligated to provide their populations with services in accordance with the local political culture. Second, if a certain aspect of the government's responsibility is covered by an outside agent, it frees government money for other purposes.

Yet as noted before, the Palestinian Authority's position in the OPT does not fit this template. While governments are normally in a position to make indirect use of humanitarian aid, the Palestinian Authority cannot. One reason is that its budget is so small: in 2002, it was a mere 0.42 percent of Israel's national budget. A second is that it is unable effectively to monitor or plan foreign donations, and a third is that in the absence of sovereignty, the Palestinian Authority is not in a position to control or supervise the distribution of aid. Most of it is provided directly to NGOs, and as a result the NGO sector has more money and influence than the Palestinian Authority itself.

However the Palestinian Authority does view humanitarian aid as a tool for fostering development, a goal which coincides with those of the international agencies disbursing the aid (Hanafi and Tabar, 2004: 19–21, 41–59). This approach is evident, for example, in statements of the Palestinian Ministry of Planning (PMoP). However, the underlying goal of both the donors and the Palestinian Authority is to help the Palestinians break free from Israeli domination, and create a separate independent state (Le More, 2005). As a result of the Palestinian Authority's weakness and the strong role played by international agencies, the OPT has become one of the places where the distinction between humanitarian aid and development aid is most clear.

Despite the idiosyncrasies of the Palestinian case, to put humanitarian aid to the OPT in context it is necessary to conduct a comparison with other places. In other countries, and specifically in Israel (as will be discussed below), the distinction between foreign aid and humanitarian aid is less clear-cut.

IS AID REALLY NEEDED?

Since aid to the OPT is so political, the question arises whether it is actually necessary. Since it is not the intention of this book to advocate the cessation of aid, it is important to briefly review the needs of the Palestinian population, and to determine whether famine is a real threat in the OPT. Certainly, the OPT is not undergoing a humanitarian crisis involving mass starvation and death tolls equivalent to the world's most poverty-stricken areas in Africa and Asia. However, malnutrition is becoming more common there, and there has been a steep decline in food security and a rapid increase in the poverty rate.

One of the best indicators of crisis is people's own sense of urgency. A survey taken by the PMoP in 2003 attempted to ascertain how Palestinians view their own social and economic needs. People were asked to rank the most urgent needs for their households. Food was ranked by over 26 percent of the respondents as the most urgent household need throughout the OPT, more than any other (PMoP, 2003). However, when the same people were asked what the most urgent need of their community or locality as a whole was, their responses were drastically different, as can be seen in Table 2.1.

The difference is very evident. Food assistance has dropped from the number one necessity for individual households to the fifth most urgent necessity (even below the "no need" response, except in Gaza) for the community or the locality.

Table 2.1 Distribution of Palestinian households by the most important need of locality and region (September 2003)

Locality's most important needs	Gaza Strip %	West Bank %	Palestinian Territory %
More jobs	63.7	38.0	46.9
Infrastructure projects	20.8	19.4	19.9
Healthcare services	6.5	20.1	15.4
No need	2.6	9.2	6.9
Food assistance	3.7	5.8	5.1
Education services	2.7	7.5	5.0
Total	100.0	100.0	100.0

Source: Palestinian Ministry of Planning (2003).

The survey therefore shows us that the Palestinians themselves are well aware of the fact (which is often associated with the writings of Amartya Sen) that hunger is not simply the result of a food shortage, but arises from a crisis in people's entitlement to food. They believe that there is sufficient food in their locality, or that it is possible to import enough food, but they find it difficult to obtain enough food for their own needs. The survey also indicates that although many Palestinians encounter difficulties in obtaining food, their collective goal continues to be empowerment rather than alleviation of immediate suffering. The conclusion to be drawn from all this is that in order to stave off starvation, the right course of action is to ensure that each household has access to sufficient nutrition, rather than just increasing the total amount of food available.

The worries that food security is deteriorating in the OPT were affirmed by the Executive Report of the Food Security Assessment compiled by the United Nations in 2003. The report argued that food often fails to reach consumers, even though food supplies are sufficient to feed the population. It cited the closures, curfews, and checkpoints as the main causes of food insecurity, leading to steep increases in food prices. Average food prices jumped by 8 percent in 2003 alone, while at the same time average income plummeted (UN, 2003: 25–7).

The report revealed that 1.4 million people in the OPT suffered from food insecurity in 2003, and 1.1 million more were in immediate danger of food insecurity, adding up to 70 percent of the Palestinian population. The ones hurt the most were those living close to the Wall of Separation, and the residents of the Gaza Strip. To cope with the hardship, many families that did not receive aid had to deplete their savings and devise resourceful strategies just to survive. Many families (called "chronic poor") were restricted to one or two meals a day without fruit, vegetables, or meat (UN, 2003: 16–17). In 2006, 18.5 percent of Palestinians were defined as living in chronic poverty (UN, 2008a).

The report also showed that throughout the OPT chronic malnutrition had already reached rates of between 6.7 percent and 17.5 percent; 80 percent of children had an iron deficiency, and 87 percent a zinc deficiency; 73 percent of women of reproductive age had an iron deficiency, and 75 percent a zinc deficiency. Moreover, freshwater resources in the OPT measured per capita were only a third of those in Israel. Land expropriation by the Israeli settlements was also making it increasingly difficult for households to supplement their diet with produce from a kitchen garden (UN OCHA, 2008a).

The United Nations report of 2003 has become rapidly outdated, however, as swiftly moving economic events in the OPT made the humanitarian situation even worse than before. The Palestinians elected the Hamas party to government in the election of January 2006, and in retaliation Israel withheld taxes due to the Palestinian Authority, while the United States organized an international boycott of the Hamas government. Since the Palestinian Authority is the largest employer in the OPT, the result was an immediate deterioration of the income of the Palestinian public sector workers, and many households that used to have a steady income suddenly became vulnerable to food insecurity (USA Today, 2007).

The economic and military siege of the Gaza Strip after Hamas took over control there in June 2007 has made even humanitarian shipments into the Strip extremely difficult. The humanitarian situation in the Gaza Strip has been deteriorating ever since, with a brief respite when Palestinians were able to breach the border and enter Egypt in order to stock up on supplies (BBC, 2008).[1] The UN reported a decline in medical services and shortage in medical supplies, rampant unemployment, poverty and chronic poverty, an acute shortage of drinkable water, and a steep increase in food prices, on top of the deaths and injuries from Israeli attacks (UN OCHA, 2008b). The Israeli attack on the Gaza Strip from December 27, 2008 until January 18, 2009, with continued lower-intensity fighting even after that, has devastated the infrastructure in Gaza, undermined health services, food distribution, and water distribution even further, and destroyed about 20,000 Palestinian homes. Over 1,300 Palestinians were killed in the attack, and over 5,300 injured, compared with three killed and 182 injured in Israel (UN OCHA, 2009).

To illustrate the present situation, Israeli brigadier-general Zvi Fogel has even admitted that "there is no death by natural causes in Gaza" – that is, death typically results from a combination of poor water quality, lack of food, woefully inadequate health services, and frequent bombings of civilian neighborhoods. This officer has become convinced that old age is no longer a possible cause of death in Gaza (Feldman, 2007). Once it has been established that aid is truly necessary under the current conditions, it must also be clarified

1 On January 23, 2008, tens of thousands of Palestinians from Gaza broke through the border fence separating them from Egypt and entered the Sinai Peninsula in order to stock up on food and other supplies, because of the acute shortage that has developed in Gaza since the 2005 Israeli withdrawal.

that the Palestinians are not the only ones who benefit from it – the benefits of aid to the donors and to Israel itself will be examined later on in the book.

CURRENT FOREIGN AID TO THE OPT

Billions of euros worth of aid have been sent to the OPT, in the form of food and goods, and as salaries for relief workers, in a seemingly unending effort to relieve the suffering of the Palestinian population. Aid is a political phenomenon, and, in the case of the OPT, it is both essential and damaging. On the one hand, the Palestinian economy is currently incapable of supporting the Palestinian population, and the aid keeps widespread famine and illness at bay. On the other hand, aid also undermines the Palestinians' political struggle, "normalizes" the situation of the occupation, and postpones a permanent solution.

There is a widespread myth that foreign aid to the Palestinians is the highest per capita in the world. A *Jerusalem Post* article in 2002 by Patrick Clawson, to take one example, claims that, calculated per capita, aid to the OPT is higher than the aid distributed during the Marshall Plan, and that the OPT receives the highest aid in the world. The article was later distributed on pro-Zionist websites (Clawson, 2002).

Although there is no denying that the OPT has received relatively high per capita foreign aid in recent years, this statement must be put in the proper perspective and context. As the data in Figures 2.1 and 2.2, and in Table 2.2, demonstrate, the OPT is *not* the highest recipient of foreign aid in the world. These show the total and per capita foreign aid to the OPT since the signing of the Oslo Accords.[2]

Note that before the outbreak of the second intifada, the *humanitarian* aid to Israel (which is not an impoverished country) was higher in absolute terms than the aid to the OPT. It is also clear that since the outbreak of the intifada total aid to the OPT has roughly doubled. Israel does not qualify for humanitarian support from international humanitarian organizations because of its socioeconomic

2 Sources for this data: Palestinian Central Bureau of Statistics (PCBS) <www.pcbs.org>; World Bank query service <http://devdata.worldbank.org/data-query>, UN Demographic Yearbook System <http://unstats.un.org/unsd/demographic/products/dyb/dyb2.htm>.

All the figures on aid to the OPT presented here are in gross amounts, and do not take into account how much of that aid had to be paid to the Israeli government or to Israeli companies.

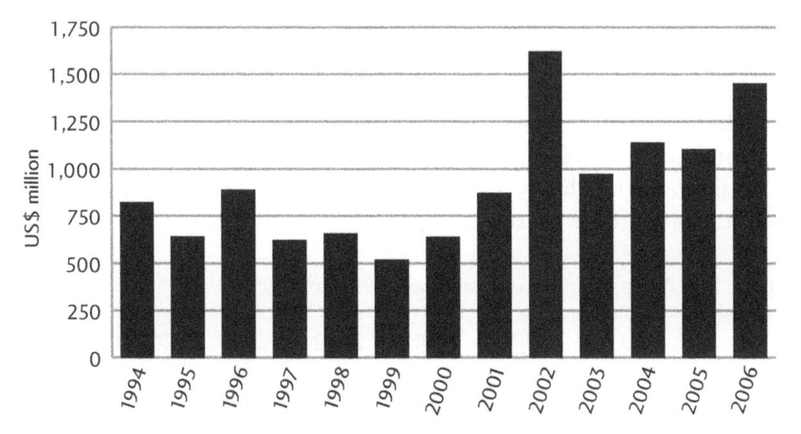

Figure 2.1 Total foreign aid to the OPT, 1994 to 2006

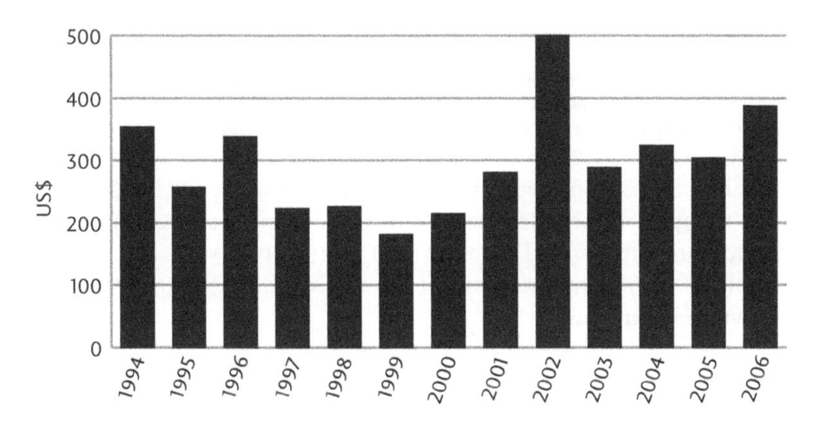

Figure 2.2 Per capita foreign aid to the OPT, 1994 to 2006

Table 2.2 Total humanitarian aid, 1999 to 2005

	1999	2000	2001	2002	2003	2004	2005
OPT	0.5	0.6	0.9	1.6	1.0	1.1	1.1
	(30)	(21)	(15)	(4)	(18)	(20)	(20)
Israel	0.9	0.8	0.2	0.8	0.4	0.5	n/a
	(12)	(13)	(76)	(18)	(46)	(46)	
World average	0.3	0.3	0.6	0.3	0.3	0.4	0.4

Notes:
The figures are in US$ billion, approximated to the closest US$100 million.
The global position (out of 209 countries) is in parentheses.
Source: World Bank query service <http://devdata.worldbank.org/data-query>.

level (Dagoni, 2005). Nevertheless, it still receives large amounts of humanitarian aid. This provides a clue to the significance of foreign money in the political economy of the region.

However, what interest us here are not merely the absolute figures of total aid, but also a comparison of per capita aid, since the OPT's population is much lower than most countries in the world. The per capita comparison, therefore, is shown in Table 2.3.

Table 2.3 Per capita aid (world rankings), 1999 to 2005

	1999	2000	2001	2002	2003	2004	2005
OPT	182 (16)	215 (13)	281 (6)	500 (7)	289 (9)	324 (8)	304 (10)
Israel	148 (21)	127 (23)	27 (84)	115 (25)	66 (43)	70 (46)	n/a
World average	10	10	9	11	12	14	16

Notes: the figures are in US$ per capita, rounded to the closest dollar.
The world position (out of 209 countries) is in parentheses.
Source: World Bank's query service <http://devdata.worldbank.org/data-query>.

When aid is considered in per capita terms, the OPT's position goes up by 14 places. Between 5 and 15 countries received more per capita humanitarian aid than the OPT in any given year. The highest recipients of humanitarian aid in the world from 1994 to 2006 are shown in Figure 2.3.

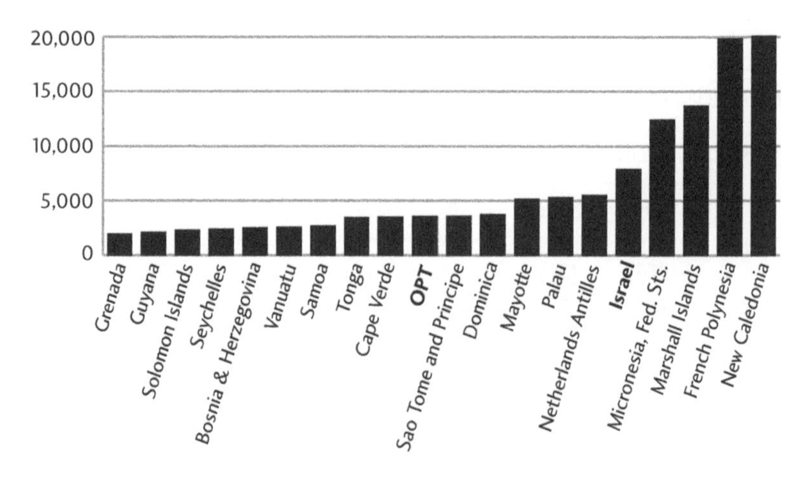

Figure 2.3 The 20 largest countries in receipt of per capita aid (in US$ million): cumulative figures, 1994 to 2006

These figures imply that the Palestinians are receiving substantial aid in addition to their locally earned income, which nonetheless is of little help in staving off the rapid deterioration of the Palestinian economy. Comparing the ratio between aid and a country's gross national income (GNI), we can get a better perspective on the actual role of aid in that country's economy. The ratio between aid and total GNI might be called "aid dependency." (See Table 2.4.)

When we look at aid as a percentage of GNI, Israel drops significantly in place, as it is one of the countries with the highest per capita income in the world. In contrast,, the Palestinian economy is one of the most aid-dependent in the world. This dependency reached a peak in 2002, when the second intifada and the attacks by Israel brought the Palestinian economy to a halt, and many households became dependent on food aid, which was increased to meet the surge in demand.

The above figures show a mild process of recovery of the Palestinian economy after the initial shock of the second intifada, and the aid dependency seems to be returning to pre-intifada levels. However, the figures in Table 2.4 only cover the situation up to 2005, just before the Palestinian elections of January 2006, in which the Hamas party took the majority of the vote, and after which the OPT were beset by an Israeli and international boycott and sanctions (Nashashibi, 2007). This second shock has led to another setback for the Palestinian economy, and has kept the dependency on aid at high levels. Oxfam estimated that 85 percent of the population of Gaza were dependent on aid in 2007 (Oxfam, 2007), and UN officials expressed worry that dependency on aid continued to rise after 2005 (Erlanger, 2007).

Table 2.4 Aid dependency, world rankings, 1999 to 2005

	1999	2000	2001	2002	2003	2004	2005
OPT	9.8% (41)	12.2% (31)	23.0% (10)	49.0% (3)	27.2% (11)	28.7% (10)	25.0% (14)
Israel	0.9% (114)	0.7% (113)	0.2% (130)	0.7% (109)	0.4% (116)	0.4% (130)	n/a
World average	0.2%	0.2%	0.2%	0.2%	0.2%	0.2%	0.2%

Notes:
The world position (out of 209 countries) is in parentheses.
Source: World Bank query service <http://devdata.worldbank.org/data-query>.

COMPARISON WITH ISRAEL

Whereas the Palestinian economy has become highly dependent on foreign money to maintain basic subsistence levels, Israel's economy has been based on capital importation from its very inception. Foreign donations, compensation, and aid were among the most important building blocks of the fledging Israeli state, and enabled Israel to maintain high imports that other countries of similar socioeconomic levels could not afford (Alexander, 1992).

Despite the many difficulties it has experienced with its absorption of massive immigration and almost constant involvement in warfare with its neighbors, Israel continues to compare itself with high-income countries in Western Europe and North America. Although Israel falls short of these countries when it comes to quality of life, it is financially very strong, with significant per capita income and a large influence on international markets, disproportionate to the country's size.

It is important to clarify that Israel's strong economic position does not mean that all Israelis are rich. Israel suffers from one of the worst rates of inequality in the Western world, and much of its income is consumed by the military-industrial complex and never reaches the general population (Ram, 2004; Shalev, 2004). According to the World Bank's World Development Indicators for 2007, Israel ranks as the 65th most equal country (sorted by the Gini coefficient). This makes Israel more unequal than all other developed countries in the world except the United States. This unique economic situation stems from Israel's reliance on a constant inflow of capital. This capital, which is usually donated rather than lent, finances Israel's imports, government deficits, and military costs.

Other than income from exports, which is the most common source of foreign capital in most countries, Israel's foreign capital comes from three main sources:

- aid from the United States (mostly military aid)
- aid from Jewish communities worldwide[3]
- compensation payments for the Holocaust, a large proportion of which is appropriated by the state rather than disbursed to the actual victims and their families (Pfeffer, 2008).

3 It is impossible to measure the total amount of donations to Israel from Jewish communities, since the donations are often given to specific institutions, companies, or government agencies, or even directly to individuals.

It is true that in per capita terms, Israel has been receiving less humanitarian aid in recent years than the OPT, but it has been receiving other forms of aid, and it has been receiving them for a much longer period of time. US aid has been accumulating since 1949, although the amounts were increased significantly in 1973. It consist of grants, loans (usually with preferred loan conditions), loan guarantees, and other forms of assistance (Clyde, 2002). Most of the aid comes in the form of military assistance, but Israel is the only country given a permit by the United States to use portions of the grant money to purchase military equipment from local industry (Yom, 2008). If interest is added to the calculation, the total aid that Israel received from the United States from 1973 to 2008 is over US$200 billion, about three times the current annual budget of the Israeli government.[4]

Compensation from Germany continues to flow to Israel even today, 63 years after the end of the Second World War, although it is declining. From 2005 to 2007 compensation was at an average of US $732 million annually, about 1 percent of the Israeli government's annual budget, although the funds do not all flow directly to the Israeli government (ICBS, 2008a). Foreign aid and compensation were not included in the calculations of humanitarian aid above, because of the World Bank's definitions of humanitarian aid and general foreign aid. If these figures are added to the humanitarian aid Israel receives, Israel's position as a recipient of aid changes dramatically (see Table 2.5).

Israel was the biggest recipient of foreign aid in the world until

Table 2.5 Total aid (world ranking, including all foreign aid to Israel)

	1999	2000	2001	2002	2003	2004	2005
OPT	0.5 (31)	0.6 (22)	0.9 (16)	1.6 (5)	1.0 (19)	1.1 (21)	1.1 (21)
Israel	3.8 (1)	4.7 (1)	3.6 (1)	3.6 (1)	3.6 (2)	3.6 (2)	3.3 (3)

Notes:
In US$ billion, approximated to the closest US$100 million.
The global position (out of 209 countries) is in parentheses.
Source: World Bank query service <http://devdata.worldbank.org/data-query>.

4 This calculation is based on an interest rate of 3.5 percent annually. The Israeli government budget is reported by the Israeli Ministry of Finance <http://www.mof.gov.il/mainpage_eng.asp>; based on 2007 prices.

Table 2.6 World rankings for per-capita aid, foreign aid to Israel included, 1999 to 2005

	1999	2000	2001	2002	2003	2004	2005
OPT	182 (17)	215 (14)	281 (7)	500 (8)	289 (10)	324 (9)	304 (11)
Israel	613 (7)	753 (7)	563 (5)	548 (6)	538 (8)	528 (7)	480 (5)

Notes
The figures are in US$ per capita, rounded to the closest dollar.
The world position (out of 209 countries) is in parentheses.
Source: World Bank's query service <http://devdata.worldbank.org/data-query>.

2003, when it was overtaken by Iraq. In 2005 it was also overtaken by Nigeria. Israel is also one of the highest recipients of aid in per capita terms. What is most surprising is that Israel receives more per capita aid than the Palestinians, refuting the myth that Palestinians are the highest recipients of per capita aid.

SOURCES OF FOREIGN AID

The largest share of humanitarian aid funds to the OPT are distributed through UNRWA, followed by the World Food Programs (WFP), which handles mostly food distribution, then the World Bank, which manages development projects (UN, 2007: 5–6; World Bank 2004b). Through these agencies, foreign aid flows to the OPT from numerous sources, including primarily (UN OCHA, 2005):

- Arab states
- the European Union
- Japan
- the United Nations
- the United States.

The largest donations probably come from European countries, although an accurate comparison is impossible because of the lack of sufficient reportage. For example, Arab states often send aid to Islamic charity organizations that do not report these donations to the World Bank or to the United Nations, and as a result there is no single organization that tallies the total aid.

BENEFICIARIES OF FOREIGN AID

If we wish to understand the reasons why the OPT is one of the regions with the highest income from aid in the world, we must analyze the key players in the aid mechanism, the ones whose participation is necessary for the flow of aid to continue. The people who benefit from this situation are discussed below.

The Palestinian population

Obviously the people who need assistance in order to survive have an interest in the continuation of aid. Even though many Palestinians believe that the aid actually helps Israel continue its occupation of the OPT (Hanafi and Tabar, 2004: 354–7), the alternative – living under a brutal occupation without assistance – is even more frightening. Furthermore, many Palestinians find employment with the aid agencies and the NGOs which receive and distribute aid, creating a class of workers who rely on aid for their employment (Hanafi and Tabar, 2005).

The Palestinian Authority

The Palestinian leadership, be it Fatah, Hamas or the Fayyad government, realizes that aid is necessary to avoid mass famine in the OPT. It is therefore crucial for any Palestinian government to maintain a semblance of political stability. Furthermore, some of the aid is directed to the Palestinian Authority itself and to its various institutions. Since the Palestinian Authority lacks sufficient sources of income to maintain itself through taxes, aid has become an essential prerequisite to its very existence (IMF and World Bank, 2007: 2, 9).

Arab and Muslim donors

Although the total amounts of aid from Arab countries and Muslim institutions to the OPT are not known, their donations are nevertheless an important source of income to the OPT. In fact, these donations played a crucial role in the victory of the Hamas party in the 2006 elections, and in its struggle to stay in government despite the international boycott imposed by Western countries (Gordon and Filc, 2005). The donors have manifold interests. Donations are used to try to prevent the Palestinians from becoming pawns of Western interests, or to promote the image of leaders in the Arab world in the public eye. Funds also allow the donors to influence internal Palestinian politics (Bahmad, 2007).

International NGO workers

The employment opportunities that NGOs offer for internationals have become very important in the current economic situation in developed countries, despite the fact that the NGO industry has only a limited supply of positions for professionals from developed countries. Since industrial production jobs in Western Europe and the United States are not increasing at the same rate as population growth – partly because of automatic processes and robotics, and partly because of intense competition from exports from countries with low wages – educated Europeans and North Americans find NGO work a viable substitute. NGO workers in the OPT find that cheap living expenses make up for the reduced pay, and that job satisfaction from doing socially important work can compensate, to a certain extent, for the difficulties that the work often entails (Strasser, 2003: 83–91).

International donors

The major sources of donations to the OPT are European countries (and to a lesser extent, the United States and Japan). These donations are not simply an expression of the donors' philanthropic feelings on behalf of the Palestinians, but stem from their political interests in the region. Since the Middle East is one of the largest sources of world oil, there is a strong correlation between the price of oil and wars in the Middle East (Bichler and Nitzan, 2006). A humanitarian crisis in the OPT can quickly undermine the political stability of the entire region and lead to a rapid increase in oil prices. Furthermore, the centrality of the Israeli–Palestinian conflict in the international media also means that countries that contribute to its resolution gain political capital as a consequence. Donors with an interest in pacifying the Middle East have an obvious reason to donate humanitarian aid to the OPT. The boost to the donor's prestige and image, hinted at by the quote at the beginning of this chapter, will be explained further in Chapter 7.

Israeli workers

The high dependency of the Palestinian population on aid, coupled with the measures taken by Israeli authorities to prevent many Palestinians from reaching their workplace, getting raw materials, or shipping out finished products, is turning the Palestinians into ideal consumers, who cannot compete with Israeli industries. Aid therefore helps the Israeli workforce avoid competition from an adjacent population whose wages are normally much lower than the Israeli standard. Competition could potentially arise both from Palestinian workers who find employment in Israel and from cheap goods imported to Israel from the OPT. Both forms of competition are blocked by Israel's checkpoint policy. Yet aid provides work to Israeli workers in companies that export to the Palestinian market, since a large proportion of aid is used to buy goods from the Israeli market.

Israeli companies

The benefits mentioned above for Israeli workers also apply to Israeli companies, which enjoy the same lack of competition from the Palestinian workforce. In addition to these benefits, Israeli companies also benefit from being called upon to provide consumer goods to the Palestinian population. Much of the demand for Israeli consumer goods is funded directly by aid. The OPT is Israel's second-largest export market (after the United States), with exports worth US$2.3 billion in 2007 (ICBS, 2008a). Because Israeli trucks can usually cross the checkpoints on their way to supply Palestinian stores (or they can deliver their cargo in the back-to-back method[5]), Palestinians often find it easier to import from Israel than from a nearby Palestinian community. Israeli companies also supply goods (mostly food) to the international aid agencies to be supplied to the Palestinians. Because of the Paris Protocols, importing cheaper food from nearby countries could be even more expensive, because then the agencies would have to pay customs. Buying food from Israeli companies exempts the aid agencies from paying customs. Altogether, a UN worker has estimated that 45 percent of the aid to the OPT flows back to the Israeli market (Karmi, 2005). This estimate, however, must be taken with a pinch of salt, because without a central bank or a separate currency, it is almost impossible to measure the true ratio of aid that finds its way to the Israeli economy. It is more probable that this figure is a gross underestimation.

The Israeli government

The Israeli government benefits from aid because it reinforces the Israeli economy – providing jobs to the Israeli labor market – and because some of it ends up in taxes paid directly to the government

5 The "back-to-back" system is an Israeli regulation that allows certain goods but not vehicles to cross into or from the areas under the PA's control. Trucks are brought into opens spaces under strict military supervision, and goods are unloaded from one truck and transferred to the other.

(as part of the profits mentioned above). But the Israeli government mainly benefits from the burden of responsibility that is lifted from its shoulders. As long as aid prevents mass famine in the OPT, the Israeli government can continue to shrug off its responsibility for the well-being of the Palestinian population under its effective control (see below).

BENEFITS TO ISRAEL

In 2005, imports from and via Israel represented 70.2 percent of total imports into the OPT, while exports to Israel represented 86.7 percent of total exports from the OPT. Nevertheless, the Palestinians had a trade deficit with Israel that year of US$1.58 billion (PCBS, 2009a). Since it is funded by aid, the Palestinian trade imbalance continues to contribute to Israel's balance of trade every year, providing jobs to the Israeli market, taxes to the Israeli government, and profit to Israeli capitalists.

The combination of the Israeli-controlled customs union, Israeli military forces' control of the OPT by force of arms, and the presence of humanitarian aid, contributes to a complete subjugation of the Palestinian economy to Israeli control. The customs union between Israel and the OPT (which is part of the Paris Protocols) is imposed and enforced by Israel. Since only Israeli goods are exempt from customs, they have an advantage in entering the Palestinian market. Whenever Palestinians import goods using this foreign aid, they must either buy from Israeli companies or buy from international companies and pay customs to the Israeli government. Even when goods from Jordan or Egypt might be available at cheaper prices, Israeli administrative hurdles to the movement of goods and customs force Palestinians to buy the more expensive Israeli products.

Meanwhile, the other part of the Paris Protocols, which ensures the free access of Palestinian workers to Israel in order to work there, has been ignored by Israel. Israeli forces, using the automatic "security" pretext, continue to prevent Palestinian workers from entering Israel. Closures, a policy which started in the early 1990s and has devastated the Palestinian economy (Farsakh, 2002), have effectively destroyed the parts of the agreement that did not benefit the Israeli economy.

At first glance, then, humanitarian assistance seems to be a blessing to the Palestinians, as it supports a minimum standard of living and prevents further disaster. However, the aid is in fact co-opted by Israel as a source of income that helps fund the occupation. Meanwhile, Israel still controls utilities such as water, electricity, and phone services. Israel confiscates moneys that were due to the Palestinian Authority[6] to pay for the costs of utilities, which sometimes are provided to the Palestinians at a higher cost than the price paid by Israelis for the same services (World Bank, 2004a; Rubinstein, 2004). Foreign aid to the OPT effectively perpetuates a situation in which the Palestinians are a nation of consumers who are unable to produce and unable to compete with the Israeli economy. Israel's government and various Israeli companies reap the profits, while the international community pays the bill. The Palestinians' desperate need is turned into a lever to promote the prosperity of their occupiers. Furthermore, the humanitarian foreign aid to the OPT relieves Israel of the need to face its responsibility for destroying the Palestinian economy, and allows Israel to continue its assault on the OPT without having to answer to the international community for creating a humanitarian disaster.

Despite the economic benefits it gains, Israel also interferes with the delivery of humanitarian aid to the Palestinians. Israeli soldiers are suspicious of aid workers, and see them as providing logistical support of their enemies (Levitin and Horenstein, 1993). The interference is so great that UN agents have complained that "we don't know of another conflict area in the world where we've had these problems – even in Kosovo." The UN Special Coordinator for the Middle East Peace Process (UNSCO) claims that while aid is currently indispensable, closures, which increase humanitarian deprivation and make aid more necessary, also reduce the effectiveness of aid by blocking access to those in need. The obstacles placed by Israeli authorities to the delivery of humanitarian assistance is evidence that international aid threatens Israel's continued control of the OPT, even as it perpetuates it (UNSCO, 2002: iii; Magnier, 2002; IRIN, 2008). Aid empowers the Palestinian struggle by staving off the immediate danger of starvation, and freeing resources for planning strategies of resistance. Despite piling on barriers that block aid from Palestinians and Palestinians from aid, towards the international community Israel continues to be fervent in its support of humanitarian aid.

Early in 2004, Israel's defense minister Shaul Mofaz held a meeting with representatives of the donor countries and international

6 The confiscated funds are not taken from humanitarian aid but from tax revenues collected by Israel on the Palestinian Authority's behalf, at Israel's ports and airport, or from Israeli companies that sell products to the OPT. Funds were also frozen as a form of political pressure in an attempt to topple the Hamas government.

organizations working in the OPT, and asked them to pull together and increase their donations to prevent the complete collapse of the Palestinian Authority. He asked them not to abandon the OPT now, because "we cannot shut our eyes to the deterioration of the Palestinian Authority, which could result in the disintegration of the Authority and its institutions, and will undermine the chances for peace" (Ben, 2004). This proves that the Israeli government is aware of its dependency on aid to the OPT.

It is important to remember, though, that the various benefits to Israel from the aid efforts to the Palestinians are not sufficient to make up for the enormous and mounting cost of maintaining the occupation. This cost is described in further detail later in the book.

CONCLUSION: EFFECTS OF FOREIGN AID

In a general discussion on the political and psychological consequences of continuous aid, Nancy Fraser claims that recipients of aid appear to remain unimproved by it. She claims that aid, while partially relieving hardships, addresses only their superficial effects but does not remove the underlying economic structure that creates and reproduces inequality. People enduring continuous impoverishment and receiving aid to stave off starvation and catastrophe develop an image of themselves as useless to society; eventually they see themselves as people who are receiving preferential treatment. This is exemplified by commentary like the statement that Palestinians are the highest recipients of per-capita humanitarian aid – which serves to entrench the image of the Palestinians as hopeless. Fraser states that while the economic situation of the recipients might remain unchanged, their social status continuously erodes (Fraser, 2004).

Although many Palestinians and their supporters feel that the aid has been subverted to help fund and maintain the occupation, and that it only makes a just solution more difficult to achieve, aid need not necessarily serve the interests of the Israeli occupation. The current situation of the Palestinian economy is dire, and a sudden stop to aid efforts could lead to a humanitarian catastrophe. Israel might recognize its responsibility towards the occupied Palestinians in the face of such a catastrophe, prompted by international pressure more than by moral commitment. But even if it does, it is unlikely to succeed in preventing an immediate catastrophe, since it is not yet prepared to meet the daily needs of the 3.8 million Palestinians under its control. Aid currently serves the function not only of preventing that catastrophe, but also of keeping desperation at bay, and giving

Palestinian activists a chance to review their non-violent options for struggle against the occupation.

Sari Hanafi and Linda Tabar argue that foreign aid has transformed Palestinian society. The NGOs that manage the aid have strong international connections, but lack a unified strategy to achieve local goals. Many local NGOs strive to empower the Palestinians' resistance, but in practice often limit themselves to supplying food and medicines. This is encouraged by the World Bank, which seeks to "depoliticize" humanitarian donations. Although the donors disburse money to deal with the symptoms rather than the causes of the crisis, their influence on Palestinian society is profound.

Hanafi and Tabar conclude that through these developments, as well as through compliance with the World Bank's pressure and the professional logic of managing funds, the NGOs become agents of a neoliberal agenda. Neoliberalism aligns with the NGOs in degovernmentalization of the state, and therefore undermines state-building (Hanafi and Tabar, 2004). Yet this seems to indicate that aid does have the potential to strengthen the struggle against the occupation, if international donors do not restrict the political involvement of the NGOs (Hanafi and Tabar, 2004). Although the United Nations and most other donors cannot support military action against Israel, they can provide tools for the Palestinians to develop a non-violent campaign of resistance, and help them weather the hardships that are sure to accompany such a campaign before it succeeds.

Aid does, however, have a strong potential to transform the nature of the conflict and the occupation. Years of neglecting the Palestinian economy have made Israel dependent on the donors' continued willingness to shoulder the responsibility for the Palestinians. Donors, however, need not go along with the demands of Israeli authorities. Donors have a plethora of available ways to make Israel more accountable for its illegal actions against the Palestinians. First, they could sue Israel for the loss of funds invested in development projects that have been jeopardized and sometimes utterly destroyed by Israeli measures. Publishing the facts about the limitations imposed by Israel and the damage to development and humanitarian projects could increase the political impact of these projects.

Aid can therefore help make the Israeli government accountable for its actions in the OPT. Such accountability means that Israel would have to internalize the damage that its actions inflict upon the Palestinian population, and the chances of achieving a just resolution of the conflict and an end to the occupation would increase significantly.

3

INFLATION IN THE OPT

The overall system of closures, checkpoints, and obstacles that hinder movement (including first and foremost the Wall of Separation and the fencing-off of the Gaza Strip: see especially Chapter 6) has redefined the Palestinian economy. One of the best ways to illustrate how the restrictions of movement have affected the Palestinian economy is by comparing prices in Israel and in the Occupied Palestinian Territories (OPT), and the rise in prices over time.

Although the Palestinian Authority runs its own budget, collects some taxes, and implements economic policies, it does not have its own separate currency. The Israeli shekel continues to be the currency in use by Israelis and Palestinians alike.

Nevertheless, prices in Israel and the OPT do not follow the same trends, and there is much to be learned from comparing the inflation rates in the two areas. Since Israel and the OPT are geographically adjacent, we might expect that competition between merchants would cause prices in the two areas to converge – why would any Palestinian or Israeli agree to buy a product at a certain price if the same product can be found more cheaply within a short distance? Thus, the price disparities between the two economies tell an interesting story about the constraints on free trade between Israel and the OPT.

Like many other countries, Israel suffered from hyperinflation in the early 1980s, and adopted a restrictive monetary policy to fight it. Inflation also affected the Palestinians in the OPT, who were powerless to fight it as they had no monetary authority. Inflation eroded the purchasing power of workers in the OPT, as well as that of Palestinian workers in Israel. A change of policy took place in 1985 with the "stabilization plan," which put Israel on the path to adopting an increasing neoliberal agenda and embracing the "Washington consensus" economic policies (Spivak, 2008a).[1] Inflation was indeed

1 The Israeli finance minister in 1979 boasted of receiving advice from Milton Friedman himself, signifying the strong swing in Israeli economic

checked and brought under control, although Israelis paid a high price, in the form of restrictive policies in welfare, labor rights and public spending on health and education (Spivak, 2008a).

During the 1990s (the Oslo years), inflation in Israel as well as the OPT fluctuated, but remained mostly at a single-digit annual level. Although at that time Israel also began to implement large-scale restrictions of movement and the number of Palestinian workers entering Israel dropped year by year, Israeli companies could still bring their wares into Palestinian markets without restriction. As a result, prices in Israel and the OPT followed a more or less parallel path, the gaps between them remaining steady.

The second intifada in October 2000 marks the point where Israeli and Palestinian inflation parted ways. The recession in the Israeli market brought about by the second intifada cut consumer spending, and consequently Israel experienced negative inflation for the first time in its history in 2003. With the inflation rate at -1.9 percent, deflation for the first time became a cause of worry to policymakers, who were concerned that it could inflict losses on industrial companies stuck with large stocks of goods that they could not sell at production prices, leading to layoffs, unemployment, and a further reduction in purchasing power, which could feed into the deflationary cycle. However, while average Israeli inflation was negative in 2003, the average inflation in the OPT remained positive and high.

It is somewhat surprising that the OPT experienced high inflation, for when there is a drop in income, according to orthodox economic theory, prices also are expected to fall. Income fell more sharply in the OPT than in Israel, even as inflation moved in the opposite direction. The combination of a rapid fall in income and a rapid increase in prices is called stagflation, an economic phenomenon which has befuddled economists since 1973 (Nitzan, 2001). In the OPT, however, stagflation seems to have become a matter of routine. The reasons for this are deeply tied to the current phase of the Israeli occupation. As will be explained shortly, the stagflation in the OPT was largely caused by the rapid rise in transport costs.

INFLATION IN ISRAEL AND IN THE OPT

Figure 3.1 demonstrates the change in prices in Israel and in the OPT. Prices are measured using the Consumer Price Index (CPI).

---

policy towards the neoliberal side of the spectrum (Bichler and Nitzan, 2001).

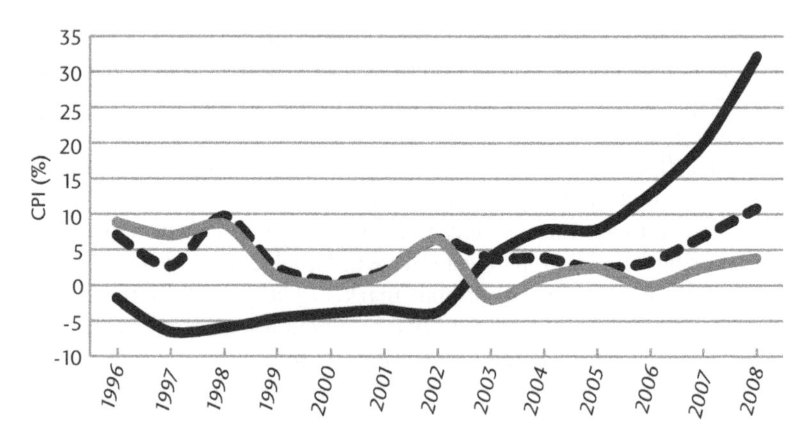

Figure 3.1 Comparison of inflation, Israel and the OPT

Sources: ICBS (2009), PCBS (2009a).

The figure also shows the widening gap in inflation between the two economies.

It is easy to see that inflation has not followed the same course in the two economies. Prices rose faster in Israel than in the OPT until 2002, mostly as a result of the growing gap in purchasing power between Israelis and Palestinians, which meant that people in Israel could pay more. At the time of the divergence in 2002, inflation in Israel and the OPT was the same, but afterwards prices in Israel began to fall, while prices in the OPT continued to rise. As a result, the purchasing power of Palestinians compared with Israelis quickly eroded. The gap in Figure 3.1 means that an average product, which was sold for the same price in both Israel and the OPT in 1995, has become more expensive for Palestinians than it is for Israelis. Although in 2005 inflation was once more at the same rate in both Israel and the OPT, the gap began to widen again in 2006. By 2008, the same product would have been 32 percent more expensive in a Palestinian city than in an Israeli city.

In Israel, prices dropped because of the constantly diminishing income of most consumers. The recession in the Israeli economy that followed the second intifada led to a drastic redistribution of income in Israeli society. The income of low-waged working people and people who are dependent on government aid has fallen, while big business has enjoyed soaring profits. Low-income earners have felt the full brunt of the recession, whereas the upper echelons of Israeli society have actually seen their income grow, although this increase has not been able to offset the overall reduction in consumption, because the wealthy tend to invest their spare income rather than consume it immediately. Low consumption of consumer goods leads to a drop in demand, and to a drop in the prices of consumer goods (a lower CPI). Financial assets such as stocks and bonds are not included in the consumer price index (CPI) and therefore do not contribute to the official inflation figures.

WHY IS PALESTINIAN INFLATION SO HIGH?

As the Palestinian economy is so tightly linked with the Israeli economy, it might be assumed that fluctuations in prices, for example, would take the same direction in Israel and in the OPT. However, the widening gap between prices in Israel and the OPT tells a different story.

Clearly, rising prices in the OPT are not the result of an increase in personal income. In fact, the average personal income of Palestinians fell by 23 percent in 2002, and by a further 23 percent in 2003 (World Bank, 2003: 28). As consumption and imports fall, Palestinians must rely more heavily on their local production and on foreign aid. Yet how is it possible that prices are rising, even though there is less available income to spend on goods?

The Palestinians' ability to produce has been severely hampered by Israeli attacks and closures, especially during the second intifada. Private property and infrastructure worth US$643 million was destroyed by the Israeli army between 2000 and 2002 (World Bank, 2003: 38–42). This created shortages of supply, granting greater monopolistic power to the Israeli companies, as well as the Palestinian companies that retained the ability to produce and distribute their goods.

According to the World Bank, the primary driving force behind rising prices in the OPT is transportation costs. The following example, which tracks a shipment of imported consumer goods on its way to the OPT, illustrates how Israeli policy impedes imports and raises transportation costs.

A single container, filled with US$4,000 worth of kitchenware, was delayed in an Israeli port for 40 days, at a cost of US$50 per day for storage. Israeli regulations require multiple pallets even when transporting a single container, so that the container (which is half a pallet's length) was loaded on a truck towing two trailers, increasing the cost of transport. The truck had to wait three nights at the crossing before it was allowed to meet with a Palestinian truck waiting on the other side of the crossing. The container had to be loaded from truck to truck in conformance with the notorious "back-to-back" regulations, designed by the Israeli authorities to prevent trucks from crossing the border. Needless to say, containers intended for the Israeli market do not face such hurdles, as they are released from customs quicker and delivered freely anywhere in Israel. When the container was finally unloaded, Israeli forces would not allow it to be returned empty to Israel, which forced the importing company to pay the shipping company US$2,000 compensation.

In total, then, this single container of goods valued at US$4,000 incurred costs of US$443 for storage to the Israeli port authorities, US$2,000 for transportation, and US$2,000 for the container. When the container was finally opened, it was discovered that US$1,500 worth of goods had been stolen during the long process, which took nearly two months, while the goods were supposedly being guarded by Israeli forces. The importing company ended up paying US$8,443 for US $2,500 worth of goods, or 337.7 percent of their value. Even without the theft, the company would have paid over twice the value of the goods (Massar, 2003).

This is an extreme example of how the limitations on transportation, imposed by Israel, can dramatically increase the costs of goods imported to the OPT, but it serves to demonstrate the various means by which the occupation affects inflation in the OPT. Palestinian importers know that every shipment of goods is at risk of encountering one or more of the problems mentioned above, and the result is a higher cost of living for Palestinians.

Adam Hanieh, a researcher into the Palestinian economy, has also argued that the restrictive regime imposed by the occupation encourages local monopolies, and that the small Palestinian economy is plagued by a few powerful monopolies, which raise prices at a whim. These monopolies have mechanisms, connections, and influence, which affords them better access through the checkpoints, often in cooperation with Israeli companies (Hanieh, 1997).

Transportation costs are therefore the key to understanding the rise in prices. It is important to note that the costs of transporting people have risen even faster than the costs of transporting goods. Since people must carry separate permits, comprised of several documents, and even then still have to undergo prolonged individual security checks, lines are long and travel times protracted. For most Palestinians, the costs of transport accumulate because of both the cost of bringing goods to market, and the cost of reaching the market to purchase these goods (World Bank, 2003: 46–50).

During the second intifada, Israeli soldiers confiscated a huge number of cars, both private cars and taxis. These confiscations, based on arbitrary decisions, have contributed to delays and to the cost of transportation, as well as to the scarcity of vehicles (ARIJ, 1999).

WHO BENEFITS FROM PALESTINIAN INFLATION?

Classical economic theory stipulates that if all prices rise, there is no real effect on the market. That is because wages are also "prices" – the price of labor. Therefore, inflation simply increases the numbers of coins or bills in transactions, without changing the amounts of the commodities exchanged. However, when the prices of different commodities change by different amounts, or when prices change by different amounts in different areas, then price changes have a real effect on the social distribution of wealth.

As shown above, inflation was not uniform in Israel and the OPT, but there are also many regional differences that were not mentioned above. Regional differences in prices in different areas of Israel and the OPT are significant, but not well measured by either the Israeli or the Palestinian bureau of statistics. Because of the growing gap in accumulated inflation between Israel and the OPT, the already wide difference in purchasing power between Israelis and Palestinians has been widening further.

In Israel, the average monthly wage rose from NIS6,323 in 1999 to NIS8,094 in 2008, an increase of 28 percent, but since the cumulative inflation during this time was 16.7 percent, purchasing power increased by 9.67 percent (ICBS, 2009). In the OPT, the average daily wage rose from NIS51.35 in 1999 to NIS77.6 in 2008, an increase of 51 percent, but because the cumulative inflation during this time was 36.03 percent, purchasing power grew by only about 2.6 percent (PCBS, 2009a).

Note that wages are measured as monthly wages in Israel and as daily wages in the OPT. This is mainly because Palestinians often find it harder to find regular employment that guarantees their working every day. The constant risk of a road being closed, of a "flying" checkpoint appearing unexpectedly on the way to work, makes Palestinians unsure whether or not they will be able to get to work on any particular day. This makes the daily measurement of wages a more relevant and useful tool than a monthly measurement of wages. As a result the Israeli Central Bureau of Statistics measures the wages of Israelis on a monthly basis, while the Palestinian Central Bureau of Statistics measures the wages of Palestinians on a daily basis. A true comparison of the two figures would require accurate estimates of the average number of work days for Israeli and Palestinian workers, but this is not available.

The comparison in purchasing power is therefore limited by the fact that it relies on official figures of wages and prices. Many Palestinian workers work for Israeli employers without permits, and try to remain clandestine because of the illegal nature of their work. Researcher Leila Farsakh has demonstrated that closures force more Palestinians to work without permits, and that Palestinians who work without permits usually receive much lower wages than those who carry permits. The wages of workers without permits are not included in statistical surveys, but witnesses report that such wages are as low as half of the wages of workers with permits (Farsakh, 2002).

Nonetheless, this comparison demonstrates that through diverging inflation, a result of Israel's tight control over movement in the OPT, Israelis are able to get a higher return for their labor, while Palestinians receive a lower return for each hour of work they put in. Israel's extensive control over Palestinian imports and exports ensures that Israeli companies (employers, importers, and exporters) are in a position to take advantage of any difference in prices between the Israeli and Palestinian markets. Israeli companies are free to trade with Palestinians or with other countries, and they can choose the best deals, to buy cheap and sell dear. Palestinians do not have that choice, and are therefore more likely to be left holding the short end of the stick in such deals.

Inflation, then, is a mechanism that redistributes wealth. In the decade described here, it served as a mechanism for the redistribution of income in favor of Israelis and to the detriment of Palestinians. The Israeli policies that create inflation in the OPT through restrictions of movement are not necessarily implemented with business interests in mind, and it is unlikely that any such forethought goes into every decision to put a checkpoint or other restriction in place. But Israeli businesspeople can nonetheless react to these policies and use them to their advantage.

Also, as a result of the inflation gap, more of the foreign aid to the OPT is appropriated by Israeli businesses. Humanitarian agencies must spend a large amount of their funds in Israel, buying food, medicine, and raw materials, and paying for the transportation costs to deliver the goods to the OPT. When prices rise in the OPT, it reflects the greater difficulty of getting these goods to the OPT, and it means that Palestinians receive fewer goods for each dollar of aid, while Israeli companies provide fewer goods and services for each dollar of aid spent in Israel.

THE OCCUPATION'S EFFECT ON ISRAEL'S CURRENCY

As Figure 3.1 shows, the Israeli inflation rate declined from nearly 10 percent in the early Oslo years to about a third of that level a decade later. The tight monetary policies of the Central Bank of Israel during the mid-1990s contributed to the lower inflation rate, and to the increased purchasing power of the Israeli shekel.

As I showed in Chapter 2, the international community's massive aid efforts on behalf of the Palestinian population of the OPT have been constrained by the Israeli authorities, and as one result of these constraints aid has been funneled through Israeli companies. Food and other supplies purchased from Israeli companies, transportation costs and storage costs paid to Israeli companies, and the taxes paid to Israeli authorities – all must be paid in Israeli currency. Donors of aid have had to convert massive amounts of foreign currency at the Central Bank of Israel to Israeli currency, and their aid efforts have indirectly caused the foreign currency reserves at the Central Bank of Israeli to swell (see Figure 5.2, page 81). In effect, Israel has been able to export the occupation, to turn the misery of Palestinians into a source of foreign currency inflow.

The differential inflation in Israel and the OPT allows Israel to leverage the exportation of the occupation, as the increase in prices in the OPT makes the aid funds less effective in providing goods and services to the Palestinians, but more effective in boosting the Israeli economy. Just as developed countries benefit from a trading advantage over developing countries through manipulations of currency exchange values, Israel has a subdivision in its own currency enabling it to preserve and expand the trade deficit between Israel and the OPT in favor of Israel.

This process signifies a new level of sophistication in the structures of exploitation. Israel is exploiting the Palestinian economy via remote control, through international donors who spend money to aid the Palestinians. These donors are unwittingly helping Israel finance its mechanisms of control and repression, as well as its war machine.

Despite its sophistication, this system of exploitation has its limits. By withdrawing its settlers from Gaza in September 2005, the Israeli government created a reality in the Gaza Strip in which aid could continue to reach Gaza, but almost nothing else could do so. The economic and military siege imposed on the Gaza Strip has turned it into the most aid-dependent region in the world. All this aid has had to go through Israel, contributing to Israel's economy. When the

Hamas party took over the Gaza Strip in 2007, it incorporated the tunnels into its economic policies, and encouraged Gazans to dig more tunnels and maintain the existing underground tunnels through which goods could be imported directly from Egypt without having to cross through Israeli customs. This loosened Israel's economic noose. The tunnels were used to smuggle not only weapons, but mainly food, livestock, consumer goods, and other necessary items that were not allowed through the official passages (Hass, 2008).

Goods from Egypt were not donated, but bought with the only currency that the people of Gaza had – Israeli currency. The main source of Israeli currency in Gaza is PA workers who continue to receive their salary from the Palestinian Authority (in Israeli currency) as long as they refuse to work for the Hamas government. The flow of Israeli currency, not channeled through customs, to Egyptian merchants (who converted it into Egyptian money) created an opposite economic effect to that of aid. It meant that Israel was "importing" the occupation, and its foreign currency reserves were being jeopardized. Although the tunnels were hardly large enough, and the people of Gaza hardly wealthy enough, to reverse or even significantly slow down the flow of foreign currency into Israel's coffers, Israel had no remote-control solution for the strategy this signified.

The worry that such trade could expand and seriously undermine Israel's economy can be seen as one of the reasons for Israel's 22-day offensive against Gaza in December 2008 and January 2009. Israeli forces bombed the Gaza Strip, and ground troops invaded it and encircled Gaza City. Despite the massive shelling, 1,434 dead Palestinians and thousands of wounded Palestinians, Israeli forces were unable to defeat the Hamas government, incite a regime change, or bring the rocket fire from the Gaza Strip to an end. From the very beginning of the attack, the tunnels were one of the main targets, and persistent Israeli attacks after the ceasefire have also focused on them. As its official reason for bombing the tunnels, Israel continues to accuse Hamas of smuggling weapons through them.

4

ECONOMIC COST OF THE OCCUPATION TO ISRAEL

At this stage, it should be clear that the Israeli occupation of the Palestinian territories has had devastating effects on the Palestinians, denying a majority of them even the semblance of a normal life. One question that needs to be addressed, however, is how the occupation has affected and continues to affect Israel, the occupying country.

In order to answer that question, we must divide the occupation into three periods of time:

- early occupation: 1967 to 1986
- late occupation (years of resistance): 1987 until today
- privatized occupation: 2002 until today.

Note that there is an overlap between the two last periods, because the realities of the late occupation have continued to intensify in the Gaza Strip, but since about 2002 the process of privatization has taken the occupation in a different direction in the West Bank.

During the first period, from 1967 to 1986, Israel's control over the OPT was achieved with minimal efforts by the Israeli military. The few troops stationed in the OPT were enough to control the civilian population with relatively few instances of fighting (compared with other military occupations around the world: Gordon, 2008b: xvi–xviii). The costs of maintaining the occupation during that time were low, and the Israeli economy also profited from the occupation for the following reasons:

- Taxes collected by the Israeli government from Palestinians exceeded the expenditures of the Israeli institutions in the OPT (Swirski, 2005: 11–42).
- The Palestinians were a captive market for Israeli goods,

especially low-quality goods unfit to be sold in the Israeli market (Strassler, 2005).
- Israeli employers hired Palestinians at very low wages, thus boosting their profits (Swirski, 2005: 11–42).
- Israel obtained illegal settlements for Israelis in the OPT expropriated land and water resources from the Palestinians (B'tselem, 2002).
- Israeli construction companies set up quarries in the West Bank and Gaza Strip; over decades of occupation, they have depleted a significant proportion of the Palestinian natural resources (Rinat, 2008).

The early period of the occupation was therefore certainly profitable for Israel. However, this changed during the 1980s. The settlement expansion became a growing drain on the Israeli public budget (as will be explained below), and the Palestinian resistance to the occupation took on new proportions with the first intifada. Israel had to send out more troops and equipment to fortify the settlements, checkpoints, and military installations in the OPT. Exports to the OPT were cut almost in half, and tourism to Israel dropped (Gordon, 2008b: 166–8). The occupation ceased to be profitable in the 1980s, as the costs of maintaining it became larger than the income it generated. The negative impact on the Israeli economy reached a peak during the second intifada, when Israel fell into a deep recession. The income generated by controlling the OPT did little to compensate for the mounting costs of the occupation.

The third period of the occupation overlaps the second, as both of these trends continue to this day. After the second intifada, the Israeli military and political leadership tried to adapt to the US-led fashion of "war on terror."[1] This adaptation included changes to Israel's military structure, as well as a massive privatization of many of the military's roles, including maintenance of the checkpoints (Buhbut, 2008) and defense of the settlements (Cohen, 2008), among others. In addition, there was a withdrawal of Israeli settlers from the Gaza Strip, and construction of the Wall of Separation began.

1 Following September 11, 2001, Israeli politicians began to market Israel as a country at the forefront of the war on terror, and argued that the Palestinian movement for national liberation from Israeli occupation is, in fact, part of the "world Islamist terror movement." Binyamin Netanyahu, who was Israel's prime minister from 1996–9 and again in 2009, said that the 9/11 attacks were good for Israel, because they helped sway international public opinion in Israel's favor (Ha'aretz and Reuters, 2008).

The new structure did not reduce the costs of occupation for the Israeli government, but it did create numerous business opportunities for private security companies. These private security companies – some formerly government-owned and later privatized, others set up by retired Israeli officers – are well positioned to obtain contracts with the Israeli government, selling their wares to the Israeli army. Later, they can use the fact that they already supply their products to the Israeli army as a selling point when negotiating with potential buyers around the world. Their "expertise" in equipment, services, and techniques, which have already been used to "fight terrorism," helps them convince buyers to pay high prices for their products (Klein, 2007a).

Since the mid-1990s, international aid efforts to the OPT have also created another source of income for the Israeli economy (see Chapter 2). This income has not been estimated yet, but as I shall show in Chapter 5), the burden of the occupation has taken its toll on the Israeli economy, even with the income generated to Israel from aid to the Palestinians.

ECONOMIC DISCOURSE ON THE COST OF OCCUPATION

In parallel to the three periods of time described above, there have been three trends in economic writing on the occupation.

During the first period, Israeli mainstream economists rarely dealt with the effects of the occupation on the Israeli economy, focussing more on the effects of the occupation on the Palestinian economy. At the time, there were many indications that the occupation was beneficial to the Palestinian economy (see for example Bergman, 1974: 1–3). Meanwhile, how the occupation affected the Israeli economy was a topic covered mostly by Marxist economists, who applied theories of imperialism to argue that the occupation is a source of profit for the Israeli economy (see for example Khouri, 1980).

During the second period following the first intifada, it became increasingly impossible to ignore the mounting cost of the occupation to the Israeli economy (which will be detailed below). Furthermore, Israel's heavy hand in quelling the Palestinian resistance, while simultaneously pushing forward with illegal settlement expansion, has meant a high level of government intervention in the economy. Such intervention has become increasingly unpopular in the eyes of neoliberal economists. After the Oslo peace negotiations in the early 1990s, neoliberal economists began to argue with increasing vehemence that the occupation is a burden on the Israeli economy, and that peace could lead to improved economic conditions in Israel (Hever, 2006c). These writings reached a peak at the time of the outbreak of the second intifada in October 2000, which led to one of Israel's deepest recessions.

The third period has added a layer of complexity to the discussion. Although government spending on the settlements and military operations in the OPT has not diminished, several private businesspeople have found ways to exploit the situation to their advantage. They began to develop a new business sector of "homeland security," focusing on surveillance, sophisticated armament, perimeter security, specialized training of security personnel, and other such activities. These new companies (some of them actually old, but with new "homeland security" products) found the Israeli Ministry of Defense to be a willing customer, and soon began to export their products all over the world as well,[2] contributing to Israeli exports and to stock prices on the Tel-Aviv stock market. Also, while its neoliberal policies (including tax cuts and slack regulation) have lured international companies to increase their investments in Israel, the Israeli government has used the "security emergency" argument to push through rapid neoliberal reforms with minimal social resistance (see Chapter 5). All of these factors have contributed to a period of high growth in the Israeli economy.

Although peace negotiations with the Palestinians have come to a standstill, and Israel's military opponents (mainly Hamas, Iran, and Hezbollah) have proved that they can pose a significant and ever-increasing challenge to Israel's regional military dominance, the Israeli economy seems to be prospering. Macroeconomic indicators such as employment, GDP, and exports have all been on the rise. Economists have therefore changed their tune, arguing that security and political issues are unrelated to economic issues, and that sound "free-market" economic policies can generate sustained growth even in the middle of a state of conflict (Landau, 2008). This reversal of opinion will be explained in greater detail in Chapter 5.

---

2 Because of the clandestine nature of this industry, information on the extent of such exports is limited to what the companies are willing to reveal for commercial purposes. However, over 45 such companies hawked their wares at a trade show in Tel-Aviv for "counterterrorism" technology (Mitnick, 2004).

GROWING AWARENESS OF THE COST

Most of the writing dealing with the cost of the occupation appeared between the beginning of the Oslo negotiations and the end of the second intifada. One of the most comprehensive works was written by the Israeli sociologist Shlomo Swirski, who attempted to summarize various estimates and sources on the cost of occupation (Swirski, 2005).

Swirski's book marked the culmination of a trend in Israeli writing about the adverse effect of the occupation and the high cost of the settlements. Ariel Rubinstein (2005), Arie Arnon, Israel Luski, Avia Spivak, and Jimmy Weinblatt (1997), Dan Ben-David (2005), Eitan Berglas (1989) and Haim Ben-Shachar (in Laviv, 2003) are among the celebrated Israeli economists who began stressing the economic burden of the occupation to the Israeli economy, even before the second intifada. Most of these economists lean towards a right-wing economic perspective. As a result of their objection to the occupation, however, they associate themselves with the Israeli moderate left. All of them have warned that the occupation is an expensive project which is dragging down the Israeli economy.

The surge of research on the economic costs of the occupation includes a study by Dror Tsaban (2003), an extensive research project conducted by the *Ha'aretz* newspaper (2003), a paper by Naor Gamliel (2005), and two studies by the Adva Center (Swirski, 2008a; Swirski, Konor-Attias, and Etkin, 2002). Swirski summarizes some of these studies in an attempt to provide a broad perspective on the subject. They suggest that the costs of the occupation apply to Israeli society as a whole, as a form of foregone utility from lost investment opportunities, and that many aspects of the Israeli economy have been strained as a result of resources being spent on maintaining Israeli control over the OPT.

Recognizing that the occupation has not always been a burden to the Israeli economy, Swirski attempts to trace the decisions that have caused an increase in its costs over the years. His main finding is that the Israeli decision to prevent the development of the Palestinian economy has contributed to the Palestinians' commitment to resisting the occupation, and it is as a result of this resistance that Israeli companies have lost their opportunities to continue to profit from the captive Palestinian market. The violent conflict has dissuaded Israelis from hiring Palestinians, and Palestinians have tried to boycott Israeli goods (Swirski, 2005: 96–7).

Swirski also acknowledges that the impact of discussing the cost of the occupation to the Israeli economy is limited at best, since the effects of the occupation on the Israeli economy, severe as they may be, are still minor in comparison to its effects on the Palestinian economy. The concept of "cost" can apply to the Israeli economy, because it is the price borne by Israel for the decision to keep the OPT under Israeli control. For the Palestinians, however, the correct term is not "cost" but "damage," for they have not chosen to live under occupation, and are therefore more fittingly described as the occupation's victims rather than its customers.

Yet the Palestinians are not passive victims in this story. Swirski notes that the main reason for the high cost of the occupation is that the Palestinians struggle against it, forcing the Israeli authorities to invest large sums of money to keep them under control and to safeguard the illegal settlements (Swirski, 2005: 49, 54). The choice of many Israelis to maintain the occupation despite its costs will be discussed in Chapter 7.

BREAKING DOWN THE COSTS

It is impossible to separate the cost of the settlements from the cost of the occupation itself. Military outposts and forts established to defend the settlements also become sources of oppression and subjugation of the local Palestinian population. It is easier to confiscate lands for building more settlements in the areas where the Israeli army exercises more control. These new settlements expand rapidly, and settlers quickly cry for more protection from the Israeli army, which readily obliges by expanding its presence. Therefore, the engine of expenditure is almost self-propelling: civilian expenses lead to military expenses, and vice versa (B'tselem, 2002).

An inherent flaw in research of this type is that the necessary data from the Israeli army and the Ministry of Defense are unavailable. These data, which are essential for a comprehensive analysis, remain withheld under the pretext of national security, making it impossible to conduct an accurate calculation of how much money Israel actually pays for the occupation (Lan, 2005).

The only option is therefore to make do with the available data, itemize the bill, and draw up a list of expenses set against income. The cost of the occupation is made up of numerous fragments, pieces of a puzzle which must be collected together. Trying to aggregate these numbers is risky. It requires an extrapolation of data that is available only for selected years and should only be considered as an approximation of the true cost. Nevertheless, it is important to make the attempt and offer a figure that can serve as a rough estimate and basis for future debates. The estimate offered by Swirski in 2005 was about NIS100 billion (about US$23 billion), but that did not take into account price changes and accumulated interest. Furthermore, it was based on a rough impression, garnered from the figures and reports that Swirski put together, and not on a methodical tally (Swirski, 2005).

THE HIDDEN FACTS

The difficulty in obtaining the relevant data does not stem from any lack of effort by the various researchers who have looked into the cost of the occupation and published their findings, but from the Israeli government's intentional policy of keeping the facts obscured. Data about the occupation is systematically concealed by the Israeli government (Blau, 2009). One example of this clandestine spending is the municipal subsidies to settlements. After the Oslo agreements, Israel began to secretly funnel millions of shekels to the settlements every year through the Ministry of the Interior. These transfers came to as much as NIS66 million annually. In 2004, the sum transferred to the settlements by the ministry was identical to the total sum allocated to impoverished municipalities within the Green Line.

A defiant minister leaked the details of this process to the press. Half of the sum was labeled "Oslo grants," the other half "Intifada grants." The names indicate that the justification given for these grants was to compensate settlers for enduring the Oslo Process, in which Israel had discussed the possibility of evacuating settlements (the grants were used as a bribe to keep the settlers from protesting against the negotiations, although as such they were not effective and the settlers did, in fact, protest), and for the hardships of living in a Palestinian area where the population is in rebellion against the Israeli occupation (Gamliel, 2005; Strassler, 2004).

Ironically, even government ministers are unable to access the actual data regarding the cost of the occupation, as is evident from the experience of several who tried, but failed (Strassler, 2004). Even simple pieces of information such as the municipal boundaries and jurisdictions of settlements were withheld by the Israeli government until 2005, when they were disclosed following a petition by the Association for Civil Rights in Israel (ACRI, 2005).

There are two reasons for the clandestine manner in which fund transfers are made. One is to avoid public outrage inside Israel at the favoritism that the settlers enjoy. The second is to avoid international outrage over Israel's violations of international law. The special subsidies given to the settlements encourage people to move to the settlements, thus violating the Fourth Geneva Convention which forbids the transfer of civilian population to an occupied territory. To hide the extent of the incentives that the government creates for would-be settlers, the subsidies are distributed into countless special budgets, one-time grants, ad hoc funds and so on, creating a financial maze that can only be navigated with great difficulty.

CAREFUL CALCULATION

Calculating the actual costs of the occupation to Israel requires a great deal of extrapolation. Often, data for only one year or a few years are available, at the prices which were current at that period. Thus, the first step of the calculation is to convert the figures into (for example) December 2007 price equivalents. The next step is to estimate the accumulated cost for the entire period of the occupation. If data is available for only a limited number of years, the figures must be multiplied, based on the assumption that Israel has been subsidizing the settlements during the entire period from1970 to 2008. I am assuming here that costs between 1967 and 1969 were relatively negligible.

Simple multiplication will not do, however, because subsidies are proportional to the size of the population that is being supported by the government. The annual cost must be adjusted to fit the changes in the settlements' population.[3] As there are no accurate figures for the settler population between 1970 and 1975, the calculations here have used an estimated average population of 1,600 settlers, half the

3 The decision to base the costs on the estimated settler population in the OPT leads to a higher emphasis on more recent costs. In the *Ha'aretz* estimate, for example, it was estimated that the costs in the first decade were half of those in the second decade of the occupation (Ha'aretz, 2003). My estimate is that since the settler population increased by a factor of ten, so did the costs. The reason for basing the costs on population is that many of the subsidies are granted on a per-family or per-individual basis.

As regards spending which could be more cost-effective in large cities than in isolated outposts, it should be noted that settlement growth usually follows irregular patterns, thus burdening the military with more complex areas to secure and utility companies with complex infrastructure requirements. This erratic growth prevents central planning of settlement growth, and causes waste in the distribution of resources and infrastructure (Sasson, 2005: 127, 143, 183, 341).

amount listed for 1976. It has been assumed that the settler population has grown steadily – ignoring, for the sake of simplicity, the surges and lulls in the rate of growth of the settlements – and that there were no settlers prior to the occupation.[4] Figure 4.1 shows the number of settlers in every year (Jerusalem Centre for Israel Studies, 2003 and 2006; Peace Now, 2007: 1).

For example, the extra cost of education services to settlers in 2003 was estimated at NIS118 million (already adjusted for 2007 prices, see below). In order to apply that cost to the entire period from 1970 to 2008, the amount must be divided by the number of settlers for 2003, namely 407,000. This means that the government paid about an extra NIS290 per settler, on average, every year. By adding up the total education subsidies paid every year between 1970 and 2008, based on the number of settlers that lived in the OPT each year, and adding interest (for the hypothetical investments that could have been made if the money had not been used for settlement subsidies), we can calculate an estimate of education subsidies of NIS5.8 billion for the entire period.

This kind of extrapolation was made whenever appropriate. When it was not appropriate (for costs or forms of income that only existed during certain years), I have explained which years I extrapolated for.

It is important to note that the costs mentioned here are only those paid by the Israeli government, excluding individual expenses on perceived or real security needs, private losses as a result of investments in occupied lands, and donations to the settlements. The discussion also focuses only on monetary costs. This obviously leaves much of the cost of the occupation in the dark, because the Israeli economy has obviously lost a great deal as a result of personal hardships, pain, and suffering caused by the Palestinian resistance to the occupation, as well as the deterioration of Israel's rule of law

4 The data on the settler population in the OPT refers to the West Bank (including East Jerusalem) and Gaza Strip only, as this discussion does not encompass the Golan Heights. Unfortunately, the largest non-governmental organization (NGO) in Israel that surveys the size of the settlements, Peace Now, does not count the settlers that are illegally living in East Jerusalem (Peace Now, 2007: 1). This is because Peace Now has adopted the Israeli perspective according to which annexed land is no longer occupied, which of course is not the case according to international law. In order to complete the statistics, information on the settler population in East Jerusalem was added (based on the Jerusalem Centre for Israel Studies, 2003, 2006).

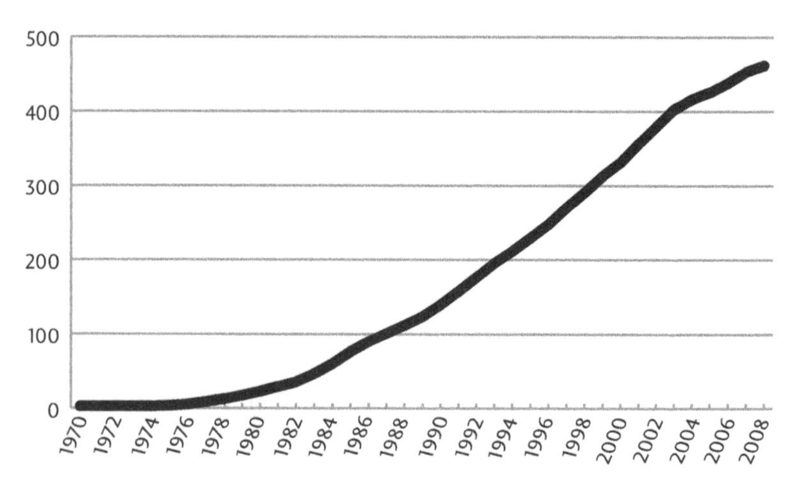

Figure 4.1 Settler population (thousands)

and transparent government practices as a result of the clandestine funding of the settlements for a period of decades.

THE CALCULATION

Interest

When discussing the concept of the "cost of the occupation," the hypothesis is that had there been no military occupation of the OPT, the Israeli government could have allocated its funds in different ways and developed the Israeli economy instead. The cost is therefore measured not only in simple nominal terms, but also as forgone utility to the Israeli economy.

It could be argued that economic investment in the settlements also has its own returns. This is indeed true, and the rapid expansion of the settlements is a telltale sign that the investment has borne fruit. Yet the question here is what could have been saved, in resources, if Israel had relinquished the OPT. In order to answer that question, we must assume that the saved funds would not simply have been laid aside unused, but would have been incorporated into Israel's government budget and used for public services, for paying off debt, and for national projects.

Also, in the event of an Israeli withdrawal from the OPT, the investment in the occupation would be largely lost to Israel, in which case it would indeed become a straightforward loss to the Israeli economy. For that reason, it is important to add interest to the calculation. There is no accurate way to determine what would have been the return on investing moneys in civilian projects in Israel instead of funding the occupation. In this calculation, the Bank of Israel interest rate is used as an approximation of the rate of return (since this is an approximation of the average interest rate available to Israeli investors: ICBS, various years). Interest was added only to estimates that did not already include an interest value. After adjusting for interest, all the figures are given in 2007 prices.

Income

The costs to Israel's government of maintaining the occupation must be compared with the income it generates, in order to get an idea of whether the bottom line is positive or negative. For the purposes of this calculation, only costs paid directly by the Israeli government were tallied, although on the income side estimates were also made for income to other non-government authorities in Israel. This is because it is difficult to determine which percentage of the income of private companies and institutions from the occupation is later appropriated by the government through direct and indirect taxation. Since what actually concerns us is the cost paid by the Israeli public, it can be assumed that some of the income generated by non-government Israeli authorities reaches a part of the Israeli public.

The income generated to the Israeli economy from the occupation can be divided into several categories:

- **Social security:** prior to the Paris Protocol, the Israeli government levied taxes on Palestinian workers who worked in Israel and in the settlements. Social security payments between 1968 and 1993 were estimated at NIS1.327 billion. The services normally provided in return for this tax were not available to the Palestinian workers. This figure was calculated by economists Stanley Fischer and Thomas Shelling (Swirski, 2005: 79–91).
- **Wage additions:** Kav Laoved, an Israeli workers' rights organization, found that NIS953.65 million was confiscated in various other forms of wage additions between 1984 and 1992. For example, Palestinian workers in Israel were charged with a "security tax" to pay for the costs of monitoring them at the workplace (Swirski, 2005: 79–91).
- **Union fees:** Palestinian workers were forced to pay union fees to the Israeli Histadrut (the federation of labor unions in Israel),

even though the Histadrut offered them no protection or assistance. These fees were estimated at NIS567.96 million (Swirski, 2005: 79–91).

- **Economic exploitation**: income was also generated through the exploitation of Palestinian cheap labor, the captive market, and water and land resources. Economists Shimshon Bichler and Jonathan Nitzan (2001: 176–8) estimated that this exploitation accumulated to 10 percent of Israel's gross domestic product (GDP) in 2001, or NIS58.99 billion.[5]
- **Transfers to the Palestinian Authority**: in order to keep the calculations as accurate as possible, it is important to account for the fact that since 1994 Israel has been obligated to transfer to the Palestinian Authority funds collected on its behalf. The sums include customs, tariffs, value-added tax (VAT), and taxation of Palestinian workers (Swirski, 2005: 29). These transfers are not really a "cost" of the occupation, since these are only sources of PA income that are collected by Israel. Israel levies administrative fees and commissions before transferring the funds to the Palestinian Authority, and even allows Israeli companies to collect debts for services rendered to the Palestinian Authority or to Palestinian municipalities directly from these funds before they are transferred to the Palestinian Authority, without an arbitration process (Swirski, 2008b: 9). In order to keep the calculation as accurate as possible, transfers to the Palestinian Authority should be subtracted from the income that Israel made from controlling the Palestinian market. They are, in effect, a partial "refund" of the profit that Israel makes from the occupation. For 1996–2006, the sum of payments was NIS29.34 billion. It is not extrapolated backwards, because Israel only began to make these payments in 1996 (Israeli Revenue Authority, 2007: 230–2).

Settlement subsidies

Transferring civilian population to live in an occupied territory is a violation of the Fourth Geneva Convention, to which Israel is a signatory. Although the Israeli government does not force Israeli citizens to live in the settlements, the many economic incentives

---

5 Since this estimate applies to economic growth and development that has been funneled from the Palestinian economy into the Israeli economy, interest calculations are not applied to it, since the alternative uses for the resources are already encompassed in the calculation.

offered to settlers and to settlement municipalities are part of the reason for the rapid migration of Israelis to the OPT.

The subsidies are divided into several categories:

- **Agriculture:** the World Zionist Organization (WZO), ostensibly working for the benefit of the Jewish people, has been used systematically as a primary apparatus for investments in the settlements. Funded heavily by the Israeli government, the WZO spends money developing agricultural projects in the settlements that are owned by Jews. Swirski estimated that between 2000 and 2002 alone, NIS454.13 million was spent by the WZO on agricultural projects in the settlements (Swirski, 2005: 60–2).
- **Education:** the Israeli government invests more in schools in the settlements than in average schools inside Israel. Incentives to teachers, transportation for children, and fewer pupils per classroom all contribute to the excess expenditure on education in the settlements, as opposed to the expenditure on average Israeli pupils. Relly Saar has estimated that the extra funds came to NIS118 million for 2003 alone (Swirski, 2005: 58–9).
- **Healthcare:** the settlements enjoy an extensive over-investment in healthcare. Isolated settlements have a clinic for every 50–100 residents, far beyond the ratio of clinics inside Israel. Furthermore, medical staff receive benefits for operating in the settlements, and extra costs are incurred by special security measures, armored vehicles, guards, and so on. Swirski quotes the *Ha'aretz* estimate of NIS2.07 billion for the extra healthcare costs in the settlements until the year 2002 (2005: 58).
- **Housing:** these costs include government subsidies for housing in the settlements, and subsidized loans and grants to settlers to buy their houses. Swirski estimates this cost at NIS3.39 billion between 1990 and 1999 (2005: 56–7).
- **Industry:** industrial zones built inside the settlements for the benefit of the settlers were bolstered by extra subsidies of NIS280 million, accumulated between 1997 and 2001, according to an estimate by Dror Tsaban. This refers only to government expenditures, not private investments (Swirski, 2005: 63).
- **Municipalities:** in recent years, the Israeli government has implemented cuts in the budgets of local municipalities in Israel, except for the settlement municipalities, which have continued to receive funding above the Israeli average. Some of the budgets were used by the settlers to fund demonstrations and campaigns against evacuation (Strassler, 2004; Yoaz, 2005a). Swirski estimates that

a total of NIS2.7 billion was provided in the 1990s as extra funding to the municipalities of the settlements. This means that settlements received more than double the equivalent per capita funding for municipalities within the Green Line (Swirski, 2005: 55–6, 149).

- **Roads:** a special network of bypass roads, for the exclusive use of settlers, allows access to every isolated settlement, while dividing the Palestinians into isolated and blockaded enclaves. Road construction in and to the OPT settlements far exceeds the rate of construction inside Israel. The journalist Ze'ev Sheef estimated that between 1993 and 2002, a total of NIS1.47 billion was spent on road construction for the settlements, but the true costs remain hidden because the budget for bypass roads was transferred to the Ministry of Defense in order to conceal it (Gamliel, 2005; Swirski, 2005: 62–3).
- **Tax benefits:** settlers also receive tax breaks simply for having their permanent address in a settlement. The biggest tax break that settlers receive is a discount in income tax. A report in *Ha'aretz* estimated that settlers received discounts worth a total of NIS1.69 billion until 2003, although other reports (such as Gamliel, 2005) estimated that tax breaks were almost double that amount (*Ha'aretz*, 2003). The more conservative estimates are used here.
- **Water:** Israel has invested a great deal in creating a water infrastructure for the settlers, based mostly on exploiting the mountain aquifer in the West Bank and preventing the Palestinians from using it. It is important to note that Palestinian water consumption per capita is a third of Israeli water consumption (Lein, 2000: 35–41). The expense on water infrastructure beyond the average water costs for the Israeli population within the Green Line was NIS562 million in the decade up to 2003 (*Ha'aretz*, 2003).

Security costs

The settlement subsidies still attract Israelis to move to the settlements, but Palestinian resistance to the Israeli occupation has created additional costs for the Israeli government in maintaining Israeli control over the OPT. The Palestinian resistance, violent or nonviolent, has been met with the use of overwhelming force by Israeli authorities, and although the damage inflicted upon Palestinians during the conflict certainly has been greater than that suffered by Israelis, the economic cost to Israel should not be underestimated.

Since 1967, in order to secure Israeli control over the OPT and to safeguard Israeli citizens from the violent aspects of the Palestinian resistance, Israeli authorities have pursued policies of spatial control through surveillance, patrols, fences, walls, checkpoints, and permits. This complex system of spatial control has become the largest component of Israeli expenditures in the OPT (Gordon, 2008b: 116–47). The investment of money, equipment, labor, and effort, and the use of force by the Israeli authorities in the OPT, have not been confined to "maintaining the security" of Israelis. This is an effort to perpetuate the hierarchical relations in the OPT, to keep Israel in complete control of movement, knowledge, and economic activities in the area (Azoulay and Ophir, 2008: 97–109, 163–98).

Furthermore, a great deal of effort is spent trying to keep the Israeli and Palestinian populations separated – not only to prevent Palestinians from entering Israel and interacting with Israelis, but also to prevent Israelis from entering Palestinian communities and interacting with Palestinians.[6] Also, the Israeli authorities strive to project the image that Palestinian violence is under control and can be contained by use of force. Although in this book I don't discuss the loss of human lives as a result of Palestinian resistance to the occupation, it is important to calculate the compensation paid by the Israeli National Insurance Institute (NII) to those injured by Palestinian resistance or to the families of those killed by Palestinian violence.

Security costs are particularly difficult to estimate, because the expenditures are distributed among many budgets, some of which are confidential. For example, the budget for settlement roads mentioned above used to include a clause for "security," comprising 19 percent of the overall allocation. But when road construction for the settlements was transferred from the Ministry of Transportation to the Ministry of Defense, the budget became confidential, and as a result the security component is now hidden (Gamliel, 2005).

Security costs are calculated here only for activities such as guarding the settlements, or actions taken in the OPT with the intention of maintaining control over the area and the people, and of preventing or defeating Palestinian violence against the settlements or against Israel. Since the Israeli authorities do not publish these figures, an estimate is used. The components of this estimate are:

---

6 Brigadier General Yair Golan, who was at the time the commander of the Israeli forces in the West Bank, gave a lecture on the Israeli mechanisms of control and separation at the Van Leer institute on April 20, 2007. In that lecture he said that separation and not security was the main reason for building the Wall of Separation, and that security could have been achieved more effectively and more cheaply by other means.

- **Special additions to the defense budget:** the special budgets for military actions in the OPT have exceeded NIS30.6 billion since 1989, in addition to the regular defense budget, part of which covers actions in the OPT anyway (Swirski, 2008a: 16–18). In addition, there is the budget of the Unit of Government Activities in the Territories (COGAT), which since 1994 has been in charge of coordinating military activities in the OPT. This unit's budget was NIS3.42 billion for the years 1994–2008, based on the budget reports of the Israeli Ministry of Finance.
- **Compensation to civilians hurt by Palestinian violence:** between the years 1980 and 2003, compensation to those directly injured or killed in Palestinian attacks totaled NIS2.776 billion. According to Swirski, before 1980 there were very few injured and dead on the Israeli side, so there is no point in extrapolating this sum backwards (2005: 100).
- **Police and internal security:** by far the biggest security expenditure of the Israeli government on the occupation was for police and internal security, because of the massive efforts required by the Israeli government to contain the resistance to the occupation, and to keep its control over the OPT and over dissenting voices within Israel. The Israeli internal security forces are charged with "fighting terrorism," and fighting crime is only their second priority (Swirski, 2005: 84–7). The average rate of annual increase in the various government budgets dedicated to internal security (for the police force, the border police, the prison authority, and other forces), has more than doubled since 1968. Creating a hypothetical extrapolation of these budgets for the years 1968–2008 based on the annual growth rate of these budgets before 1968, and comparing it with the actual budgets approved by the Israeli governments for these years, reveals a wide discrepancy.

  In the years 1968–2008, the Israeli government invested a total of 17.3 percent more on these budgets than it would have been expected to spend without the increased burden brought by the occupation. After applying interest (see below), this becomes the largest portion of the cost of the occupation. This cost is divided as follows: 4.2 percent for construction of extra jails and police stations, 7.4 percent for extra expenses for the border police, 14.9 percent for extra expenses for the prison authority, and 73.5 percent for other security-related expenses. These figures are based on Israel's national budget books collected from 1948 and until 2007.

  Such expenses include purchasing armored vehicles, arming

and training settler militias (which organize patrols in the settlements where they live), surveillance gear, fences and walls, and a plethora of weapons and ammunition for uses ranging from suppressing demonstrations to assassinations and house demolitions (Swirski, 2005: 84–7).

- **The Wall of Separation:** although the Wall's main purpose is not security, but separation, it certainly falls under the category of "security costs." It is a military project, patrolled by soldiers or private security companies. Surveillance equipment and remote-controlled armaments are installed upon it. The Wall is not a permanent fixture, but is constantly being contested by Palestinian, Israeli, and international activists who argue that its route has been declared illegal by the International Court in Hague.[7] The Wall's route is also contested by settlers and military officers, who are attempting to incorporate as many settlements and strategic assets as possible into the Wall's western side (Azoulay and Ophir, 2008: 92, 217, 252-253, 257, 266). As a result, the course of the Wall is constantly being changed, and sections of it have been destroyed and rebuilt, turning it into a very expensive project. Furthermore, the Wall's route snakes around settlements and cuts deep into the West Bank, creating a longer route, at higher cost. The Wall's route in 2004 was already double the length of the Green Line (which is the international border between Israel and the West Bank, Ynet, 2004).

  The Wall's total cost is therefore estimated at about NIS13 billion (Swirski, 2008a: 18). This calculation does not take into account compensation that Israel has paid to Palestinians whose lands were confiscated for the purpose of building the Wall. This is because the vast majority of Palestinians have chosen not to apply for compensation (because asking for compensation could be interpreted as accepting the confiscation as legal), and because those few who did apply have received compensation mostly in the form of state lands in the occupied West Bank (Yoaz, 2005b).
- **Redeployment in Gaza:** the "Disengagement Plan," which was implemented by Israel in September 2005, has evacuated Israeli settlers from the Gaza Strip, but that did not end Israeli control over the Gaza Strip. Once the settlers were removed, this enabled the Israeli army to use massive shelling against the civilian

7 See the International Court's press release, July 2004, at <http://www.icj-cij.org/icjwww/ipresscom/ipress2004/ipresscom2004-28_mwp_20040709.htm>.

population in the Gaza Strip and to block all movement into or out of it, allowing only the entry of essential humanitarian supplies, without endangering Israeli settlers. Shelling began in late 2005, immediately after the withdrawal of the settlers. The withdrawal from Gaza cost Israel over NIS11.25 billion, based on a study conducted by the Alternative Information Center (Hever, 2005c). Of this sum, about one-third represents the cost of relocating military installations, and the other two-thirds was compensation to the settlers. As the number of settlers evacuated from the Gaza Strip amounted to about 3 percent of the total settler population, the hypothetical cost of compensating the remaining settlers in the West Bank, based on the Gaza withdrawal precedent, would be prohibitive. This is discussed below in greater detail.

SUMMING THE COST

The various costs above do not constitute an exhaustive list, but they can serve as a basis for an estimate of the overall burden that the occupation poses to the Israeli economy. Adding interest to the above figures, the costs total as follows:

Income from the occupation:	NIS39.64 billion[8]
Settler subsidies:	NIS104.46 billion
Security costs:	NIS316.21 billion
Total (net) cost:	NIS381.02 billion.

These totals include the extrapolation for the entire period 1970–2008, with adjustments for price changes and for interest. The totals do not, however, include the benefits to the Israeli economy from international aid to the OPT, nor from the US aid to Israel, which has largely corresponded with the years of the occupation.

SECURITY IMPLICATIONS

The security costs are nearly triple the settler subsidies. The fact that security costs far outweigh all the other civilian costs means that the main reason for the occupation's costliness is Palestinian resistance. The Palestinians are the true force that is driving Israel out of the

8 After deducting transfers to the Palestinian Authority between 1996 and 2008.

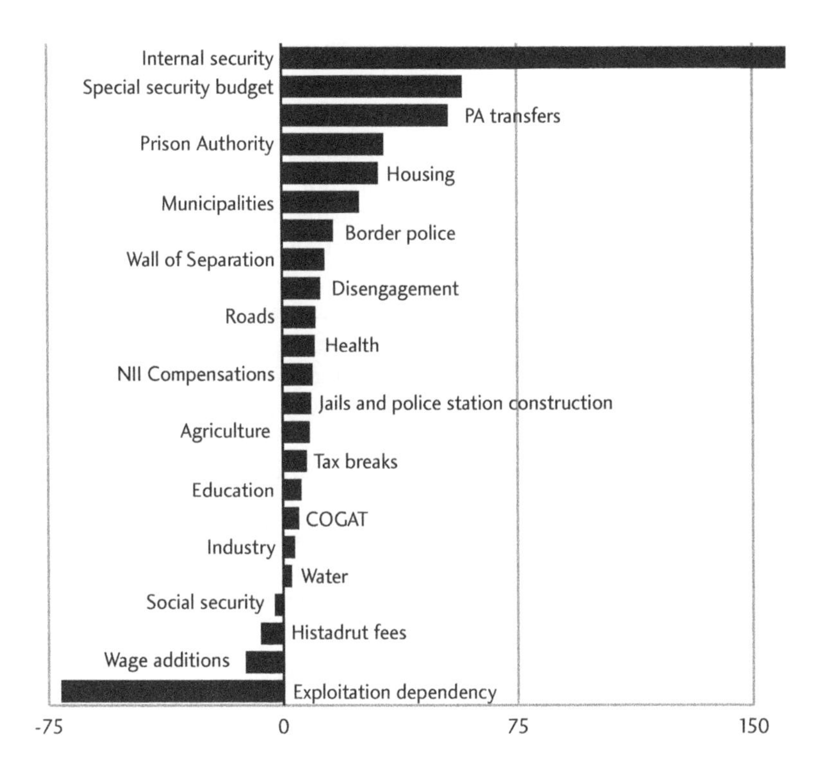

Figure 4.2 Costs of the occupation (in NIS billion, 2007 prices)

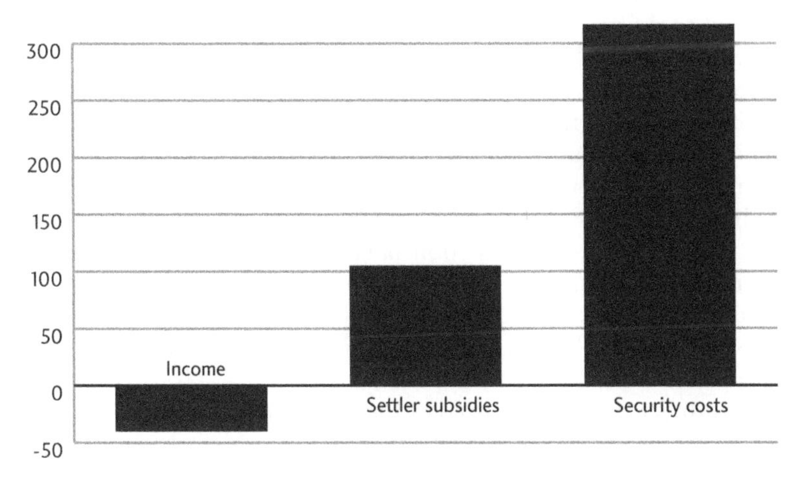

Figure 4.3 Total cost of the occupation (in NIS billion, 2007 prices)

OPT, making every move by Israel in the OPT difficult and expensive, and turning the occupation into an increasing burden for Israel.

This point cannot be overstated. The fact that the armed resistance to Israel's occupation by the Palestinians is an effective means of eroding Israel's economic strength may not be, in itself, a justification for violence. It does, however, indicate that the effectiveness of armed struggle is not limited to the battlefield (where Palestinians almost always lose), but is also relevant in the economic sphere. In that sphere, the struggle is not about who can inflict the most damage on the other side, but who can last longer.

The Palestinians certainly suffer greater economic hardship than Israelis as a result of the occupation. However, the only economic requirement they have in order to keep the struggle going is the ability to stay alive, which is assisted by international aid. Israel, on the other hand, needs a much more elaborate system of technological and military superiority, social cohesion, and popular support in order to keep the trappings of the occupation in place, and those requirements depend on Israel's continued economic growth.

COMPARISONS OF TOTALS

The different studies upon which these calculation are based gave varying estimates of the total cost of the occupation, based on different assumptions about the right way to perform the calculation. At the lower end of the estimates is the one published by *Ha'aretz*. It is limited to the years 1970 to 2003, and does not include the security costs and accumulated interest on the sums involved. The total estimate is NIS50.62 billion (in December 2007 prices). At the upper limit, estimates of the cost of the occupation reach as high as NIS600 billion, but without compensating for the income generated by the occupation for Israel.

If we proceed, however, with the above calculations, we find that the first 41 years of occupation have cost the Israeli government over NIS381 billion as of 2008. This is not a static cost, but rather a constantly growing expenditure. Thus, a more useful number is US$6.84 billion (NIS26.3 billion), which is the annual cost of the occupation as of 2008.

The direct expenses incurred by the occupation currently comprise 8.72 percent of Israel's budget. According to this calculation, the government spends an average of NIS40,890 on the average Israeli citizen, but more than double that amount – NIS 93,100 – on the average settler (135.03 percent more). In the years from 2003 to

2008, the Israeli budget grew by an average of 2.3 percent annually, while the number of settlers has risen by an average of 7.13 percent annually since 1991. This trend is unlikely to continue, since if it does, by 2038 more than 50 percent of the Israeli budget will be being spent to maintain the occupation of the OPT.

But such a long-term projection is bound to be inaccurate, and extremely unlikely to come true. No developed country can sustain a budget burden of 50 percent to fund the occupation of a foreign territory. Therefore it is not very useful to ask, "What will happen if the cost of the occupation becomes 50 percent of the Israeli budget?" A more useful question is, "What will happen between now and 2050 that will stop the rate of increase in the cost of the occupation?"

I do not pretend to know the answer to this question, but certainly as the occupation becomes increasingly more expensive, the political pressure for change will grow stronger. Whether it will eventually convince Israel to withdraw, prompt Israel to reform its mechanisms of control and find ways to cut costs, incite Israel to perform genocide, or bring about the collapse of the state of Israel – only time will tell. These options and the likelihood of their coming to pass are discussed in Chapters 7 and 8.

COMPENSATIONS

When Israel evacuated the Jewish settlements in the Gaza Strip in September 2005, the government implemented a complex system of compensation to the evacuated settlers. Settlers were compensated for the value of the real estate they left behind, for the jobs they had, for businesses that used to operate in the settlements, and for the discomfort of relocation. Although settlers are considered criminals under international law, and although it was their choice to live in the Gaza Strip, the Israeli government could not deny that it had encouraged Israelis to settle in the OPT, and it had to take responsibility.

Fewer than 8,000 settlers were evacuated, but the cost of compensating them was immense. Supporters of the withdrawal in the Israeli parliament pushed for high compensation in order to help the evacuation go smoothly (effectively bribing the settlers to leave without a struggle). Those opposed to the withdrawal pushed for even higher compensation, once they realized that they could not stop the evacuation, in order to set a precedent of unaffordable compensation and thus prevent future evacuations. Eventually, the average settler received more than NIS1 million, equivalent to about €200,000 (Hever, 2005c).

The implication of this precedent is that should Israel decide to evacuate the illegal settlements in the West Bank, where 471,000 settlers lived in 2008, it will have to deal with their demands for compensation. The settlers could use the precedent of the Gaza withdrawal and demand that the same formula be applied to them, which would mean that compensation could reach NIS471 billion, certainly more than the Israeli government can afford to pay, and more than 1.5 times its annual budget.

On the other hand, if the settlers are not evacuated and the cost of occupation continues to grow, Israel could end up paying even more. When the calculations of the cost of the occupation made above are considered, the Israeli government would be making a sound economic decision if it chose to borrow enough money to fund compensation for the settlers, and then paid interest on the loan instead of paying for the settlement subsidies and settlement security. Such a decision would save money for the Israeli government at interest rates of over 5 percent, even disregarding the fact that evacuated settlers would probably spend their compensation money in the Israeli economy and generate tax revenues for the government.

The current political situation in Israel is hardly congenial to such calculations. The cost of the occupation is not acknowledged by the government, nor is it often discussed in the Israeli media. The leaders of the settlers have become increasingly militant and are willing to use force even against Israeli authorities to prevent evacuations (thus making them even costlier), and the very idea of evacuating the settlements and returning to the 1967 borders is still unacceptable to most Israelis, as can be inferred from statements by elected Israeli politicians. The results of the February 2009 elections in Israel further demonstrate this point, with the far right having increased its strength and newly elected prime minister Binyamin Netanyahu arguing that he is opposed to the idea of a two-state solution.

WHO ACTUALLY PAYS THESE COSTS?

All of these costs are paid by the Israeli government through the state budget, either directly or through state institutions such as the WZO or the Israeli Lottery Institution (Gamliel, 2005). Economic or personal losses of private individuals are not taken into account in this chapter, although they have often been considerable. Most of the budget is funded with taxes that the government levies from the public.

However, it is necessary to keep in mind that, in addition to the

Israeli citizens who bear the burden of funding the occupation, two additional groups of people help to pay for it. One is the Palestinian population. The profits generated by Israeli companies through the exploitation of the captive Palestinian market, and the different forms of income that Israel enjoys at the Palestinians' expense (see above), have contributed to funding the occupation, as well as convincing many Israeli businesspeople to support the occupation (Swirski, 2008b: 3).

The second group is US citizens, whose tax money is used to support Israel's military endeavors. The current high rate of US aid to Israel began six years into the Israeli occupation of the OPT, and it has been sustained for 36 years, making Israel the highest recipient of US aid in the world. This aid has had a crucial role in keeping the Israeli economy afloat, despite the strain caused by the constant conflict with the Palestinians (Bowles, 2003).

PROFITS OF THE OCCUPATION

The profits of the occupation are too widespread and diffuse to be fully discussed here, but it is important to understand them when analyzing why the occupation continues. In fact, the concept of "cost" that has been used here may be misleading. The occupation has not only caused significant economic damage, it has involved a substantial redistribution of income. Whenever the government has spent extra money on funding the occupation, people and organizations have taken a cut. The redistribution is very difficult to follow, since Israeli companies systematically hide their operations in the OPT. Government tenders for construction in the settlements are intentionally obscured, and the names of the companies that win the tenders are not published (in contrast to tenders for construction projects within Israel).

The listing of settlement subsidies may have given the impression that settlers benefit from the occupation, and that they enjoy better living conditions than the average Israeli citizen. In some settlements this is indeed true, but the subsidies to settlements are not distributed equally among all the settlements. Most of the illegal settlements in East Jerusalem, for instance, fall within the municipal boundaries of Jerusalem and thus do not receive special benefits, except for cheaper housing. Also, settlements that are in more isolated and dangerous parts of the West Bank, or those that are relatively far from Israeli urban centers, confront settlers with daily difficulties that subsidies cannot fully compensate for.

Some of the biggest profiteers from the occupation are Israeli military companies and "homeland security" industries, which use their ability to employ former Israeli officers, or to claim to have experience in "fighting terrorism," as a marketing tool. They sell their products to Israel's Ministry of Defense, later boasting that their products have been used and tested against real human beings. Since the Palestinians do not offer much organized military resistance to the Israeli forces, Israeli companies have begun to specialize in surveillance techniques, perimeter defense, biometric identification, and data mining. There was a rapid rise in the market value and business of the military-surveillance sector of the Israeli economy after the September 11, 2001 attacks. Military exports from Israel exceeded US$4 billion in 2004, not counting "homeland security" exports (Klein, 2007a; Zuriel-Harari, 2005).

However, the profits from the occupation are certainly not limited to Israelis (individuals or companies). There are many international companies and governments that have a vested interest in the continuation of the occupation. In addition to companies that provide Israel with weapons, construction equipment, and services needed to maintain the occupation, the most notable profiteers from the occupation are international oil companies and arms manufacturers. As long as the occupation continues, the levels of violence in the Middle East cannot subside. The Palestinians serve as a symbol for many political groups in the Middle East (including terrorist groups), and Palestinian refugees in Arab states in the Middle East continue to constitute an important pool of candidates for recruitment to these organizations.

Israel's aggression, and the aggression towards Israel, have only served to increase the levels of violence and uncertainty in the Middle East. Each cycle of violence raises the price of weapons and generates uncertainty regarding future oil production in the Middle East, hence raising the price of oil as well. Studies conducted by Jonathan Nitzan and Shimshon Bichler (2002: 24–7, 198–273; 2006) have shown that wars in the Middle East (to most of which Israel has been a party) have dramatically increased the relative profits of weapon and oil companies.

Although the Palestinians in the OPT are neither oil producers nor large-scale weapons importers, the Palestinian refugees scattered in Arab countries support an end to the Israeli occupation. This is the basis for the long-standing hostility between Israel and Lebanon, with repeated Israeli attacks against Lebanon from 1978 to 2006.

CONCLUSION

In monetary terms, funding its occupation of the OPT has been the most expensive project undertaken by Israel since 1967. The reason is that Israel chose to suppress the economy, welfare, culture, human rights, and dignity of the Palestinians. The Palestinians have not sat by idly as Israel exploited and suppressed them, and their efforts to break free from Israel's control have forced Israel to spend more on security than on anything else, and in consequence to assume all the trappings of a militarized state, constantly on guard against the resistance of the oppressed Palestinians.

So far, the Palestinians have been unable to shake off the Israeli occupation. The occupation continues because Israel still has the means the perpetuate it and defeat Palestinian resistance. Although the Israeli economy is showing the strain, US funds and arms continue to reach Israel, and allow it to maintain its military superiority and violent control of the OPT.

The ongoing efforts by Israeli authorities to keep the Palestinian resistance suppressed, however, are costing Israel precious resources. The burden of the occupation has begun to take its toll on Israeli society, and the effects are already starting to show, as I will try to demonstrate in Chapter 5.

5

TRENDS IN THE ISRAELI ECONOMY

If the cost of the occupation to the Israeli government is summed, it remains smaller than the total aid that Israel has received from the United States since 1973. The argument could be made that if Israel had withdrawn from the Occupied Territories, allowed the Palestinian refugees from 1948 to return and made peace with its neighbors, the United States would have had no reason to support Israel any more.

Israel plays an important role in the US strategy in the Middle East; it is mostly a military role, which requires constant conflict, escalation, and retaliation (Keinon, 2006). According to this logic, the occupation can actually be seen as a profitable venture for Israel, a kind of export business for which the Israeli government receives payment in US dollars, but pays in Israeli currency.

However, to argue that the occupation is being fully paid for by the United States is to ignore the fact that the cost of occupation is rapidly increasing. The annual cost of the occupation to the Israeli government has already reached over twice the annual aid that Israel receives from the United States (see Chapter 4). This means that even if US aid used to exceed the cost of the occupation, that is no longer the case. Since about 1999, Israel has been paying more for the occupation than it receives from the United States The argument that the occupation is paid for by the United States also ignores the fact that not only has the occupation transformed the Israeli economy in many ways, it has eroded Israeli social cohesion. Not all the costs of the occupation to Israeli society are measurable in financial terms. In this chapter I describe these non-monetary costs.

In 2008, Israel celebrated the 60th anniversary of its independence. Israeli politicians and journalists extolled the virtues of the Israeli economy, painting a picture of a fast-growing market that is swiftly closing the gap with the world's richest countries. The Israeli economy, according to many Israeli economists and policymakers, is somehow able to prosper despite the constant state of military conflict in which Israel is embroiled. Booming business is somehow able to ignore the security risks, political uncertainty, and other long-term effects of the 42 years of military occupation of the West Bank and the Gaza Strip. Israelis have also celebrated the seeming immunity of the Israeli economy to the global financial crisis which erupted in 2008, arguing that Israel's conservative, regulated, and cautious financial system has softened the impact of the crisis, turning Israel into one of the few safe havens during the collapse (Rimon, 2008). The vice-chairman of the Central Bank of Israel said in November 2008 that "The global financial crisis finds Israel in the best condition it was in since the founding of the state." (Levy, 2008b).

On closer scrutiny, however, the Israeli economy seems to be undergoing a different process altogether. Israel suffers from growing levels of inequality, with wealth concentrated in the hands of the few, a looming crisis in public services offered by the state, and the country's socioeconomic structure in a fragile state.

REPORTS ON THE ISRAELI ECONOMY

The *Economist* report

In April 2008, the *Economist* published a special report on Israel entitled "The next generation." The 14-page report argued that the prosperity of the Israeli economy may be only skin deep, and that beneath the surface Israeli society is suffering from deep-rooted, unresolved problems which could lead to a crisis. Written by foreign correspondents, the report benefited from the advantage of perspective. Its insights shed light on the long-term effects of Israel's political and military policies on its economy and social integrity.

However, as I will show below, the report failed to stir a response in Israel. Although many Israeli scholars have been pointing at the cracks spreading across the Israeli floor, very little has changed in government policy to confront these problems, and the momentum of past policies continues to carry Israel towards what seems to be an impending crisis. That crisis has already begun, and in the remainder of this chapter I will try to shed light on its true extent.

Adva Center report

In June 2008, shortly after the *Economist* report, the Adva Center for Information on Equality and Social Justice in Israel published a report entitled *The Cost of Occupation*. It once again challenged the argument that the Israeli economy is prospering, and like the

Economist report, clearly stated that the Israeli economy is buckling under the burden of the military occupation of the Palestinian territories (Swirski, 2008a: 16–18).

WHY DOES ISRAEL APPEAR STRONG?

The main reason that the Israeli economy appears to be a success story is the macroeconomic indicators published by the Israeli Central Bureau of Statistics, the Central Bank of Israel, and other institutions. These indicators are aggregate measurements, which means that they sum up or average data relating to the entire country. The macroeconomic indicators that are cited as evidence of Israel's rapid growth are GDP growth rate, the falling unemployment rate, rising exports, and the strengthening of the Israeli currency and foreign reserves. Before considering the claim that the Israeli economy is weak, we need to review the arguments why it is considered strong.

Growth

Following the slump brought about by the second intifada, Israel has experienced a relatively high growth rate in gross domestic product (GDP). In the years 2003–07, the average annual growth rate in real GDP was 4.66 percent, which is considered very high (CBI, 2008b). During that time, the value of the stocks listed on the Tel-Aviv Stock Exchange rose by 374 percent (Tel-Aviv Stock Exchange, 2008). Between the years 1997 and 2006, Israeli GDP grew by a total of 43 percent (Swirski, 2008a: 8–11).

Unemployment

Unemployment also appeared to be declining in Israel during the years 2004–08. The government has taken credit for the lower official unemployment rates, and attributed them to its economic policies.

The economic journalist Nehemia Strassler has pointed out that in the first quarter of 2008, according to the Israeli Central Bureau of Statistics unemployment reached its lowest rate in 13 years, falling to 6.3 percent, only slightly above the OECD average of 6.1 percent (OECD, 2008). This is indeed an impressive drop from the peak of 10.3 percent that was reached in 2003. Strassler argues that this reduction can be attributed to the government policies of budget austerity, privatization, and tax cuts. By cutting welfare benefits to poor families, government officials believe they can prevail on unemployed people to accept any job available to them. By privatizing government companies and cutting taxes to employers, they believe they will create a more efficient market in which more jobs will be available (Strassler, 2008).

Exports

Ever since its foundation, Israel has imported more than it exported, and suffered from a trade deficit that can be sustained only with the assistance of foreign inflows of money. Such inflows have come mostly in the form of aid from the US government, Holocaust compensations from Germany, and donations from Jewish communities around the world.

However, during the 1990s this deficit, and consequently Israel's dependency on foreign capital, shrank considerably. Israel was one of the most prominent countries in the world in taking advantage of globalization. Israeli companies extended their foreign holdings and also attracted foreign investments. During the 1990s, Israel became one of the biggest per capita exporters and importers in the world (Ynet, 2005). Foreign trade thus became one of the important aspects of the Israeli economy.

These changes had everything to do with the Oslo peace negotiations and the peace agreement with Jordan. As a result of these events, the Arab boycott on trade with Israel was largely lifted, and many international investors began to do business in Israel. Yet the changes in the Israeli economy as a result of increased foreign trade affected mostly the top echelons of Israeli society (Swirski and Konor-Attias, 2005: 6–11).

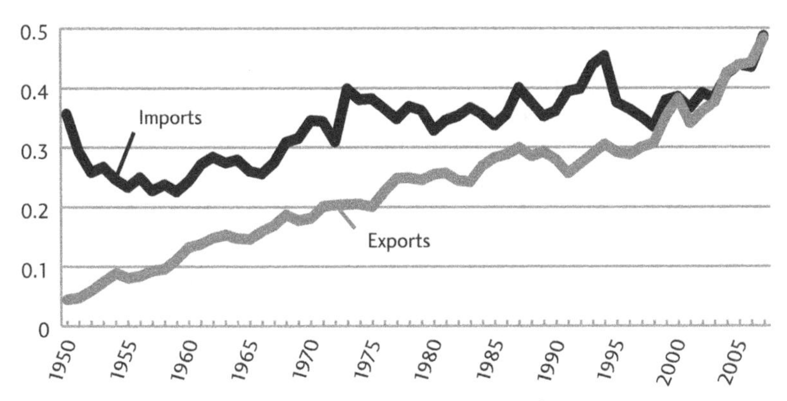

Figure 5.1 Israeli imports and exports as a percentage of GDP

Source: ICBS (2008a).

Although Israel still runs a trade deficit, it has shrunk significantly to less than US$3 billion in 2007 (ICBS, 2008a).

Strong currency

The Israeli shekel has also increased in strength in the past few years, giving Israelis abroad greater buying power, and indicating that many speculators have faith in the Israeli economy. To a large extent, this is due to the massive aid efforts by the international community aimed at the Palestinians in the OPT (see Chapter 2). Since all aid must be converted into Israeli currency, Israel is effectively exporting the occupation, and this has the effect of strengthening its currency (see Chapter 3).

Between January 2003 and March 2008, the Israeli currency grew in strength in comparison with many other currencies, with the notable exception of the euro (CBI, 2008a):

NIS vs. US dollar: +34.67 percent
NIS vs. euro: -11.14 percent
NIS vs. British pound: +8.54 percent
NIS vs. Japanese yen: +12.55 percent
NIS vs. Jordanian dinar: +34.47 percent
NIS vs. Egyptian pound: +58.56 percent

A stronger currency confers on Israeli business owners the ability to exert influence abroad, and to expand their businesses more easily into other countries.

Foreign currency reserves

Also attesting to the strength of the Israeli economy are the growing amounts of foreign currency reserves held by the Central Bank of Israel. These reserves are in effect the foreign currency "treasure chest" of the Israeli state. Despite the fact that Israel runs a trade deficit, the inflow of foreign money through channels other than trade is sufficiently strong not only to finance the deficit, but also for surplus currency to be diverted into the Central Bank of Israel's coffers.

The main boost to the foreign reserves came in 1996, following the loan guarantees given to Israel by the United States. By 1997, the loan guarantees totaled nearly US$10 billion (USIA, 1996).

Another period of rapid growth in the foreign reserves began in 2006. This period of growth can be linked to the results of the January 2006 Palestinian elections, which the Hamas party won.

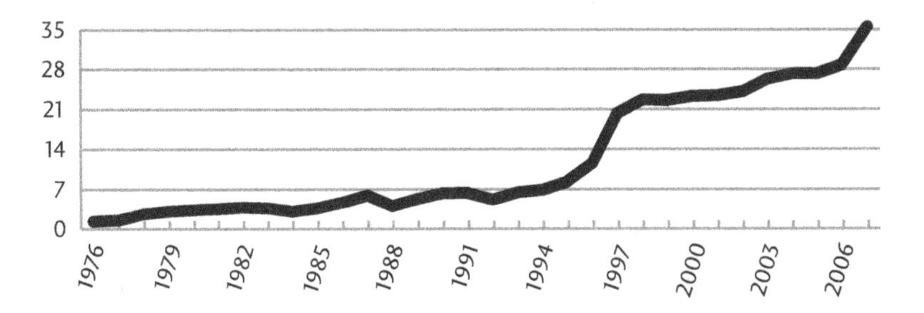

Figure 5.2 Central Bank of Israel foreign currency reserves (in US$ billion)

Source: ICBS (2008a).

Although the international community and Israel boycotted the Hamas government, aid to non-governmental organizations (NGOs) actually increased in 2006[1] (Erlanger, 2007). This increase in funding, funneled through the Central Bank of Israel, was one of the reasons for the sudden increase in reserves of foreign currency in the coffers of the Central Bank of Israel.

Now we have reviewed the main arguments why the Israeli economy is prospering, it is time to look at them more closely, and to examine the true state of the Israeli economy.

COMPARISON OF GROWTH RATE

The story of Israel's growth rate is a two-act play. In the first act, starting with the founding of the state of Israel, the Israeli growth rate was extremely high, both in aggregate terms and per capita. Between 1960 and 1972, per capita GDP grew at an average annual rate of 5.7 percent. By comparison, during these years the average growth rate in Canada, France, Germany, Italy, Japan, the United Kingdom, and the United States was 4.2 percent. If Israel had continued to grow at that rate, it would have caught up with the per capita GDP of the United States by 1990 (Ben-David, 2003).

In the second act, after the economic crisis of 1973, Israel's growth rate declined. Israel had fought a difficult war and failed to win,

1 International donors shifted their funding to NGOs, which were tasked with providing services that usually fell under the Palestinian Authority's responsibility. Meanwhile, the European Union and the World Bank instituted the Temporary International Mechanism (TIM) to pay salaries to public servants in essential roles. Finally, the Hamas party was able to raise money from donors that did not join the boycott.

and following that war, oil prices around the world skyrocketed. In the years from 1973 to 2005 the Israeli growth rate fell to an annual average of 1.81 percent, below the average of the OECD countries.[2] This means that as Israel was in the process of closing the gap with the most developed countries in the world, the process was disrupted, and the gap between Israel and the most developed countries actually began to grow, leaving Israel behind (Ben-David, 2003). The Adva report on the cost of the occupation demonstrated that Israel's actual growth rate was lower than the world's average, and lower than US and European annual growth rates between 1997 and 2006 (Swirski, 2008a: 8–11).

Although growth rates in Israel increased dramatically after the second intifada, this process was not unique to Israel. Between 2003 and 2007, Israeli GDP grew at an average annual rate of 4.66 percent, compared with 4.59 percent in the entire world and 6.02 percent in the Middle East (World Bank, 2008). It could therefore be argued that the high growth rate in Israel during these years was mostly a result of international trends and the benefits that Israeli business-people were able to obtain through the global market. This argument has been further developed by Shimshon Bichler and Jonathan Nitzan, who have demonstrated that the Israeli stock market is more correlated with international stock markets than it is with the Israeli domestic economy, and that inflated stock prices have contributed to the appearance that Israel's economy is growing (Bichler and Nitzan, 2007).

Finally, the growth rate by itself is a poor form of measurement of actual economic prosperity. GDP measures the total value of goods and services produced within a specific territory in one year. The measurement of this value is based on the total income of all companies, institutions, and individuals operating within the territory, from which sum all the costs are subtracted. This measurement of the economy has come under criticism by many contemporary scholars because it fails to differentiate between the growth of positive components such as infrastructure, education, and welfare, and the growth of negative components such as natural disasters, car accidents, and pollution (Saporta, 2001). This criticism is especially pertinent to Israel's case.

GDP measures economic transactions using prices cited in invoices and company financial reports, but makes no distinction between

2 The Organisation for Economic Cooperation and Development (OECD) includes 30 of the world's most developed countries.

different kinds of transactions. To take an example of two people selling their houses, one in order to buy a bigger house and the other in order to pay for an expensive medical operation, in terms of GDP the two will contribute the same amount, even though one is now better off and the other worse off than before.

Times of crisis and war actually tend to increase GDP, because wars involve monetary expenditures. People fleeing from dangerous areas spend money on transportation and hotels, hospitals work at full capacity to treat the wounded, and insurance companies (or the government) are charged with compensating people for damaged property.[3] In fact, Israel's state of continued conflict and outbursts of escalating violence along its borders could in fact be a contributing factor in the short term to its growth rate, although this state of affairs certainly does not contribute to the well-being of Israel's citizens or to the long-term growth of the Israeli economy (Abu-Bader & Abu-Qarn, 2003).

It is indeed true that Israel's military spending as a proportion of GDP has fallen over the years, from a peak of about 25 percent in the late 1970s to below 10 percent starting in 1995 (although the total expenditure in numerical terms has increased over these years). However, these numbers must be taken in their proper context. The 1960s and 1970s were a period in which large military spending was the norm, and the military-industrial complex that thrived during the Cold War years was designed not only for the purposes of military build-up, but also as a means of creating jobs. These policies were known as "military Keynesianism." During these two decades the average military burden of Egypt, Jordan, and Syria ranged between 18 percent and 48 percent, and the United States spent between 4.9 percent and 9.4 percent of its GDP on its military (Abu-Qarn and Abu-Bader, 2008).

However, contemporary economic doctrines have rejected the military-Keynesian model, and high proportions of military spending are no longer considered either normal, or a way to generate growth

3 The Adva Center estimated that at least NIS36.6 billion were earmarked specifically for military operations in the OPT from1989 to 2008. This sum only includes government spending through the Ministry of Defense, and does not include the budget of COGAT, the budget of the Ministry of Internal Security, compensations by the National Insurance Institute, private spending on security, and the cost of Israel's wars with its neighbors – wars that are directly related to the occupation. It also does not include NIS 22 billion for the 2005 withdrawal from the Gaza Strip and construction of the Wall of Separation (Swirski, 2008).

and employment. Israel, however, seems to be slow in adjusting to this new reality. Whereas during the 1960s Israel was spending a smaller amount on its military than its neighbors (Egypt, Jordan, and Syria), today it spends a higher proportion of its GDP on its military than any of its neighbors (Abu-Qarn and Abu-Bader, 2008).

Wars are being fought with smaller armies, and with a great deal of reliance on private companies to provide services to the fighting forces, sometimes even to do the fighting themselves (Nitzan and Bichler, 2006). In addition to the heavy spending on the military by the Ministry of Defense, Israel has an army of private security operatives who stand guard in restaurants, supermarkets, shopping malls, bus stations, and many other public places. All these security guards are paid for by the public through higher prices of consumer goods.[4] There is no data on the amount of private money that is spent on security, but we can safely assume that if the public and private expenditures on security are added together, the burden of Israel's security spending is among the highest in the world.

Although the heavy military burden on the Israeli economy does reinforce the Israeli military industry, it is a factor that risks the prospects of growth for the Israeli economy in the long run. This is because many economic transactions in Israel are more expensive than in other places in the world, because of the extra cost of security. That makes economic activities more expensive, starting from the simplest act of shopping. Israelis who spend money thus receive less in return than Europeans and Americans, as they are also paying for the salaries of the security guards in the shopping venues.

Lastly, it is important to ask who the real gainers are, the ones who experience actual growth in their economic strength. Economic policies implemented to encourage growth have included massive cuts in government social spending on the lower classes (Swirski, 2008a: 19–28). As a result, inequality has risen over the years of the occupation, and has reached its highest level in Israel's history. The poverty rate is climbing steadily regardless of growth. That means that only the upper echelons of Israel's society are prospering, while the majority of the population are being left behind (*Economist*, 2008; NII, 2008).

Figure 5.3 shows how poverty has increased in Israel over the years, especially the proportion of children living beneath the poverty

---

4 In 2003, the Ministry of Industry, Trade and Labour estimated that there were 46,500 private security guards employed in Israel. This number is higher than the number of combat soldiers in regular service in the Israeli army (Handels, 2003: 3).

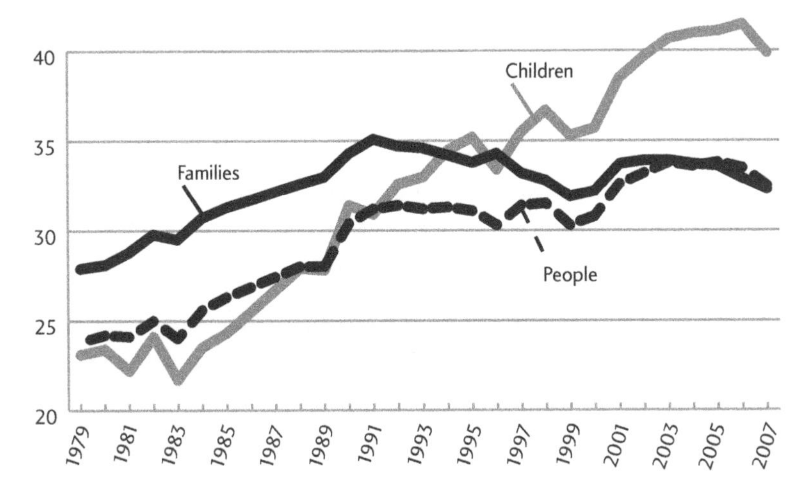

Figure 5.3 Poverty in Israel, 1979 to 2007

Note: figures are before taxes and transfer payments.
Source: National Insurance Institute (2008).

line. Except for occasional years in which poverty has declined, such as 1996, 1999, 2004 and 2007, poverty in Israel has increased overall for families, individuals, and especially for children. Furthermore, poverty is more pervasive in Israel than in any OECD country except Mexico (NII, 2008).

THE ISRAELI EDUCATIONAL SYSTEM IN DECLINE

One of the Israeli economy's sources of strength is the high-tech industries that Israel is famous for. In 2006, 46 percent of the net industrial export (excluding diamonds) was classified as "high-tech" exports (ICBS, 2008b). The main input into the high-tech industry is human capital, and therefore the industry is highly dependent on the educational level in Israel. Yet Israel's educational system is in a state of crisis. Massive strikes by schoolteachers and university professors in 2007–08 demonstrated that educators are dissatisfied with their wages and working conditions, yet there was only a marginal improvement in these conditions after the prolonged strikes, largely because public opinion did not support the educators' struggle and the different labor unions failed to present a unified front (Wold, 2008; Zelinger, 2007).

Public investment in schoolchildren and in university students has fallen steadily since the 1970s, leading to the ongoing erosion of the public education systems and encouraging the development of a massive private education system, including "upgrades" to public schools in wealthier regions, and private colleges that charge high tuition fees (ICBS, 2007). While most developed countries have responded to the changes in the global economy with massive investments in education, Israel has not, and the gap in education levels between Israel and the OECD average is widening rapidly (Swirski, 2008a: 25–7). That is one of the reasons that Israeli academics are leaving Israel in large numbers, and the best students and scholars emigrate at a much higher rate than in other countries. Israeli economist Dan Ben-David found that there is a strong correlation between the number of years of study an Israeli accumulates and their chances of emigrating from Israel. He also found that the share of Israeli academics working outside Israel is comparable to those of Third World countries (Ben-David, 2008).

Israel's position in international exams has fallen dramatically over the years. In 1963–64 Israel had the highest grades in international math tests for 13-year-olds, but by 1999 Israel had the lowest such grade among all the industrialized states (Ben-David, 2002).

Another important trait of the Israeli educational system, and in fact one of the main reasons for its decline, is the deep levels of inequality embedded in it. In the same math tests mentioned above, Israel was ranked in the 50th place, out of 53 countries, in the level of equality of grades' distribution, making Israel one of the countries with the highest levels of inequality in its educational system (Ben-David, 2002). There is deeply entrenched discrimination in Israeli education, and non-Jewish schools suffer the highest levels of discrimination (Human Rights Watch, 2001). In several cases during Israel's early years, authorities even prevented certain Palestinian citizens from being accepted to academic institutions when they suspected them of harboring undesirable political beliefs (Cohen, 2006: 245).

This discrimination takes a plethora of forms – less budget per pupil, smaller and crowded classrooms, safety problems in the schools, fewer schooling hours, worse treatment of teachers, and insufficient supervision. Nowhere are the problems and inequalities of the Israeli educational system more apparent than in East Jerusalem, which has been neglected by the Israeli authorities and has entered a downward spiral of decline in quality and quantity of services (Hever, 2007b). In effect, the Israeli government has created parallel educational systems, providing high-quality education for certain small parts of society, and poor-quality education for all the other social classes in Israel. The high-quality education is available mostly in the upper-class communities largely populated by Jews of European descent, where parents are able to pay extra money for their children's schools.

One of the reasons for the inequality and decline in Israeli educational services is the low priority assigned to education in the Israeli political discourse, which places security and national pride at the top of its agenda. The educational system is used as a tool to spread Zionist beliefs, to prepare schoolchildren for military service, and to entrench a hierarchical structure that preserves the dominance of Jews and the Jewish state. Focus on skills, academic excellence, and critical thought takes a lower priority (Resnik, 1999; Spiegel, 2001: 2, 6, 8).

Despite these problems with its educational system, Israel has been able to develop a successful high-tech sector that contributes to exports. However, if the rapid deterioration of the Israeli educational system continues unchecked, the effects on the high-tech industries, on worker productivity and on other economic aspects will quickly be felt. The high reliance of Israel's leading industries on education means that the current educational policies and trends in quality and quantity of education spell a grim future for the Israeli economy (*Economist*, 2008).

THE ISRAELI POLITICAL CRISIS: CAUSE OR SYMPTOM?

One of the reasons cited by the *Economist* for the instability of the Israeli economic system is the instability of the country's political system. The report listed structural problems in the Israeli political system which create paralysis in government and pose problems with regard to effective representation (*Economist*, 2008). However, the report's analysis of the Israeli political system is very technical, and misses the idiosyncrasies of Israeli society. The paralysis in the political sphere should be seen as a symptom rather than the cause of the current crisis in Israel.

The crisis does not stem from the flawed planning of Israel's political system, but from the internal contradictions in the Zionist movement, which are pulling at the very seams of Israeli society. From its earliest days, the Zionist movement failed to come to grips with the fact that the land of Palestine was already inhabited, and that its population is not Jewish (Shlaim, 2000: 25–48). This has led Zionist leaders to pursue conflicting agendas and focus on short-term planning.

The Zionist movement aspires to be a democratic movement, even as it simultaneously engages in disenfranchising the indigenous population it hopes to displace (Gordon, 2008a). It aspires to maintain a Jewish majority, while at the same time nurturing aspirations of territorial expansion into areas that are populated by Arabs. It has striven to create a safe haven for Jews throughout the world (Yftachel, 2002), but has instead, through reliance on military strength as a substitute for diplomacy, created one of the most dangerous places for Jews to be in the world, and certainly a place where many Jewish citizens do not feel safe. The Palestinians' resistance to Israel's policies of ethnic domination have made even innocent and uninvolved Israeli citizens the occasional targets of terrorist acts. And Israeli institutions, as part of their strategy of gaining legitimacy with Israeli citizens, encourage the prevalent sense of insecurity and existential fear, because it helps in suppressing any opposition to non-democratic policies (Rose, 2005).

These contradictions have intensified in the course of Israel history. The occupation of 1967 gave impetus to the internal conflict between those concerned about security and maintaining a Jewish majority and those who aspire to the "liberation of the Promised Land." War-weariness has heightened the conflict between those who would like to enlist ultra-Orthodox Jews in the Israeli army in the name of sharing the burden and those who argue against it, contending that it might endanger the already fragile alliance between different Jewish groups. Globalization processes have created a contradiction between the desire to be part of the global community on the one hand, and the decision to keep defying international law and ignoring international pressure to end the occupation on the other hand. Finally, the neoliberal discourse has created a contradiction between the individualistic approach it promotes and the national solidarity and collective effort that the Zionist movement demands of its members (Shafir and Peled, 2002: 278, 307, 342).

For many Israelis, these contradictions have become very personal. If the Ministry of Finance calls on citizens to "fend for themselves" and take personal responsibility for their livelihood in the absence of welfare, why should they waste the best years of their lives in the Israeli army? Indeed, the number of young Israelis who enlist in the army is falling,[5] but data on conscription rates is kept confidential.

5 Conscription is obligatory in Israel for Jewish and Druze citizens, yet many young candidates for conscription find ways to avoid military service, including feigning medical or mental problems, or other problems that make a person "unfit" for duty in the eyes of the Israeli army. Women are

The *Economist* published the conscription rates for the 1980s, which pointed to a steady decline. There are many indications that the conscription rates continue to fall. The August 2007 draft was called the smallest draft "in many years" (Shenfeld, 2007). In 2009, the commander of the Israeli army department of manpower revealed that only 74.2 percent of Jewish men and 56 percent of Jewish women enlist every year. If that figure is adjusted for the entire population of Israeli (not only Jewish) citizens, it means that only about 49 percent of Israelis enlist. It is necessary also to factor in the number of non-Jews who enlist in the Israeli army. There are no published figures for the proportion of non-Jews who join the Israeli army, but it is widely known that only a very small minority do so. With a majority of Israelis no longer enlisting in the Israeli army, the willingness and motivation of other young Israelis who come of age to enlist is also falling (Pfeffer, 2009).

The contradictions rife in Israeli society are causing the growing alienation of the population from the political system, leading to a lower voting turnout. The elections of 2006 and 2009 had the lowest turnouts in Israel's history (Ynet, 2006). Furthermore, the ills of the political system are also apparent in the numerous corruption scandals that have surfaced over the past few years. Just in the years 2006–08, the Israeli president had to step down following accusations of rape, the minister of finance was accused of theft, and five separate investigations were launched on suspicions of corruption against the prime minister (Stahl, 2008) – and this is only a partial list. Meanwhile, the government has focused its efforts on firing whistle-blowers (Zino, 2007), attacking the legitimacy of the state comptroller (Bengal, 2007), and jeopardizing the independence of the court system (Persico, 2008), thereby undermining the institutions that exist to curb corruption.

NOT A DEMOCRACY

Its determination to maintain the occupation of the OPT, and to foster the notion of a "Jewish state" in the rest of the area controlled by Israel, has prompted the Israeli government to set aside civil liberties and the democratic process in order to keep pursuing projects of "national interest." The results of this process are part of the toll that the occupation and ethnic superiority policies exact from Israeli society.

---

allowed to claim exemption on the grounds of their religious beliefs.

Although Israel claims to be a Western-style democracy, it eschews many of the vital components that make up such a democracy. It has no constitution. It has a different set of rights for Jews and non-Jews. It exists in a constant "state of emergency," which allows the government to violate civil rights in the name of security. The military and the police hold prisoners without trial. Government agencies keep many secrets from the citizens and use violence to repress dissent and criticism. The Israeli military executes people without trial, and Israeli soldiers are very rarely tried for the deliberate killing of innocents (Maor, 2006).

However, the clearest evidence that Israel is not a democracy is the simple fact that not every adult under Israeli rule gets to vote. Israel exerts effective control, a monopoly on the legitimate use of violence (to borrow Max Weber's definition of a state) and even administrative authority over the West Bank and the Gaza Strip, where 3.8 million Palestinians are subject to Israeli rule, though they are not Israeli citizens and cannot vote in Israeli elections. The approximately 267,000 Palestinians living in East Jerusalem in 2008 were officially annexed by Israel in 1980, yet they still do not have the right to vote in Israeli elections (PCBS, 2005b).[6] Consequently, although Jews comprise only 49.74 percent of the total population under Israeli control, they have 75.57 percent of the votes to the Israeli parliament (ICBS, 2008a; PCBS, 2009a). This ensures that although Jews are now a numerical minority in the land controlled by Israeli authorities, the Zionist parties remain the only ones capable of forming majority coalitions in the Israeli parliament.

It could be argued that Palestinians are represented by the elected bodies of the Palestinian Authority, but what followed after the January 2006 elections to the Legislative Council disproves that claim. The Israeli government refused to acknowledge the results of those elections and acted to dislodge the democratically elected Hamas government in the West Bank, and placed the Gaza Strip under siege when it found itself unable to dislodge the Hamas leadership from there (BBC, 2006; B'tselem, 2007b).

Furthermore, the Palestinian Authority is not a sovereign government, and occupied Palestinian subjects in the OPT are still under the direct and indirect control of Israeli authorities. The latter continue to produce identity cards, movement permits, and magnetic cards for

---

6 This figure is an estimate based on the 2005 report by the Palestinian Central Bureau of Statistics, updated according to an estimated annual rate of growth of 3.617 percent, which is a continuation of the past growth rate.

Palestinians, to control their movement to and from the OPT, and to dominate their trade with other countries. And there are many other fields in which Israeli authorities have refused to relinquish power (Gordon, 2008b: 173–7).

At least until there is a truly sovereign Palestinian state where Palestinians enjoy self-determination, Israel cannot claim to be a democratic state.

DEMOGRAPHICS – THE SOCIOECONOMIC STANDING OF NON-JEWS

One of Israel's deepest contradictions deserves a special focus, and that is its attitude towards and relations with the non-Jewish citizens of the country.

Most of Israel's non-Jewish citizens are Palestinians, and they have been forced to live in a state that defines itself as the "state of the Jews," and allocates to them the status of second-class citizens. Non-Jews in Israel are at best tolerated by the authorities, and at worst suffer from the authorities' efforts to dislocate them from their lands. Such efforts include land confiscation, refusal to grant building permits, refusal to allow family reunification, the denial of access to certain communities and jobs, and discrimination in public services. Though they are usually better-off economically and have more rights than Palestinians in the OPT, they are far from equal citizens with full rights in Israel (Farah, 2006).

From the very founding of the state of Israel, massive land confiscation, which continues to this day (Falah, 2003), and the state's appropriation after 1948 of the properties left behind by the dislocated Palestinian refugees (Fischbach, 2003: 7–57) have formed part of the basis of Israel's wealth. Beyond the outright confiscation of land, the Israeli government and other institutions have implemented discriminatory policies to reallocate the public wealth away from the non-Jewish population, creating a deeply divided society. Some examples of this inequality are:

- The average wage of a Palestinian citizen in 2006 was 57.7 percent of the wage of a Jewish citizen (Swirski, Konor-Attias, and Abu-Khala, 2008: 15).
- Unemployment among Palestinian citizens in 2006 was 18.56 percent higher than among Jews (Sikkui, 2007: 54).
- The poverty rate among Jews was 15.2 percent in the first half of 2007, compared with 54.8 percent among non-Jews (NII, 2008).

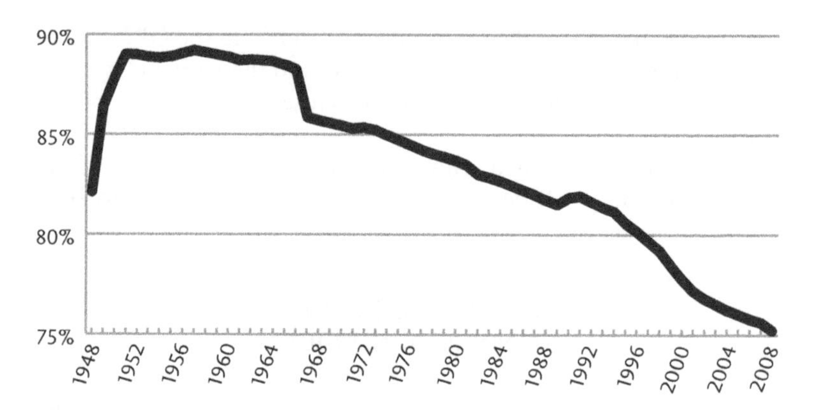

Figure 5.4 Proportion of Jews among Israeli citizens

Sources: ICBS (2008a), PCBS (2009a).

The low productivity and low job participation among Palestinian citizens is a ball and chain shackling the legs of the Israeli economy, with a large part of the population unable to achieve its potential. This phenomenon has already been acknowledged by senior Israeli economists, such as the chairman of the Central Bank of Israel in a lecture delivered in November, 2007 (Fischer, 2007).

Despite the efforts by Israeli agencies to encourage Jewish immigration to Israel and curb the expansion of the Palestinian population, these discriminatory policies have ultimately failed and the proportion of Jews in the Jewish state is declining steadily, even when considering only citizens of Israel, as shown in Figure 5.4. One reason for this, as mentioned in the *Economist*, is that "many Jews from the diaspora already view Israel as spiritually impoverished and uninviting" (*Economist*, 2008).

What the expansion of the non-Jewish population in Israel under the current regime means is an expansion of the underprivileged social groups in Israel, and inevitably the expansion of poverty as well. The *Economist*'s report (2008) pointed out that the continued discrimination against a growing part of the Israeli population is one the main threats to the future prospects of Israel as a stable and prosperous country.

Furthermore, the non-Jewish citizens of Israel, especially the Palestinians among them, are not content to remain second-class citizens. Although the Israeli authorities have tried to sow division among these groups, to reward individuals who demonstrate loyalty to Israel and to partially compensate households whose lands have been confiscated, these rewards have been far from sufficient to overcome the discrimination levels, and many of the supporters of the Zionist leadership of Israel among the non-Jewish Israeli population have become disappointed and disillusioned (Cohen, 2006: 23–54).

Over the years, resentment has grown among these repressed groups, who have gradually become more articulate in their demands for emancipation, economic equality, and cultural autonomy (Rabinovitch and Abu-Baker, 2002). In recent years, the Palestinian citizens of Israel have launched a series of campaigns demanding the alteration of Israel's very nature as a Jewish state and their own equal place within that state. Prominent among these efforts were *The Future Vision of the Palestinian Arabs in Israel* (National Committee for the Heads of the Arab Local Authorities in Israel, 2006), *The Democratic Constitution* proposal by Adalah (2007), and *The Haifa Declaration* (Mada Al-Carmel, 2007).

These statements and declarations have come in response to the fact that the Israeli leadership continues to ignore the rights and the political voice of non-Jewish citizens. After decades of being repressed and ignored, many Palestinians are ready to struggle for their rights in new ways, in open defiance of Israel's regime. Over 800 Palestinian citizen demonstrators were arrested by the Israeli police during the Israeli attack on the Gaza Strip in December 2008 and January 2009, many of them being held in jail for over two months. In January 2009 the Israeli parliament also disqualified two political parties representing Palestinians from running for election, a decision that was later overruled by the Israeli High Court. These are indications that the Israeli authorities feel threatened by the Palestinian political struggle within Israel (Weill and Azarov, 2009).

This challenge to Israel's political regime also has implications for Israel's prospects of economic growth, as the *Economist* noted (2008), because Israel's integration into the global economy hinges on its image as a Western democracy, and that image is marred by the suppression of minority rights.

THE TRUE FACE OF THE LABOR MARKET

It is indeed true that Israel's official unemployment rate has dropped significantly from the peak it reached in 2003 to "only" 6.3 percent in the first quarter of 2008. Yet this is still far from the 3.6 percent unemployment rate the country had from 1961 to 1965 (ICBS, 1966).

Furthermore, this figure is the official unemployment rate, calculated according to an ICBS survey in which participants were asked whether they were actively seeking work. The actual questions, the duration of the search, and other factors have changed over time. Two changes in the ICBS methodology of measuring unemployment, in the years 1978 and 1985 respectively, have each reduced the official unemployment figures, and consequently these by no means indicate a true increase in employment (ICBS, various years).

According to the *Manpower Surveys* published by the Israeli Central Bureau of Statistics, the average weekly hours of employment per worker dropped from 37 in 2003 (the peak of Israel's unemployment) to 35.9 in 2006. Accounting for the increase in the labor force, but also for the increase in the total population, the result is that the average Israeli worked 1 percent fewer hours in 2006 than in 2003 (including people not in the workforce). That means that although official unemployment has dropped, the actual amount of work performed by the average Israeli has fallen, and therefore unofficial unemployment has, if anything, increased (ICBS, 2008a).

The fact that the average working week of an Israeli has become shorter is a good thing on the surface, because more leisure is certainly the preferred way to reduce unemployment. However, this holds true if the leisure is dispersed in a more or less equal manner. In Israel, however, many workers continue to work long hours in a constant struggle to make ends meet, while many others are unable to find a full-time job or even a part-time job that meets their needs, and work for only a few hours each month. Underemployment is not registered by the Israeli employment offices, and people are considered to be employed even if they only work for a few hours a month (Ben-Shakhar, Schuldineger, and Toker-Maimon, 2006: 6–10).

From 2000 to 2003, years of high unemployment, the government decided to revoke the unemployment status of many unemployed people and classify them as "job refuseniks." It accomplished this by restricting the rights of unemployed people and forcing them to accept any job offered to them, even one that makes them leave their children unsupervised or requires hours of travel to and from the workplace. Anyone who refuses even a single job offer is branded a "job refusenik" and loses their benefits. The social benefits to unemployed people have also worsened since the 1990s (Frenkel, 2001: 3–8). As a result, there has been a sharp increase in the number of income support[7] recipients. People whose unemployment benefits

7 Income support is Israel's most basic form of welfare, which is given to households that have no other income, or to households that do not meet a certain minimum income level.

were revoked have been forced to subsist on income support instead, a much lower stipend than before (NII, various years).

Furthermore, in 2005 Israel implemented a "welfare to work" program (first called *Mehalev* and later *Orot Letaasuka*,[8] and inspired by the Wisconsin Program that was implemented in parts of the United States), which came under widespread criticism for its failure to reduce poverty and for encouraging corruption. The program is intended to force recipients of income support to participate in workshops, to remain under continued supervision, to do "volunteer" community service without pay, and to agree to the first job that they are offered. Program participants who were classified as "uncooperative" had their income support benefits revoked. The program was started in four cities and has expanded continuously since its inception. Palestinian citizens and East Jerusalem Palestinian residents have been included in the program in especially large numbers (Adut and Hever, 2006).

It is therefore not surprising that many Israelis of the lower socio-economic classes have had no choice but to agree to low-paying jobs with fewer hours just to survive. The Commitment organization has argued that if those who had given up looking for a job, and those who had insufficient employment and were seeking more hours of work, had been included in the unemployment figures, the unemployment rate for 2006 would have been 14.7 percent rather than 8.4 percent. That means that the unofficial unemployment in Israel is 43 percent of the actual unemployment, and that the official figures grossly underestimate unemployment levels (Ben-Shakhar et al., 2006: 6–10).

ISRAEL'S FOREIGN TRADE BALANCE

As mentioned above, Israel's trade deficit has shrunk considerably in recent years. Part of the boom in Israel's exports has to do with the export of military technology and surveillance technology and equipment (Klein, 2007b: 423–42). Israel markets itself as a country that maintains a high level of security for its citizens despite the constant state of conflict in which it is embroiled – a kind of "fortress" state. Israeli companies (some of them state-owned) use this image to market Israeli-made security systems in the world (Klein, 2007a). Indeed, in 2006 Sibat, Israel's office for military exports, reported the highest demand

8 The Hebrew meanings of the names are "From the Heart" (*Mehalev*) and "Lights for Employment" (*Orot Letaasuka*).

for Israeli military exports in history – a record sum of US$4.4 billion (Koren, 2007). But Israel's military exports depend on Israel's image as a secure country surrounded by enemies. The question that remains, then, is whether Israel can keep up this image for much longer.

Israel's reduced trade deficit, plus the sustained aid from the United States, compensations from Germany, and donations by Jewish communities around the world, have led to a growth in the foreign currency reserves of the Central Bank of Israel (see Figure 5.2). Since the 1990s, aid to the Palestinians has also boosted Israel's foreign currency reserves (see Chapter 2). This money represents the greater purchasing power of Israelis in the world. However, imports have also increased significantly (see Figure 5.1). As a result of these two trends, Israel has become increasingly dependent on foreign trade.

Figure 5.5 demonstrates that the ratio between the foreign currency reserves of the Central Bank of Israel and imports to Israel reached a peak in 2003, but has been dropping ever since. The first rapid increase in Israel's reserves came following the US loan guarantees of 1996. Even the bursting of the dot-com bubble in 2000 did not stop the accumulation of foreign currency, mainly because of the increase in aid that came in the wake of the second intifada. But as the intifada began to take its toll on the Israeli economy, the ratio between Israel's foreign currency reserves and its imports began to deteriorate. While Israel's trade with the rest of the world kept increasing, accounting for the higher imports, the inflows of foreign capital could not keep up.

That puts the Israeli economy in a more vulnerable position, where international sanctions, boycotts, or other obstacles to trade could have a profound impact on it. In 2003, in the hypothetical scenario that its exports dropped to zero, Israel would have been able to keep importing for 208 days until running out of foreign currency. In 2006

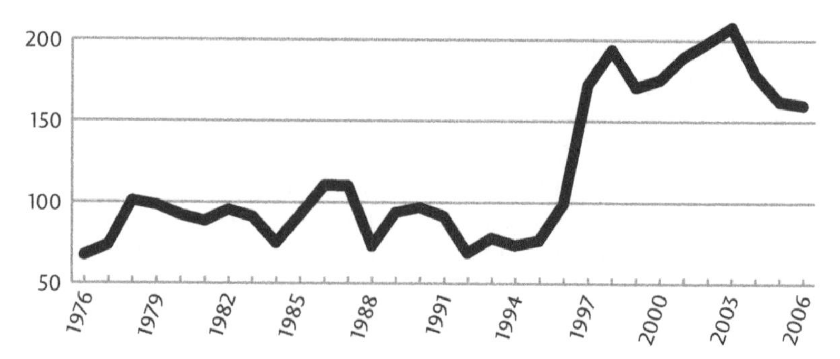

Figure 5.5 CBI reserves in days of imports

Sources: ICBS (2008a), CBI (2008b).

that number dropped to 160 days, a 23.1 percent decrease. Although Israeli exports are unlikely to come to such an abrupt halt, this hypothetical scenario merely serves to emphasize that the Israeli economy is more vulnerable than before to changes in its foreign trade status.

Merrill Lynch has warned that because the Israeli economy is highly tied to the United States,[9] the recent decline of the US economy has created new threats to the Israeli economy. It emphasized Israel's vulnerability to trends in global markets, and the leverage that various countries can apply to Israel through economic sanctions (Tobias, 2008). Furthermore, the drop in tourism to Israel between 1995 and 2005, from 2.5 million tourists to 1.9 million, demonstrates that Israel's image as a successful fortress state is not convincing enough to keep tourists coming and bringing foreign currency into the Israeli market (Swirski, 2008a: 9).

The threat of boycott, divestments, and sanctions against Israel is indeed gaining impetus. The calls for a boycott have been multiplying among Palestinian organizations (Badil, 2005) and Palestinian solidarity organizations.[10] Also, more questions are being raised over the legality of cooperation with Israel and Israeli companies in projects that perpetuate the occupation or develop the illegal settlements in the West Bank. These include:

- the decision by the International Court of Justice that the Wall of Separation violates international law
- the decision by the United Nations to create a register for the damage caused by the Wall
- several legal proceedings against Israeli officers suspected of committing war crimes
- legal struggles against companies that trade in settlement products or build in the settlements.

Not only is the list too long to be included here, it would quickly become outdated as new cases are regularly being brought against Israel and companies that provide illegal services to it. *Al Majdal* magazine surveyed boycott campaigns that took place in 17 different countries in 2008, and even that is only a sampling of the campaigns around the world (Badil, 2008).

---

9 It reports that about a third of Israel's GDP is tied to the United States, and 35–40 percent of Israeli exports go to the United States.

10 See for example the Global BDS Movement website of the Boycott, Divestment and Sanctions Campaign National Committee: <http://www.bdsmovement.net/>.

Moreover, it is not only for moral reasons that internationals boycott Israel. Companies that care only about their profits also have reason to be concerned about dealing with Israel, because Israel's illegal occupation of the OPT might have repercussions on third parties as well. Companies that trade with Israel could be subjected to a consumer boycott, or find themselves facing trial for collaboration with war crimes. As the political and economic pressure on Israel mounts, companies could also be hurt financially by the inability of Israeli companies and the Israeli government to pay their debts. This could become a real possibility if Israel is ever forced to pay compensation to Palestinians who have been hurt by the occupation. The Adva Center has argued in consequence that the occupation is the main reason for Israel's low credit rating, compared with other countries with similar levels of per capita GDP (Swirski, 2008a: 12).

Since the 1990s, Israeli companies have been shifting many of their investments overseas, taking advantage of Israel's tax laws and easily corruptible officials, but doing business all over the world (Dayan, 2008; Spivak, 2008a). Part of the reason for the shrinking of Israel's trade deficit is the fact that Israeli companies prefer to invest money abroad, where business enjoys a more stable and secure atmosphere (Swirski, 2008a: 13). These companies could easily move their headquarters overseas, bringing about a rapid capital drain on the Israeli economy – something that could quickly negate all of the Israeli economy's achievements mentioned at the top of this chapter.

ISRAELI ECONOMIC DISCOURSE OF BLISS

During the 1990s many Israeli economists argued fervently that Israel's military conflict with its neighbors and with the occupied Palestinians was bringing down the Israeli economy. Economists were worried about the vast sums of money that were going into the defense budget and illegal-settlement construction. They were concerned about Israel's image in the eyes of the world community, and the lost potential for trade within the Middle East. Economists argued that peace is not merely a goal in itself but also a source of economic prosperity in the form of "peace dividends." These voices grew louder when the second intifada struck, as economists realized that the conflict had plunged the Israeli economy into recession (Hever, 2006c).

In the wake of the second intifada, however, the Israeli economy quickly began to change. As described in greater detail above, the neoliberal reforms that were implemented during the crisis have made Israel a more convenient place for the wealthy to do business, sparking an increase in the growth rate of the Israeli economy. While the government has granted billions of NIS to factory owners (Maoz, 2008), at the same time it has introduced massive cuts in welfare, which have helped to conceal the true levels of unemployment. This has encouraged foreign investors to pour money into the Israeli market, which explains at least part of the high growth rate that the Israeli economy enjoyed from 2004 to 2008.

The new economic situation led to an abrupt change in the rhetoric of Israeli economists. The "peace dividends" discourse was discarded and replaced by a different notion – that the conflict's effect on the Israeli economy is insignificant (for example, see Sharabi, 2002; Myre, 2006). The new discourse argues that the Palestinians do not matter that much, and that the "right" policies by the government (that is, neoliberal policies) can lead to prosperity regardless of anything else (Landau, 2008). Ezra Sadan, a former CEO in the Israeli Ministry of Finance, has argued that Israel's prosperity owes much to the peace treaty with Egypt from 1979, but that the continuing conflict with the Palestinians has had negligible effects on the Israeli economy (Sadan, 2004). Consequently, Israeli economists have adopted an extremely optimistic approach to the Israeli economy, repeatedly arguing that it is in the best condition it has ever been in Israel's history (see for example Landau, 2008).

In March 2008, the Tami Steinmetz Center for Peace Research held a conference on the effects of Israel's 41-year occupation of the OPT on Israeli society. The conference had one economic panel to deal with the economic effects of the occupation on Israel, and all the panelists agreed that they were negligible. They brushed aside the fact that the OPT is Israel's second-biggest export market, arguing that since the OPT's GDP is so small, it cannot have a large effect on Israeli GDP. By virtue of this position, the economic panel in the conference stood out – as experts on every other aspect of contemporary Israeli society (media, culture, social solidarity) argued that the occupation is one of its defining features.[11]

The responses in the Israeli media to the report by the *Economist* were a good example of this approach by economists. Despite the fact that seven of the report's 14 pages were dedicated to issues relating to the occupation, the treatment of minorities, and military matters,

11 The conference took place on March 31, 2008, at Tel-Aviv University. The economists participating in the debate were Dan Ben-David, Ezra Sadan, and Efraim Kleinman.

these issues were not reflected in the responses and criticism of the report by Israeli economists and journalists. The economic newspapers *TheMarker* and *Kalkalist* argued that the main reason cited by the *Economist* for the woes of the Israeli economy was the political system (Rollnick, 2008; TheMarker, 2008; Taig, 2008). *Globes Magazine* argued that the reason cited by the *Economist* was the vestiges of socialist systems in the Israeli economic system (Avigad and Kol, 2008). *Ha'aretz* argued that the main reason cited by the *Economist* was the crisis in the educational system (Ha'aretz, 2008). Economist Avia Spivak argued that Israel's dire situation is a result of the government's diminishing role in directing the economy (Spivak, 2008b). *Ynet* magazine published an article forcefully rejecting the entire report (Plotsker, 2008).

This is just a sampling of the many articles that responded to the report by the *Economist*. The interesting feature is the unspoken agreement among nearly all the respondents to leave out of the debate the most burning political issues raised in the report – the occupation, the Palestinians' right of return, Israel's Jewish nature – to simply skip over them as if they were not there.

To ignore the essential problems and internal contradictions that plague the Israeli political and economic systems is a fateful choice, since the issues that are being ignored are not likely to disappear on their own. More than any economic indicator (inequality, deterioration of public services, and so on) – the absence of an internal discourse to address the threats to the Israeli economy is perhaps the biggest threat of all. It leaves Israelis unequipped and unprepared to deal with the inevitable consequences of the colonial project which continues to be cultivated in their backyard, with their consent.

CONCLUSION

The Israeli economy is definitely less stable and prosperous than the mainstream macroeconomic indicators would appear to suggest. Moreover, Israel also lacks the mechanisms to correct these problems. Social solidarity is very weak in a country where national and ethnic distinctions are more important than class identity.

A major reason for the paralysis in Israeli institutions is that "security" issues always override the need for social change, and neoliberal officials have almost unlimited power when it comes to implementing economic policy. These officials maintain that the Israeli economy is a success story because that argument justifies their own policies in hindsight, and because wealth continues to accumulate in the hands of a few powerful financiers. Economic elites in Israel have an incentive to keep the existing system in place.

The general Israeli public prefer not to inform themselves about the minutiae of the occupation. Israelis spend their daily lives concerned with other things, and they rarely see the impact of the occupation on their daily lives. They do not realize how ever-present the occupation is in the lives of Palestinians, and the Israeli authorities and mainstream media help the public stay willfully ignorant by releasing only sporadic and incomplete information about the OPT (Azoulay and Ophir, 2008: 24–7).

Furthermore, there are those who profit from the current state of affairs. The neoliberal policies of the Israeli government enable large companies to extract high profits with minimal regulation and taxes, and to buy government assets cheaply while the government is engaged in a rush to privatization (Morav, 2008). Those who profit from the Israeli crisis have no incentive to help in resolving it. On the contrary, they have every reason to press the government to keep up its current policies. The occupation, the conflict, and the "war against terror" have all helped to obfuscate the redistribution of wealth that has been picking up pace, leading to a less equal society, and to disarm the social resistance to this redistribution.

Due to backing from the United States and certain European countries, Israel's international standing has allowed it to pursue policies that would not be legitimate if implemented by other countries, including extrajudicial killings, collective punishment, intentional pauperization, the near-starvation of large civilian populations, and many other actions that violate international law. However, international support for Israel is not a bottomless pit, and if Israel's international standing gradually weakens, it could alter Israel's place in the global economy (Swirski, 2008a: 32).

As the quality of social services to Israeli citizens continues to deteriorate, and the crisis in the educational system worsens, the Israeli economy's prospects increasingly hinge on Israel's distinctive feature as a relatively secure country, despite the fact that it is in a constant state of conflict. In other words, only if the Israeli military forces can keep Hezbollah, Hamas, Iran, and others under control can it continue to pretend that conflict does not affect its economy.

As Israelis' motivation to risk life and limb in military service drops, as social solidarity crumbles, as more Israelis hope to leave the country, and as Israel's chief ally (the United States) fumbles in Iraq, the prospects for future Israeli victories in the region seem slim.

The emphasis on short-term security solutions, says the *Economist* (2008), is hurting the security of Israelis in the long run.

It is important to emphasize that military failure for Israel does not only concern the personal security of Israelis. It also has grave implications for the prestige of the Israeli military industry, the willingness of the United States to keep arming Israel to serve as its proxy in Middle East wars (Keinon, 2006), the willingness of tourists to visit Israel, and the willingness of educated and talented Israelis to stay in Israel when other countries offer better living conditions, better career opportunities, and more personal safety.

6

CASE STUDY: THE WALL IN JERUSALEM

INTRODUCTION

The mechanisms of the occupation itself have been transformed radically over the years. Although the Israeli authorities have continued to exercise control over the OPT, the means for doing so have changed. The way that control is exercised has defined the economic relations between Israel and the OPT over the years.

The Wall of Separation is the most prominent symbol of the decision by Israel's government to enforce separation between the Israeli and Palestinian populations. Yair Golan, the commander of Israel's forces in the West Bank, has said that the Wall is not the best or cheapest solution to provide security for Israelis, but it was chosen because it prevents the people from intermingling.[1] As a result of the Wall's construction, Palestinian merchants and workers find access to the Israeli market extremely difficult, and there are insufficient alternatives for employment and trade in the areas enclosed by the Wall.

Israel's change of policy was spurred by a combination of factors:

- The cost of maintaining military control over the OPT is mounting every year, at an average rate of about 6 percent annually (see Chapter 4), and requires an increasing investment of labor. The Wall is designed to help keep the Palestinians out with fewer checkpoints and patrols, thus lowering the cost of maintaining control.
- The Zionist ideology of Israel's political elite envisions a Jewish

1 In a lecture at the Van Leer Institute in Jerusalem, April 20, 2007.

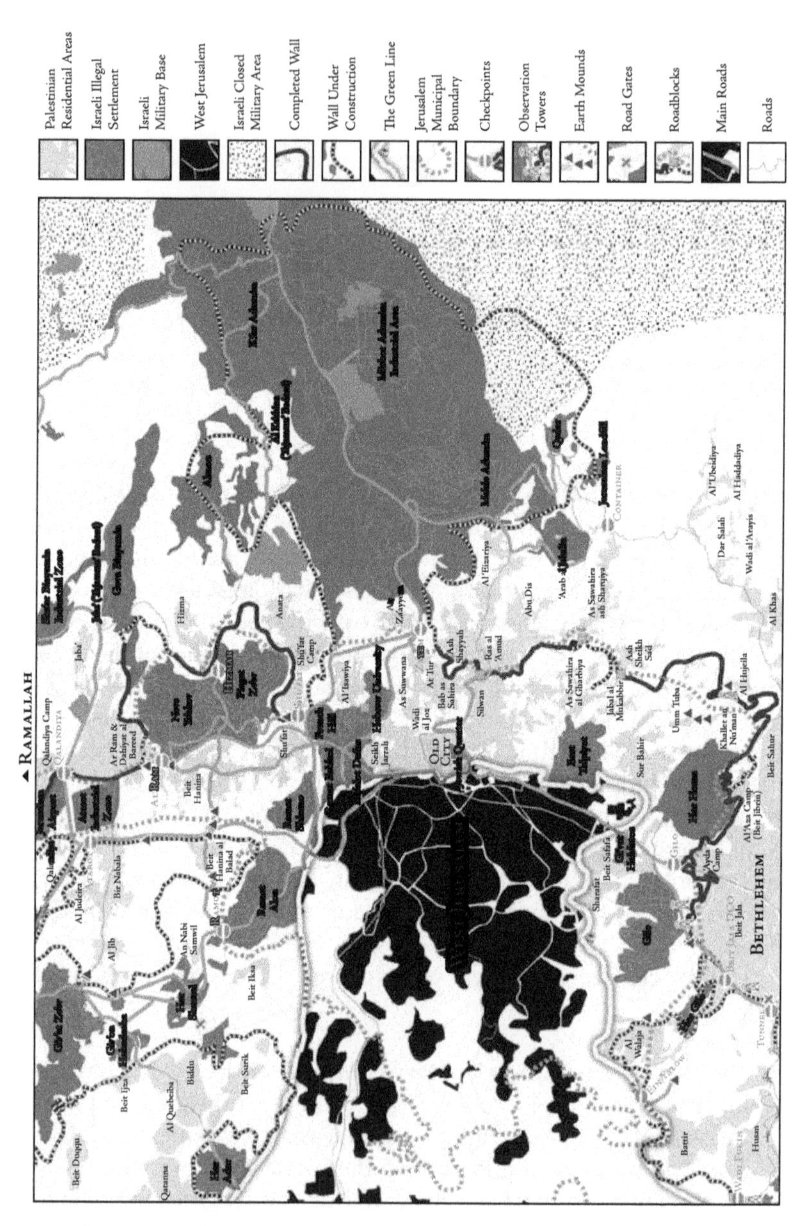

Map 6.1 The Separation Wall in Jerusalem

Many thanks to OCHA and the Alternative Information Center for permission to use this map, and to Tal Hever for editing it to suit the needs of this study.

state with a Jewish majority. Contact between Jews and Palestinians leads to business transactions, friendships, and even intermarriage, which in turns leads to cultural diversity, which is unacceptable to the Israeli leadership.
- The global support for the Oslo peace negotiations has convinced large segments of the Israeli public that Israel may be forced to withdraw from some of the areas occupied in 1967. The Wall is therefore a fait accompli, creating a new reality on the ground which could later be converted into an international border, despite the fact that the Wall is being built east of the Green Line, which is Israel's internationally recognized border.

Although the Wall is being built throughout the West Bank, the focus here is on that section of it which runs through Jerusalem. Jerusalem is but one city, but for many significant reasons it occupies a central position in the Israeli–Palestinian conflict. It is a mixed city, and the lives of its inhabitants are marked by discrimination and violence on a daily basis. Both Israelis and Palestinians want Jerusalem to be their capital, and the city's plenitude of holy sites – venerated by the three major monotheistic religions (Christianity, Islam, and Judaism) – has contributed to making its politics extremely volatile.

The Wall of Separation is continuing to be built across the entire West Bank and will ultimately extend for over 703 km. Only about 90 km of it run through Jerusalem, and yet the Wall in Jerusalem is especially important and deserves special attention. In Jerusalem, the Wall cuts deep into a developed urban area, thus affecting the daily lives of schoolchildren, workers, families, and entire communities. Studies published in 2006 found that the Wall adversely impacts 875,000 Palestinians, comprising 38 percent of the West Bank's population at the time. Of that population, over a quarter lives in the Jerusalem area (Müller, 2004: 22–3, 53–64; UN OCHA, 2006: 3).

A book written by Israel Kimhi for the Jerusalem Institute for Israel Studies in 2006, *The Security Fence in Jerusalem: Its impact on the city residents* (Kimhi, 2006), revealed detailed statistical findings about the impact of the Wall of Separation on the lives of Palestinians in Jerusalem and its vicinity for the first time. Although the raw data and analysis presented in the book is very important, the text seems to rely heavily on the popular assumptions of Israeli Zionist public opinion. These assumptions – namely, the requirement to maintain a Jewish majority and the permanence of the annexation of East Jerusalem – are not recognized by the Palestinian population or by the international community. Still, the information and analysis are both accurate and thought-provoking, and could establish the foundation for a new debate on the future of Jerusalem. This highly useful source will therefore figure prominently in this chapter.

The United Nations has already recognized the right of Palestinians to receive compensation for the damages caused by the Wall of Separation; in December 2006 it decided to establish a register of damage arising from the Wall. This chapter is intended to showcase some of that damage (UN General Assembly, 2006).

EAST JERUSALEM BEFORE THE WALL

During the 1967 war Israel occupied the entire West Bank, among other areas. Most of the territory remained under military administration, except for 70 sq. km, or 12 percent of the West Bank, which was annexed directly to Israel. This area includes the 6 sq. km of the former Jordanian municipality of East Jerusalem. The area was henceforth regarded as part of Israel, and added to the jurisdiction of the Israeli municipality of West Jerusalem. Israel has regarded East Jerusalem as part of the country for all administrative purposes, although the international community has never recognized the annexation, and equal Israeli citizenship has never been granted to the residents of East Jerusalem (UN General Assembly, 2006). In 1967, many Israeli policymakers believed that Israel would soon withdraw from the occupied territories in exchange for a peace treaty with the neighboring Arab states. However, almost all policymakers also believed that East Jerusalem merited a different approach and had to be occupied permanently (Gazit, 1985: 222–31).

The Palestinian population of East Jerusalem refused to accept the Israeli occupation. They have consistently refused offers of Israeli citizenship or enrolment in the Israeli educational system. In July 1967, a group of 20 prominent Palestinians headed by Anwar Al-Hatib – the governor of the East Jerusalem governorate before the occupation – signed a petition protesting the annexation of Jerusalem and instructing Israel not to interfere in religious matters in the West Bank for the duration of the occupation. Israel responded by sending four of the signatories into exile (Gazit, 1985: 276–8). The Israeli government continued to suppress the population's attempts to shake off Israeli control by various means (Amirav, 2007: 268).

Eventually, Jerusalem played a key role in strengthening the ties between the occupied territories and Israel. West Jerusalem was strongly attached to the Israeli economy and East Jerusalem likewise to the Palestinian cities of Bethlehem, Ramallah, Jericho, and beyond. When East and West Jerusalem were joined, economic ties between the OPT and Israel became much stronger as a result. Jerusalem became a gateway through which Palestinians from the West Bank could enter Israel almost freely (Gazit, 1985: 206–15). This situation persisted until the checkpoint regime of the 1990s disrupted that free movement.

Israeli public discourse at the time coined such phrases as "the eternal capital of Israel" and "one unified Jerusalem," which now form the rhetorical backbone of the annexation policy. These catchphrases are repeated ad infinitum by countless politicians and parties, besides being regularly cited at national events and in official publications. Despite the objection of the international community, Israel maintains that Jerusalem has been united permanently, and that both sides of the city are the capital of the Jewish state. Israel has therefore refused to accept the Palestinian demand that East Jerusalem should become the capital of the future Palestinian state, a point of disagreement which has served as an excuse for Israeli politicians to avoid negotiations with the Palestinians.

However frequently this "unification" of Jerusalem may be declared, though, it cannot change the demographic reality of the city. Jewish and Palestinian neighborhoods feature visibly distinct socioeconomic conditions. Jewish Israelis even avoid entering much of East Jerusalem, and many areas are frequented almost exclusively by Palestinians. The commercial areas, which were frequented by Israelis before the intifadas, have now also been largely abandoned by Israelis (Garb, 2005: 2).

To minimize confusion, the term IWA (Inside Wall Area) will be used to refer to those parts of Jerusalem surrounded by the Wall of Separation, and the term OWA (Ouside Wall Area) to refer to those parts of Jerusalem left outside the Wall. It is important to remember that while the entire OWA lies in the OPT, the IWA is divided between Jerusalem, which is legally Israeli, and lands that were illegally annexed to Israel in 1967 (United Nations, 1967).

Jerusalem is a city completely under Israeli control, but that does not mean that it is an "Israeli" city. According to Israel's identity card system, there are four different "types" of citizen in Jerusalem, all of which are distinguished by carrying one of four different identity cards.

Jewish Israelis

The most privileged (though not the most homogenous) group in Israeli society are the Israeli Jews, who enjoy the highest level of civil rights and who hold most of the political and economic power in Israeli society, specifically in Jerusalem. This is reflected in income distribution, positions of authority, and treatment by the Israeli court system.[2] They carry blue identity cards. Jews from all over the world can easily obtain Israeli citizenship.

The city of Jerusalem has expanded rapidly, with numerous Jewish suburban neighborhoods (built on occupied land) encircling the Palestinian areas. There are 200,000 Jewish settlers in East Jerusalem (Hoshen, 2005).

Palestinian citizens of Israel

About 20 percent of all Israeli citizens are Palestinians. These are Palestinians who remained in Israel's territory after the 1948 ethnic cleansing. Palestinian citizens of Israel are officially full citizens and share the same rights as Jewish citizens. In reality, however, they are discriminated against in politics and in the allocation of national resources. As a result, Palestinian citizens of Israel suffer from higher poverty rates than the rest of the population, and are at the same time under-represented in official positions (Khaider, 2005: 43–52). In Jerusalem, there are comparatively few Palestinians with Israeli citizenship, as most "Palestinian Israelis" are resident in areas that became part of the state of Israel in 1948. Palestinian Israelis live mostly in the northern parts of Israel, in the southern deserts, and in mixed cities such as Haifa, Jaffa, Lod, and Ramle. Only a few thousand live beyond the 1967 borders.

Formally, all Israeli citizens are supposed to have full social and political rights. In practice, Palestinian citizens ("48 Palestinians") are subjected to systemic discrimination, under-development and political oppression.

Jerusalem residents

Residents of East Jerusalem held Jordanian citizenship until 1967. After the occupation and annexation of the area, they received

2 For further information about the multitude of mechanisms that discriminate in favor of Jewish Israeli citizens in Israel, see the Mossawa Center: <http://www.mossawacenter.org>, and the Sikkuy center: <http://www.sikkuy.org.il/english/home.html>.

permanent Israeli residency which, crucially, is not full citizenship. These Palestinians are not allowed to vote or be elected to the Israeli parliament, and their children do not become citizens of Israel. As a result, they do not hold the citizenship of any country. However, they do receive social benefits like full Israeli citizens, although these benefits are often of a lower quality, and they carry blue identity cards.

Permanent residents comprise more than 90 percent of the Palestinian residents of Jerusalem, and about a third of all Jerusalem residents.

Although these individuals are unable to elect and be elected to the Israeli parliament, they have the right to vote for the municipality. Formally, they have full social rights which, in practice, are mostly embodied in social security benefits and public health insurance. Jerusalem Palestinians are subjected to deep systemic discrimination and political oppression of their Palestinian identity.

A harsh "demographic policy" aims at "Judifying" the city, and pushing Palestinian residents out. This is mainly achieved by the construction of new Jewish settlements and by bureaucratic policies intended to reduce the number of Palestinian residents of the city and its surroundings (Amirav, 2007: 191–214).

The isolation of many Palestinian residents in the OWA created by the Wall has been followed by the suspicion that the next move could be the loss of their residency status. This in fact would mean the cancellation of all social entitlements and the prevention of entry into Jerusalem and Israel.

This group has already faced a long-running Israeli policy aimed at canceling their status using a bureaucratic criterion: the common argument was that the person had moved their "center of life" to a foreign land and therefore could no longer be considered a resident of Israeli territory. Individual Jerusalemites who are now living on "the wrong side" of the Wall expect an increased chance that their status will be revoked, meaning that they will lose all social rights that come with it, and be prevented from entering Jerusalem and Israel.

Green ID and Orange ID card Palestinians

Palestinians who live in the OPT areas that were not annexed to Israel did not receive Israeli residency status. They remain subjects of the Israeli government, and under the administration of the Palestinian Authority, to this day. These Palestinians have no rights in Israel, although they often seek employment in Israeli cities and settlements. Many of the residents of outlying communities around Jerusalem carry green or orange ID cards, indicating that they are not citizens of Israel. If caught on "Israeli soil," including annexed East Jerusalem (which in reality can mean the street where they live), their presence there is considered illegal and they are likely to be arrested or deported.

OPT Palestinians lived under "civil administration" of the military government. After the formation of the Palestinian Authority, the Jerusalem outskirts became a complex mosaic of regions A, B, and C, separated by numerous roadblocks. Freedom of movement is still determined by the permanent regime of the civil administration.

The annexation, political oppression, curfews, permits policy, and roadblocks on the main highways between the Palestinian cities, have all created a disparity between Jerusalem, its Palestinian residents, and their compatriots in the OPT and in the city's outskirts. The difficulties that people face in meeting each other jeopardize their ability to maintain family, business, and other relations.

The Israeli long-term policy has aimed at erecting barriers against the residency of OPT Palestinians in the Jerusalem area. Lately, the legal prevention of the possibility of "Family Unification" (Warschawski, 2008b) was introduced in order to stop OPT spouses from becoming Israeli residents, even if their partners already enjoy that status.[3]

The reverse magnet

Before the construction of the Wall of Separation, Israel was already making constant efforts to establish a "reverse magnet" for Palestinians with Israeli residency in East Jerusalem. This was achieved through a combination of providing incentives to those who wished to leave and placing numerous obstacles in the way of Palestinians who wished to remain in Jerusalem (Kimhi, 2006: 139–43).

According to the Palestinian Central Bureau of Statistics (PCBS), Palestinians in the Jerusalem metropolitan area are divided in two along the annexation line, without any regard for the actual identification papers that they carry. The Palestinian population in the "Jerusalem governorate"[4] was estimated to be 267,000 in the annexed

3 Family members who used to be OPT residents might face further persecution. Wives who request a residency change must be over 25 and husbands must be over 35 years old, ages beyond the common marriage age among Palestinians.

4 The "Jerusalem governorate" is defined by the Palestinian Authority as the area of Jerusalem that is within the West Bank. To gauge the rate of

area in 2009, and another 167,000 in the outlying communities that were not annexed to Israel. The Wall leaves about 178,000 of these Palestinians in the IWA, and 256,000 in the OWA. By comparison, the entirety of the Wall in the rest of the West Bank leaves 67,000 Palestinians in the areas between the Wall and the Green Line, outside Israel's legitimate borders but under its control (UN OCHA, 2006: 1).

THE WALL'S HISTORY

The idea of building a wall in the West Bank to separate Israelis from Palestinians was first proposed by Israeli prime minister Yitzhak Rabin in 1992 (Dickey and Dennis, 1995). On July 18, 2001, the Israeli cabinet approved a plan to construct a "separation barrier" between Israel and the West Bank, after being urged to make a quick decision following a suicide bombing at a nightclub on the Tel-Aviv promenade on July 2 which claimed 22 victims. The bombing created the political impetus for the Israeli Knesset to move forward with the idea. However, numerous political and human-rights organizations have criticized the Wall and argued that it is a one-sided attempt to earmark Israel's future borders, ensuring that as much land – and as many settlements – as possible falls within these new borders. The flip side of this contention is that it also keeps as many Palestinians as possible outside the Wall. (Bimkom, 2006; B'tselem 2005; Physicians for Human Rights, 2005: 9–16). Even some Israelis, from Ramot (a settlement near Jerusalem) in particular, have objected to the Wall, claiming that it disrupts their lifestyles, the view from their homes, and the local nature reserves (Farouz, 2006).

Later in 2001, the Ministerial Committee on Security Affairs decided to construct a wall around Jerusalem following a December 1 suicide bombing in the center of the city. It was decided that the Jerusalem barrier would be built on the city's municipal limits. This decision implied that the Wall would include East Jerusalem, which

population growth, I drew on population growth figures of the Palestinian Muslim population living within the Green Line. According to this cautious estimate, the annual rate of growth is 3.617 percent. Some argue that the rate of population growth in East Jerusalem is actually 6 percent, on account of migration to East Jerusalem, but I opted to use the conservative estimate. Population figures presented in this chapter are as of 2009 (Svetlova, 2006).

was illegally annexed in 1967. In the summer of 2002, construction began on two sections of the Wall in the north and south of Jerusalem. Both sections extended for about 10 km. On September 11, 2002, the Israeli cabinet approved the "Jerusalem envelope" plan. Its purpose was to surround the city with walls from the south, east, and north. A year later, in September 2003, the government approved the construction of three more sections of the Wall, which together extend for about 45 km. In February 2005, the government made some changes in the Wall's route in the West Bank, in response to a high court decision following an appeal of human rights groups.

The government approved the E1 plan, which entailed including the Ma'ale Adumim enclave (see below) inside the Wall, but it did not authorize the actual construction of that section. Rather, it consulted with Israeli legal experts from different fields before embarking on construction (Bimkom, 2006; B'tselem 2005; Physicians for Human Rights, 2005: 54–5). When construction eventually began, it had a great impact on the Jerusalem residents: it connected Jerusalem with one of the largest settlements in the West Bank, Ma'ale Adumim, a town of 35,000 Israeli settlers, and annexed a vast area of approximately 15,800 acres of the West Bank which lies between Jerusalem and Ma'ale Adumim. This area also contains about 6,100 Palestinians who were trapped in their own enclaves (Bimkom, 2006; B'tselem 2005; Physicians for Human Rights, 2005: 54–5). The E1 plan meant a 14 km penetration of the Wall into the West Bank, 45 percent of the West Bank's width at that point (UN OCHA, 2006: 2). Actual implementation of the E1 plan began in May 2008.

The Wall's major effect is on the roads connecting Bethlehem and Ramallah. More generally, the Wall has extensive repercussions for the north and south of the West Bank (Bimkom, 2006). The Ma'ale Adumim enclave will seriously undermine any prospects for an independent Palestinian state, because it effectively divides the West Bank in half.

Although the plan is riddled with controversy, the motivation to build the Wall was extremely powerful, underlying the Israeli government's overall ideology (the "separation" agenda). In January 2006 the Israeli defense minister at the time, Shaul Mofaz, decided to resume the construction of the Wall in Jerusalem along those sections that had been ruled illegal by the Israeli High Court. He argued that the Wall is "temporary," although the movement of Palestinians was restricted in these areas just as it has been in other areas (Harel, 2006a).

THE CHARACTERISTICS OF THE WALL

The Jerusalem barrier is approximately 90 km long (Cohen, 2005b). In built-up urban areas, separation has been achieved via a concrete wall. In rural areas an electronic fence has been erected. Most of the Wall in Jerusalem is 6 m to 8 m high (Aronson, 2006: 4).

By and large, the Jerusalem Wall follows the 1967 annexation border, with two major exceptions: the Ma'ale Adumim enclave (still not constructed), which stretches deep into the West Bank, and the exclusion of two Palestinian neighborhoods which were annexed in 1967: Kafr A'keb and the Shua'fat refugee camp. The Palestinian enclaves are a result of two walls, one separating the area from Jerusalem and the other separating it from the West Bank, mostly for the benefit of the settlers on the other side. The Ma'ale Adumim settlement will encircle the Palestinian area of A-Za'ayem, home to Palestinian residents who are mostly of Bedouin origin. The A-Za'ayem area was thus turned into an enclave, like Abu-Dis, Azarieh, and Sawahre A-Sharkieh, another encircled Palestinian enclave in the area to the east of the Old City. The third enclave contains Anata, Ras-Khamis, and Shua'fat refugee camp, northeast of the Old City (Bimkom, 2006; B'tselem 2005; Physicians for Human Rights, 2005: 19, 54). A fourth enclave extends from Saffa to Beit Surik, enclosing 16 villages with a combined population of 59,000 (UN, 2004).

The people living in these enclaves are mostly Jerusalem residents, although they are in danger of losing their status. The enclaves can all be seen in Map 6.1 on page 104.

In the south, the Wall also threatens to cut off the village of Nahalin and other villages nearby. The current plans of the Israeli Ministry of Defense are to construct another section of the Wall to connect the border of (annexed) Jerusalem with the surrounding Jewish settlements to the south of Jerusalem. This will create another enclave of several Palestinian villages with about 22,000 residents, and also including several Jewish settlements with about 44,000 residents. The Wall will then prevent access to the Palestinian urban center in Bethlehem (Bimkom, 2006). Settlers in the area have already announced their objection to being incorporated in this enclave, despite the fact that they will retain the ability to drive through the gates in the Wall. Meanwhile, Palestinians will have to undergo long security checks and be denied access to valuable sources of employment, trade, and services in Jerusalem (Bimkom, 2006; B'tselem, 2005; Elgazi, 2005; Physicians for Human Rights, 2005: 26).

The Wall also follows road no. 443 on both sides – a road that connects northern Jerusalem with Tel-Aviv and the rest of Israel. The road has a checkpoint in it, making it hard for Palestinians to use it, and the Wall already cuts off access by Palestinians from nearby communities to the road (Rubinstein, 2006).

THE EVERYDAY EFFECTS OF THE WALL

The Wall of Separation imposes severe restrictions on the free movement of Palestinians. It prevents Palestinians with Israeli residency from being able to move freely into West Jerusalem and to the rest of Israel. It also prevents Palestinians in Jerusalem from maintaining free contact with Palestinians in the rest of the West Bank (UN OCHA, 2007: 8–23). This limitation of movement stands in violation of international law and other covenants signed by Israel. Article 13 of the Universal Declaration of Human Rights, signed in 1948 and ratified by Israel (UN, 1948), states that:

1. Everyone has the right to freedom of movement and residence within the borders of each state.
2. Everyone has the right to leave any country, including their own, and to return to their country.

Although Israel has built passages in the Wall where soldiers perform security checks and admit people with the proper papers and authorizations, Kimhi notes that they pose difficulties to the Palestinians passing through them. Security checks are prolonged and intrusive, creating long lines. Palestinians are delayed on their way to work, to study, to shop, or to receive medical treatment, and thus the passages cause growing resentment among the Palestinian population of the area (Kimhi, 2006: 15–16).

There is an inherent trade-off between the effectiveness of the checkpoints in detecting weapons and the ease of passage through them. Unless large amounts of money are spent to speed up the checking process, Israel must choose between making the checkpoints ineffective or causing resentment and suffering among the Palestinian population. The policy in practice tends to fluctuate between these two extremes, thus resulting in periodic and unexpected disruptions to Palestinian movements. The anger that accumulates as a result may lead to an increase in the number of Palestinians who wish to cross the checkpoints with harmful intent (Kimhi, 2006: 15–16).

According to the UN Office for Coordinating Humanitarian

Affairs (OCHA), there are 256,000 Palestinians in East Jerusalem who are left in the OWA (UN OCHA, 2006: 2), and are directly or indirectly affected by the Wall. The Palestinian neighborhoods in Jerusalem that have had access to them restricted by the Wall, but are not actually in enclaves encircled by it, are home to about 112,000 people. These residents already suffer from the effects of the artificial severance from their cultural, occupational, healthcare, and educational center (Physicians for Human Rights, 2005: 5–8, 23–4; B'tselem, 2005; Bimkom, 2006).

The Wall has about 60 gateways along it, but about two-thirds of them are built exclusively for Israeli settlers, and Palestinians are prohibited from passing through them. The Israeli government has not declared how many gateways are planned in total, where they will be located, or who will have access to them (UN OCHA, 2006: 2–4; UN, 2004). In Jerusalem, however, there are twelve official gateways in the Wall, only four of which are open to Palestinians, and the rest are reserved for settlers' use only, despite the fact that the settlers in East Jerusalem are there illegally (Aronson, 2006).

THE WALL IN ISRAELI DISCOURSE

To the Israeli public, it is clear that the Wall is intended to create a divide between the ethnic groups. The construction of the Wall is intended to separate Jews from Palestinians, even though in practice it mostly separates Palestinians from Palestinians. The Wall is justified by "security needs," because the discourse effectively sees Palestinians as inherently dangerous. According to this perspective, merely being a Palestinian poses a threat to the security of Jews (Kimhi, 2006: 131–2, 141–2). The Wall is therefore a denial of the political and sociological reasons for Palestinian resistance. It replaces the political discourse that promotes the creation of security through dialogue and compromise with an ethnic discourse which objectifies the Palestinians, marginalizes them, depicts them as a natural hazard, and encircles them inside a wall to keep them at bay.

In the Israeli discourse the Wall is presented as an act of fortification. After almost 40 years of occupation, the Palestinians are perceived by many Israelis as furious, hateful, vengeful, and dangerous. The Wall is supposed to keep them away. However, although the fortification discourse may give the impression that Israel is surrounding itself with a wall, in reality, Israel is surrounding the Palestinians with a wall. The proper term is not fortification, but incarceration – because the Wall is being built around Palestinian communities in the West Bank. Although Israeli officials often argue that the Palestinians as a collective deserve punishment, they refuse to use incarceration terminology, or even to suggest that the Palestinians are being "punished" by the Wall, since many of them would like to mask the hardships that the Wall imposes on the Palestinians (Newman and Biger, 2006).

Because of the annexation, Jerusalem appears to be a counter-example of the above. The Wall surrounds Jerusalem (in fact, it is called the "Jerusalem envelope" by the authorities), and on the maps it appears more like a fortification line against Ramallah and Bethlehem than a wall closing in on the Palestinians.

Additionally, the Wall is still built on occupied land, in order to incorporate the annexed areas into Israel. Jerusalem has grown so large – with all the settlements surrounding it – that the Jerusalem Wall cuts deeply into the West Bank. With the inclusion of the E1 plan, the Jerusalem Wall becomes a barrier between the northern and the southern West Bank, leaving only a narrow passage east of Ma'ale Adumim in the Jericho area. Viewed from this angle, it becomes clear that the Jerusalem Wall is part of the process of incarceration, not fortification (see Map 2).

LAND CONFISCATION

Many organizations have already discussed the illegality of the confiscation of land from the Palestinian territories. The International Court in The Hague has ruled that international law prohibits Israel from building the Wall on occupied territory (International Court, 2004). Nevertheless, the Wall's most recent route runs largely through the West Bank. Only 20 percent of the Wall's route corresponds with the Green Line, and the rest is being built inside the West Bank. About 10.7 percent of the West Bank – 154,320 acres – is trapped between the Wall and the Green Line. Of that area, 141,974 acres (92 percent) are in Jerusalem (UN OCHA, 2006: 2).

The Wall also traps many Palestinians without residency in the IWA. These Palestinians must obtain a permit simply to reach (or stay in) their own homes. They are not allowed into Israel, and cannot even go to the rest of the West Bank without crossing an Israeli checkpoint and presenting a permit. Those Palestinians who lose their permits or are denied one are permanently deported from their homes into the IWA (UN OCHA, 2006: 2). This creates a situation, such as in Al Walaje village, where a Palestinian can be sitting

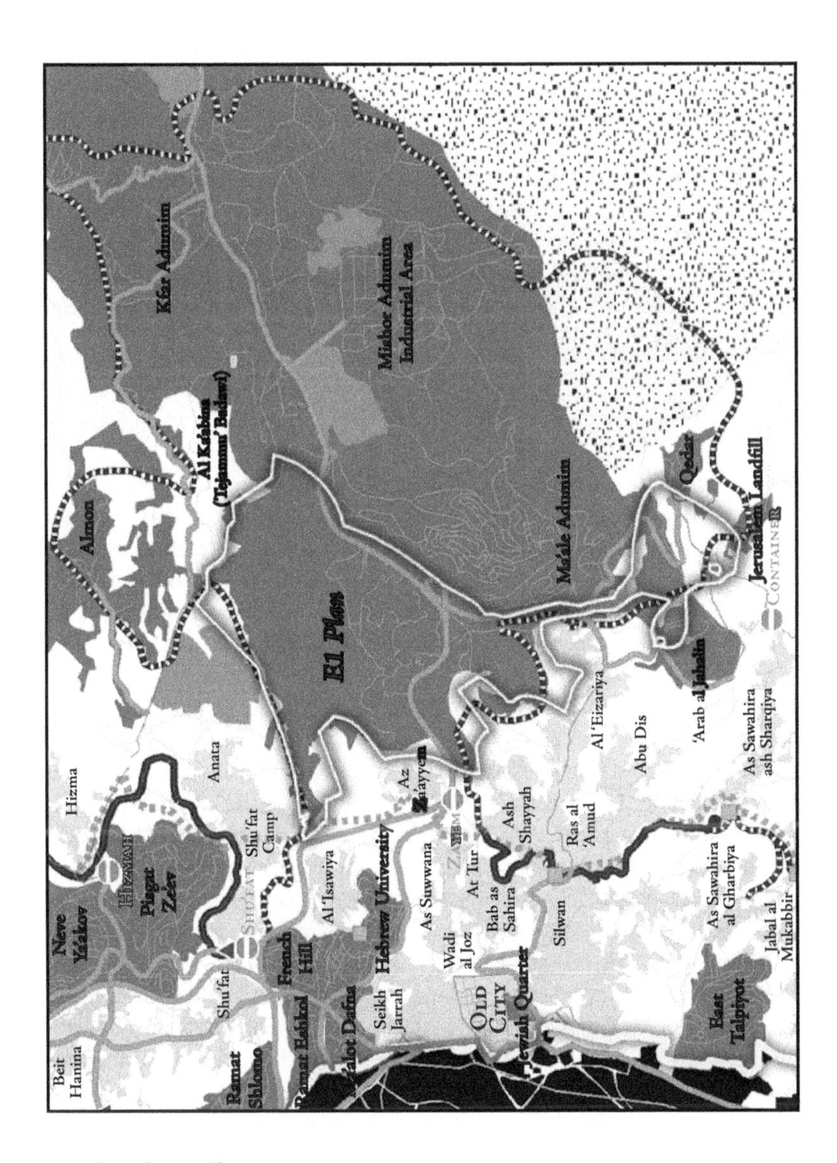

Map 6.2 The E1 Plan

(See comment on the map of Jerusalem at the start of this chapter.)

in his own living room and be "illegally present in Jerusalem without a permit" at the same time.

According to the Palestinian Central Bureau of Statistics (PCBS) (2005b), the construction of the Wall of Separation in Jerusalem has involved the confiscation of 3,360 acres and the displacement of 1,150 households comprising 5,920 people. Land confiscation is the most obvious way in which the Wall damages the East Jerusalem Palestinians, although it is not necessarily more damaging than the limitation on movement. The Jerusalem Institute for Israel Studies found that 28 percent of the people surveyed reported that land confiscation for the construction of the Wall had affected them directly (Kimhi, 2006: 76–7).

PRIVATIZATION

While Israel has already decided to privatize the main checkpoints between Israel, Gaza, and the West Bank, it is still not clear whether the checkpoints in the Jerusalem Wall will be privatized or run by the military (Rapoport, 2007). Part of the reason for the privatization is that the military wishes to avoid any bad press resulting from its soldiers mistreating the Palestinians at the checkpoints. However, allowing a private company to manage the checkpoints does not guarantee any improvement of conditions for the Palestinians who will need to cross them on a daily basis. Only 10 percent of the people surveyed by the Jerusalem Institute for Israel Studies reported that they expect that a private company will ease some of the suffering caused by the Wall. A vast majority (54 percent in total, 71 percent in the OWA) said that the passages are not a solution to the problems caused by the Wall. Therefore, the question concerning whether the passages are run by the army or by a private company is secondary (Kimhi, 2006: 15–16, 80–1).

However, although the passages may not be the solution, their mode of operation is crucial to the livelihood of all Jerusalemites. There is an essential difference between a wall that delays people's movement and a wall that prevents it altogether. The longer the lines grow in front of the checkpoints and the more humiliating and invasive the security checks become, the more likely the Wall is to have adverse affects. Leaving the responsibility of managing the Wall in the hands of a private company could easily cause a swift deterioration in the social, economic, and political situation in Jerusalem, if the company puts profit above the welfare of the people who are under its jurisdiction (Kimhi, 2006: 128–30).

"SECURITY NEED"

A recent report by the B'tselem organization examined the Wall's route in certain areas, confirming the conclusion that the Wall was not built in conformance with the specifications of satisfying "security needs," but in order to protect and annex the illegal settlements in the OPT. The report focuses on specific locations; one of them is northern Jerusalem, where the Wall surrounds the Neve Ya'akov settlement in order to incorporate it into Israeli-controlled Jerusalem (B'tselem, 2005: 44–51).

There are areas in the eastern reaches of the Wall in which it is clear that security concerns took second priority to other considerations when it was designed. The residents of Abu Dis, a large Palestinian suburb stranded east of the Wall, appealed to the Israeli High Court in March 2006. The residents argued that the Wall turns Abu-Dis and Sawakhreh into enclaves. About 41 percent of Abu-Dis's land will be separated from Abu-Dis by the Wall. Also, the residents argued that the planner of the Wall's route in their area, Dani Terzal, lives in Kfar Adumim, a settlement that he decided to leave inside the Wall (though it is even farther east than Abu Dis). They claimed that the Wall's route had been inspired by a conflict of interests, not by true security needs. Israel's High Court decided in August 2006 to reject the appeal, stating that the Wall "serves a vital security need" (Hass, 2006; Zino, 2006).

The Israeli journalist Danny Rubinstein (2006) claims that the Wall serves no security purpose whatsoever – it has been and is being built to make life more comfortable for the settlements, to provide jobs for construction companies, and to create the illusion of security for the Jewish residents of Jerusalem.

THE MAKING OF THE WORKING CLASS IN EAST JERUSALEM

Although the entire Israeli market is very stratified and suffers from high levels of inequality, in the case of Jerusalem this has many unique aspects. Palestinians traditionally form the lowest rank in the labor market, competing only with the poorest Jewish migrants for low-prestige and low-income jobs.

Israel's exploitation of cheap Palestinian labor from Jerusalem has focussed mainly on employing male manual laborers. As of 2004, only 10.1 percent of Palestinian women in East Jerusalem participated in the official workforce. This is also due to the traditional structure of the Palestinian family. Nevertheless, it is important to remember that Palestinian women perform essential work. In an area that receives minimal government services, and in particular inadequate public education, the domestic roles of Palestinian women have become more time-consuming and demanding (PCBS, 2005b). Furthermore, the implementation of the "Welfare to Work" labor reform plan (see below) is making it more difficult for women to continue to perform their traditional roles, forcing them into wage labor, without providing alternative methods of fulfilling household responsibilities. Often, the result is that women end up performing domestic services in other women's homes for a small salary, rather than doing the same work in their own homes.

GAPS IN THE EDUCATIONAL SYSTEM

The educational figures give us a clue to the class aspects of the national conflict inside Jerusalem and the unequal distribution of income. The PCBS provides many figures on the PA Jerusalem Governorate, the area of which extends somewhat beyond the annexed parts.

Although illiteracy among East Jerusalem Palestinians has fallen, it is still much higher than the Israeli average, standing at 5.7 percent among all people 15 or older, compared with 4.6 percent in Israel generally (PCBS, 2005a; IMFA, 2004). As of 2004, fewer than 1 percent of all Palestinians in the age range 6 to 35 had never attended school, whereas among their grandparents' generation (ages 65+) 40.2 percent never attended school. This major shift took place in the 1950s and 1960s during the period of Jordanian rule, continuing, albeit more slowly, during the Israel occupation and annexation period (PCBS, 2005a). Over a quarter (28.3 percent) of all young Palestinians in the 20–24 age range have less than nine years of schooling. The rate of Palestinians with under nine years of schooling rises with each higher age group, reaching over 80 percent among the 55–64 age group, who are the oldest still in the workforce. Men, who comprise the majority of the East Jerusalem Palestinian workforce, suffer from even higher rates of incomplete education. These men are the labor pool for low-status, manual, and unskilled jobs in Jerusalem (PCBS, 2005a).

The Wall creates a further obstacle to education in East Jerusalem. About 15,000 Palestinian students live in the OWA and have the right to study in IWA schools. The Wall makes their daily commute to school harder, longer, and more dangerous, and this will have even more adverse affects on the educational gaps of East Jerusalem Palestinians in the future (Kimhi, 2006: 140–2).

GAPS IN OCCUPATIONAL STATUS

The Jerusalem Institute for Israel Studies has reported that 15,500 workers (about 8.5 percent of the Jerusalem workforce) worked in unskilled jobs in 2002–03. Of these, 50 percent were Jews, meaning that Palestinians made up almost 50 percent of the unskilled labor force, even though they are only 31 percent of the Jerusalem population. Furthermore, of 27,100 workers (about 15 percent of the Jerusalem workforce) who were listed as skilled "blue-collar" workers, over 57 percent of these were Palestinian (Hoshen, 2005).

These figures show that Jerusalem Palestinians occupy mainly the lower-rung jobs in Jerusalem, yet even they do not reflect the important internal divisions among the low-status jobs. For example, security guards are almost exclusively Jewish – mainly immigrants from the former Soviet Union countries and from Ethiopia. Although these jobs provide low pay – and although the security guards are often exploited by their employers – Palestinians are never hired for these jobs, and that is one of the reasons these jobs offer a higher social status than manual jobs. There is also a certain air of importance to security guards, especially in a tense city such as Jerusalem which has known many violent outbursts.

Manual jobs that are considered "dirty," such as construction labor hired on a daily basis, are performed predominantly by Palestinians, and afford a lower occupational status than security jobs. There is a strong association in Israel between the words "manual," "dirty," and "Arab." This association has a symbolic importance in disempowering and humiliating the Palestinians. Even certain construction-related professions that have a higher status in other countries, such as floor-laying and pipe-installation, are still considered non-professional by Israelis (Kraus and Yuval, 2000).

MOVEMENT OF LABOR IN JERUSALEM AND THE QUALITY OF LIFE

The Wall is designed to limit movement. Whether it is effective in preventing the movement of armed Palestinians on their way to attack Jerusalem is highly debatable, but it is certainly effective in making it harder for unarmed civilians to perform daily tasks such as going to work, to school, to the hospital, to pray at the Al-Aqsa Mosque, or to visit family. Palestinians have reported that because they must walk to the nearest checkpoint and then wait until they are allowed through it, distances between destinations have grown considerably. A 20-minute walk has become an hour's walk (Kimhi, 2006: 53–4).

The Wall was even erected in the middle of a schoolyard in Anata, turning the school building itself into part of the Wall and lengthening the pupils' route to school considerably. Despite the hardships, the school's staff insisted on keeping the school open. Israeli soldiers assigned to defend the Wall have frequently used tear gas against the schoolchildren (Cohen, 2005a). The World Bank conducted a survey among East Jerusalem students and found that the average rating they gave to describe their travel to campus was "difficult" (World Bank, 2004b).

As the Wall was extended to include Ma'ale Adumim and the surrounding area, entrance into Jerusalem has become exceedingly difficult. In January 2006, the Israeli army prevented Palestinians from using eight out of the twelve roads entering Jerusalem, and forced them to undergo extensive security checks (UN OCHA, 2006: 2–4).

DETERIORATING HEALTHCARE SERVICES

The organization Physicians for Human Rights has published an extensive report (2005) on the effects of the Wall in Jerusalem on the health of Palestinian residents of the area. The main arguments in the report are as follows:

- Treatment of chronic patients, elderly people and pregnant women is delayed.
- Palestinians from the OPT find it hard to reach hospitals in the city.
- Ambulances are delayed at the checkpoints and entrances to East Jerusalem, even in urgent cases.
- Hospitals are experiencing a financial crisis (one of the reasons for the crisis is patients' inability to pay for treatment).

The poor quality of healthcare services available to East Jerusalem Palestinians and to West Bank Palestinians as a result of the Wall not only increases the risk of disease and suffering to the residents of these areas, but also creates a long-term drain on the Palestinian economy. Inadequate medical treatment invariably diminishes the average productivity of workers, decreases the number of productive years in a worker's life, and increases the chances that people will suffer from disabilities, making them dependent on others for survival. The overall impact of inadequate healthcare services is extremely difficult to measure, but it should not be ignored simply because it cannot be quantified.

AREAS OF SPECIAL INTEREST

It is in the nature of geographic obstacles that they do not have a homogenous effect on people's lives. Those living in certain areas have been able to avoid the brunt of the Wall's economic impact, or even to profit from that impact, while some living in more vulnerable areas have been hit harder than others.

The two striking examples of the Israeli policy to minimize the number of Palestinians on Israeli territory, which are also the two areas most adversely affected by the Wall, are the Shua'fat refugee camp and Dahiyat A-Salam. Although Israel annexed these areas in 1967 and has repeatedly claimed that Jerusalem's new borders are permanent and will not be changed, it only gave residency status to the residents of these areas, instead of granting them Israeli citizenship. As if in an attempt to correct the "demographic mistake" of the annexation, the Wall has been extended to the west of these neighborhoods, cutting them off from the rest of Jerusalem. Although the residents of these neighborhoods, about 70,000 today, still carry Israeli residency papers, the value of these documents has significantly depreciated now that a physical wall makes movement into the IWA difficult or sometimes impossible (Kimhi, 2006: 24–6). The level of damage to these areas cannot be assessed accurately. The residents of the Shua'fat refugee camp are so frustrated with the situation that 97 percent of them refused to cooperate with the survey of the Jerusalem Institute for Israel Studies and did not report how the Wall affects their lives (Kimhi, 2006: 24–6). About 21 percent of the residents of the two areas reported land confiscations, 14 percent suffered physical injury or health problems, 36 percent reported a rise in their cost of living, 11 percent reported a change of residence, and 6 percent reported increased population density. Also, residents of these areas had to find new sources of income. The number of providers per family has increased dramatically, indicating a higher reliance on child labor. However, the share of families who have no provider increased from 8 percent in 2000 to 18 percent in 2004 (Kimhi, 2006: 79–80).

Recent changes to the Wall's route leave the village of Beit Iksa surrounded on three sides by the Wall and by the settler road no. 443. The state has promised that the village will have access to the West Bank through tunnels and underground passages, which had yet to be built as of 2008 (UN OCHA, 2006: 5).

The village of Al-Walajeh, mostly populated by Palestinian refugees from Israel, is gradually being surrounded by the Wall on all sides. The village has lost its agricultural lands because of the Wall. The southern side of the village is already blocked by a road that Palestinians are not allowed to use. Israel has promised an underground passage to connect the village to the rest of the West Bank, which had yet to be built as of 2008 (UN OCHA, 2006: 5).

The village of Al-Walajeh has been subject to a series of land confiscations, house demolitions, and "flying checkpoints" (temporary unexpected checkpoints). The confiscation of lands on the outskirts of the village effectively blocks all movement to and from Al-Walajeh. In 2004 Israel declared its intention to construct a settlement, Giv'at Yael, to absorb 55,000 settlers. The sinister factor here is that, although the village still exists, the maps released by the government show that the planned settlement area includes much of its populated residential area; it would seem the intention is to expropriate the lands of the village without compensating the residents (ARIJ and LRC, 2006).

Sheikh Sa'ad, a suburb of 2,500 people on the outskirts of Jerusalem, was also left outside the Wall. The neighborhood has only one access road, which has been blocked by a permanent roadblock, concrete cubes with rubble on top of them. The only way in or out of the village is by foot, even in cases of emergency. Although Israel promised an access road to Bethlehem, that road has yet to be built (MachsomWatch, 2008). The neighborhood has no clinic or high school, and over half of the residents have abandoned their houses in the neighborhood as a result (Levy, 2005).

DIFFICULTIES IN OBTAINING GOODS

Consumption patterns demonstrate that both East and West Jerusalem, as well as the satellite cities, are a metropolitan commercial center for Jerusalem Palestinians. In 2000, between 16 percent and 25 percent of OWA Jerusalem Palestinians reported that they bought their goods in the IWA. By 2004, consumption patterns were already noticeably different because of the Wall. In A-Ram, cut off from the IWA, shopping in the IWA fell to 5 percent. Residents of Kafr A'keb and Samiramis divided their shopping between their own neighborhoods and Palestinian cities such as Bethlehem and Ramallah. The share of these residents who were able to shop in the IWA fell from 4 percent in 2000 to 1 percent in 2004. Residents of the Shua'fat refugee camp and Dahiyat A-Salam suffered limitations to their movement, as a result of which 93 percent purchased their goods within their own neighborhoods (Hoshen, 2005). The loss of sales to Israeli merchants in the IWA as a result of the Wall has not been studied.

With Jerusalem Palestinians forced to change their shopping patterns radically, the options available to them have diminished and so has their quality of life. Assuming that people make choices to buy the goods that are the most accessible, best suited to their needs, and cheapest, narrowing their options for purchasing goods is bound to have a negative impact on their standard of living. Palestinians who must now buy in the IWA, such as the Old City of Jerusalem, pay higher prices than they used to pay in the OWA or in nearby Palestinian cities. Over 51 percent of the Palestinians from the OWA have reported that the Wall has caused a sharp increase in their cost of living (Kimhi, 2006: 76–7).

ARRESTED TRADE

Even before the completion of the Wall of Separation in Jerusalem, merchants and shopkeepers noted a steep decline in business. The Old City and Salah-A-Din Street, both bustling centers of commerce, started suffering a loss in business volume as soon as the Wall's construction began. Shopkeepers have attested that they find it increasingly difficult to pay the overhead costs and taxes for their shops because they have so few customers (Kimhi, 2006: 24–5).

Although there are no estimates of the losses to the East Jerusalem economy because of the reduced trade volume, examining the diminished income of households may afford a broader understanding of the economic slowdown. Because many households own a shop and rely on it as a source of income, the figures on the slowdown in trade are in fact hidden within the figures on reduced household incomes, which are discussed next (Kimhi, 2006: 78–9).

DIMINISHED INCOME IN EAST JERUSALEM

The survey conducted by the Jerusalem Institute for Israel Studies showed that there has been a reduction in income for Jerusalem Palestinians. The percentage of Palestinians who have no income at all has doubled, while in the communities surrounding Jerusalem it has quadrupled. The number of families who earn less than NIS2,000 (US$459) per month has more than doubled (Kimhi, 2006: 78–9).

It could perhaps be argued that some of the deterioration in income is connected to the general trend of increased social gaps in Israeli society during the period from 2000 to 2004. However, if we look at the effects of the separation caused by the Wall, the findings are even more alarming.

The proportion of people earning less than NIS2,000 per month prior to 2000 was 9 percent in the areas that were later included inside the Wall, but had increased to 14 percent by 2004. Outside the Wall, the deterioration was much more severe, with the proportion increasing from 16 percent in 2000 to over 46 percent in 2004 (Kimhi, 2006: 78–9). The proportion of families who reported that they had no income at all quadrupled among people living outside the Wall from 1 percent in 2000 to over 4 percent in 2004 (Kimhi, 2006: 78–9).

In East Jerusalem as of 2004, the concept of middle earners applied to people who earned NIS2,000–4,000 per month (US$459–918). This is below the Israeli minimum wage of NIS3,585 (US$822), and about half the average wage in Israel (NIS7,333 or US$1,681), a further indication of the unequal distribution of wealth in East Jerusalem. In the areas outside the Wall, the proportion of middle earners fell from 53 percent to 37 percent between 2000 and 2004. The proportion of people who earn NIS4,000–6,000 per month fell from 23 percent to 10 percent (Kimhi, 2006: 78–9).

The lack of accurate data means that only a rough estimate can be made of the total damage caused by the Wall. My estimation uses the midpoint of each category as the baseline for the calculation (for example, NIS3,000 to represent the people earning NIS2,000–4,000 per month). For households dependent on National Insurance Institute stipends, the average stipend for a household of two parents and two or more children is used. Since the average Palestinian household in East Jerusalem has seven members, it is statistically sound to use this amount: NIS2,078 (US$477) (NII, 2005). Based on these figures, the estimated nominal reduction in the income of East Jerusalem households was 8 percent in the four years from 2000 to 2004.

In addition price changes, which have further eroded the income of Palestinian residents of Jerusalem, must be taken into account. The expenses of Jerusalem Palestinians are distributed between spending money in Israel and in the OPT, mainly in the West Bank. Therefore in order to calculate inflation we have to separate the two venues of expenditure. As a result of the Wall, Kimhi reports, the amount of shopping that Palestinians from East Jerusalem do in the West Bank, where prices are generally cheaper, has fallen from 30 percent to 27 percent (Kimhi, 2006: 91–2). Between 2000 and 2004 the Consumer Price Index (CPI) in Israel rose by 7.12 percent, but it increased by 23.7 percent in the OPT (ICBS, 2006b; PCBS, 2009a). Taking these figures into account, the real reduction in income for Jerusalem Palestinians was in fact 17.5 percent, almost a fifth.

For Palestinians in the OWA, cut off from Jerusalem by the Wall, the numbers indicate a sharper reduction in income, for two reasons. One is that their nominal income has dropped more significantly, and the second is that inflation in the OWA was higher than in the IWA. In nominal terms, income decreased by 34 percent. After taking account of inflation as well, I conclude that real income fell by 46 percent. The Wall therefore almost halved the real income of Palestinians in the OWA between 2000 and 2004.

Of course, the sharp increase in prices is very much related to the construction of the Wall, as is the difference between the inflation rates in Israel and the OPT. In Chapter 3 the relations between movement limitations and inflation were described at greater detail.

Using this estimate to calculate the total damage caused by the Wall in Jerusalem, we can multiply the average loss of income per household by the number of households. The total income loss as a result of the Wall is an average of US$4 million per month in the IWA, and US$12 million per month in the OWA. In total, the Wall in Jerusalem causes US$194 million in damages per annum. In the years from 2000 to 2009, it has already caused more than US$1.94 billion in income loss. These figures must be updated to account for the natural growth of the population, and will therefore increase further and continue to accumulate at an accelerated rate until the Wall is removed.

IMPLEMENTATION OF THE WELFARE REFORM PROGRAM

In July 2005, the Israeli government commenced the implementation of the Welfare to Work labor reform, under the name "*Mehalev*" ("From the Heart," in Hebrew), but known to all as the Wisconsin

Plan (Adut and Hever, 2006). Nearly half of the program's participants are from Jerusalem, most of them Palestinians from East Jerusalem. The plan makes it harder for the participants to receive income support (Israel's most basic form of welfare), and disqualifies them from receiving welfare unless they participate in the program for many hours every week and perform "community service" jobs without pay. Numerous reports of abuse, humiliation, and discrimination have accumulated about the treatment of the program participants, with especially disturbing reports in the East Jerusalem branch of the program (Adut and Hever, 2006).

The implications of this program for the East Jerusalem Palestinians are dire. Many families have lost the income support upon which they were dependent. Others have been forced to do "community service" jobs for less than half of the minimum wage. As the Wall in Jerusalem closes in around them, more and more East Jerusalem Palestinians discover that they are expected to replace non-resident OPT Palestinians in jobs that they can no longer reach, and to work for about US$3 an hour. Because of the Wall, Israeli businesspeople have fewer opportunities to exploit the cheap labor of OPT Palestinians. However, the Wisconsin Plan downgrades the entitlements of Israeli citizens and residents, forcing them to take the place of the non-citizen Palestinians for about the same wages (Adut and Hever, 2006).

There seems to be a contradiction between Israel's attempt to limit movement and avoid investing money in East Jerusalem,[5] and its insistence on implementing the Wisconsin Plan, which is officially intended to assist unemployed people in finding jobs. This seeming contradiction is resolved when it becomes apparent that the Wisconsin Plan is, in fact, another form of repression that effectively reduces welfare payments to East Jerusalem residents, and places them under a system of strict supervision, just like the Wall of Separation (Adut and Hever, 2006).

Following mass protests in Israel against the plan and its treatment of unemployed people, the Israeli government decided to make some changes in it. They were implemented in August 2007, and the plan was renamed "Lights for Employment." The changes were designed to help certain social groups in Israel that were most adversely affected: people close to retirement age, academics, people with disabilities,

5 See Margalit (2005) for a detailed description of the funding discrimination against East Jerusalem exercised by the Jerusalem municipality.

and single mothers. The new plan ignored the particular needs of East Jerusalem, leaving the treatment of East Jerusalem residents almost unchanged.[6]

HOUSING SHORTAGES

Construction of the Wall has required the confiscation of a large amount of land from Palestinians, and numerous houses have been demolished along its path. Furthermore, the threat of being cut off from Jerusalem has convinced many Palestinians with Israeli residency to move into East Jerusalem, to the western side of the Wall, for fear of losing their residency or to avoid the long wait at the checkpoints. This has created a sharp rise in housing density. More people per room, smaller rooms, and higher rent are all contributory factors to the erosion of the quality of life in East Jerusalem (Kimhi, 2006: 16–17, 141).

The growing density in East Jerusalem is a worrying trend to Zionists, who are striving to maintain the Jewish majority in the city. Meanwhile, house prices in East Jerusalem in the IWA rose by 30–40 percent in 2003–04 (Greenbaum, 2005). The population density per room in East Jerusalem is double that in West Jerusalem, and 30 percent of the households suffer from extreme density, compared to only 3 percent in West Jerusalem (Garb, 2005: 4).

About 73 percent of the Palestinians who participated in the survey by the Jerusalem Institute for Israel Studies reported that the Wall has affected housing costs. According to the published estimates, housing costs in the OWA fell by 40–51 percent (Garb, 2005: 4), while housing costs in the IWA rose by 50 percent (Kimhi, 2006: 45, 141). To illustrate what that means, there can be such a huge price gap between two houses of similar construction – which used to be adjacent to each other, but are now separated by the Wall – that one house costs three times as much as the other, only a few meters away.

SEVERED FAMILIES

The Wall also breaks apart Palestinian families in East Jerusalem. Almost all of the respondents to the survey by the Jerusalem Insti-

6 Based on discussions with program participants and with workers at the Community Action Center (Markaz Al-A'mal) of Al-Quds University in East Jerusalem.

tute for Israel Studies reported that they had family ties both within Jerusalem and in the outlying communities. The Wall makes it increasingly difficult to visit, provide care, and receive assistance in kind from close family members (Kimhi, 2006: 40–4). Over 40 percent of the Palestinians from the communities around Jerusalem reported that they had entered Jerusalem regularly to visit their relatives. Most of them had first-grade relatives living in Jerusalem (52 percent in total, but 76 percent of the holders of Israeli residency cards: Kimhi, 2006: 40–4). The PCBS (2005a) also found that 56.8 percent of East Jerusalem Palestinians had relatives on the other side of the Wall.

BEDOUIN TRIBES

For the approximately 3,000 Bedouin residents of the Jahalin and Ca'abneh tribes, the Wall threatens a devastating blow to their quality of life. The Jahalin have already undergone forced evacuation from their lands and were forcibly resettled by the Israeli authorities close to a landfill. The Wall means almost complete disconnection from their agricultural lands – which serve as their central source of income – as well as from services which they used to receive in the nearby Palestinian towns. Their only remaining source of livelihood will be manual labor, such as cleaning and gardening, which many young workers are performing in the Ma'ale Adumim settlement. Bimkom architects have estimated that there is almost no chance that the Bedouin will have access to other sources of employment (Bimkom, 2006).

GROWING PESSIMISM AND DISCONTENT

The Palestinians in East Jerusalem who see the Wall being built around them are trying to cope with the growing realization that it will affect every aspect of their lives and seriously threaten the lifestyle to which they are accustomed. The World Bank has found that many Palestinians in the OPT express worry and concern about the future, and has concluded that this pessimism stems from the restrictions on movement caused by the Wall (World Bank, 2004b: 3–8).

Kimhi has expressed concern that the damage to the Palestinian civilian population caused by the Wall will be detrimental to Israel's image among the international community. Although the report did not express concern about the actual suffering of the Palestinian

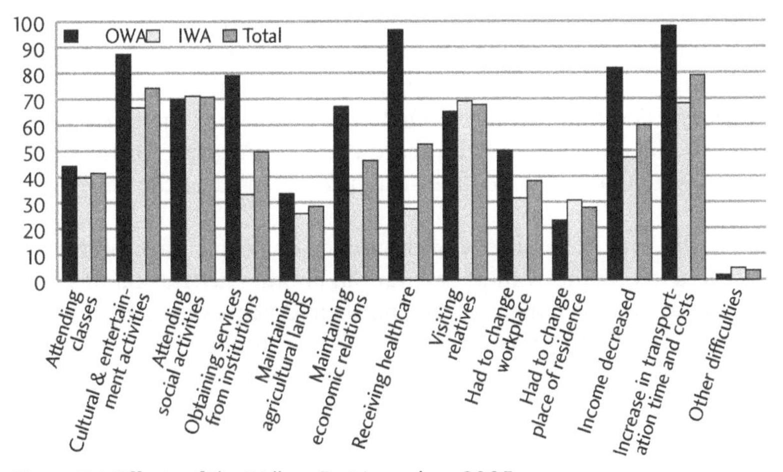

Figure 6.1 Effects of the Wall on East Jerusalem, 2005

Note: The figures represent the percentage of East Jerusalem Palestinians who reported hardship as a result of the wall.

Source: Palestinian Central Bureau of Statistics (2005a).

population, it was concerned for its possible effect in undermining Israel's position in world opinion (Kimhi, 2006: 10). Kimhi went to argue that peace in the city depends on easy passage through the Wall of Separation. However, because ease of passage is unlikely – in light of past experiences with other Israeli checkpoints in the West Bank and Gaza – he believed that unrest was likely to break out in Jerusalem (Kimhi, 2006: 24). This analysis is reinforced by the fact that over 78 percent of the participants of the survey of the Jerusalem Institute for Israel Studies said that they believed the Wall would worsen the political situation (Kimhi, 2006: 81).

The Israeli authorities recognize that the East Jerusalem Palestinians' ability to continue living a normal life is ultimately an Israeli security interest. If the daily lives of Jerusalem Palestinians are ruined, the Palestinians are more likely to resort to violence in their struggle for fair treatment. Since the Israeli government officially maintains that the occupation of East Jerusalem is permanent, it has to allow for longer-term plans than the mechanisms used to suppress and control the West Bank and Gaza Palestinians (Kimhi, 2006: 131–2, 136–7).

The first Palestinian intifada erupted in 1987 after an entire generation of Palestinians became frustrated by the wholesale loss of job opportunities following the economic crisis in Israel and the fall in oil prices, which led to loss of employment in the Gulf states. The second

Palestinian intifada erupted in 2000 after Palestinians became frustrated with the unilateral policy decisions of Israel, which subverted the spirit of the Oslo agreements and blocked all opportunities for economic development in the OPT. The collapse of the peace negotiations and the entry of Ariel Sharon into the Al-Aqsa Mosque were the triggers that unleashed the accumulated anger of the Palestinian people.

As the lives of hundreds of thousands of people have been radically altered by the Wall of Separation, another generation of Palestinians is now in danger of having their dreams of a better world shattered by arbitrary Israeli state policies. Although East Jerusalem Palestinians, with their residency status under Israeli law, are among the better-earning Palestinians in the OPT, they are also the group that can lose their income faster than any other OPT group. Their relatively high income is mostly a result of their connection to the Israeli market, something the Wall threatens to change. The danger of a third intifada is increasing steadily, as more and more Palestinians find that the Wall cannot be circumvented, and that it prevents them from continuing to receive the levels of healthcare, education, and services to which they are accustomed.

IMPORTANCE OF JERUSALEM EMPLOYMENT TO THE PALESTINIAN ECONOMY

I have chosen to present the effects of the Wall on East Jerusalem here not merely because of the importance of Jerusalem itself, but also because of the ripple effects throughout the West Bank, which have a profound impact on the Palestinian economy as a whole.

Despite the fact that East Jerusalem Palestinians usually hold low-paying and low-prestige jobs, the Palestinian economy in the OPT has nonetheless become dependent on their income, as a result of many years during which Israel prevented the independent economic development of the OPT. In fact, of all the areas of the OPT, Jerusalem has the highest average wage, mainly because of the proximity to Israel. While the average daily wage in Gaza was US$13.8 just prior to the Israeli withdrawal from Gaza in 2005, and the average daily wage in the West Bank at the same time was US$16.4, the average daily wage in Jerusalem was US$27.2. However, it should still be kept in mind for the sake of comparison that the average daily wage in Israel in 2005 was US$56.8 (PCBS, PMA, and MAS, 2006).

According to the World Bank, if the number of Palestinians from East Jerusalem working in Israel drops significantly because of the

Wall, the result will be catastrophic to the entire OPT – causing a steep increase in poverty and unemployment. In 2004 the World Bank predicted that by 2008 per capita GDP in the OPT would be either US$878 or US$1,090 (it was US$1,091 in 2004), depending on how many people were allowed to continue working in Israel. The official unemployment rate would either fall to 19 percent if workers continued to be employed in Israel, or jump to 31 percent if they were not. Poverty would fall to 56 percent or jump to 72 percent (World Bank, 2004a: iv). In 2008, unemployment rates hit 25.7 percent in the West Bank (28.9 percent in the OPT in total), and per-capita GDP had fallen to US$1,029 even by 2006, indicating that the World Bank's more pessimistic scenario had come to pass (UN OCHA, 2008d: 2, 12).[7]

The Wall's effects are felt far beyond the limits of the Jerusalem area. It would be impossible to describe them fully here, but the village of Yatta provides a telling example.

Although Yatta is located south of Hebron, close to the southern end of the West Bank and about 35 km outside Jerusalem, it has still been profoundly affected by the Wall in Jerusalem. Many of the people of Yatta who used to find employment in Jerusalem, despite the long journey from their homes, have now lost all their former sources of income. They have instead turned to an alternative source – mining for metal scraps in the Yatta garbage dump and selling them. Children 14 years old work up to ten hours or more every day, gathering about 60 kg of scrap metal, and earning about US$6.5 for a day's work (Sadaa Media, 2006).

The Palestinian Economic Policy Research Institute (MAS), the PCBS, and the Palestine Monetary Authority estimated that the number of Palestinian workers in Israel in the third quarter of 2005 was 60,000. About half of them had "Israeli residency," meaning most likely that they came from Jerusalem. These workers received a median daily wage of NIS134.6 (US$30.87), compared with the median daily wage of NIS69.2 (US$15.67) in the West Bank and NIS61.5 (US$14.1) in the Gaza Strip (PCBS, 2009a; PCBS, PMA, and MAS, 2006). Although these estimates were made for all of the Palestinian workers from the OPT who work in Israel and not specifically those carrying residency identity cards, it is important to remember that Palestinians with residency status have the best access to the Israeli job market, and thus contribute a great deal to the Palestinian economy. This is important as the West Bank suffers from

7 Figures for 2008 were yet unknown at the time of writing.

high unemployment, and the official unemployment rate in the West Bank for 2005 was 20.3 percent (PCBS, 2009a; PCBS, PMA, and MAS, 2006). The Wall threatens to change that permanently, and it is extremely doubtful that jobs can be created fast enough to provide alternative employment for the East Jerusalem Palestinians who have lost their jobs in Israel.

Kimhi voices an argument that Israeli policymakers dare not say openly – that Israel is manipulating the competition between East Jerusalem Palestinians and West Bank Palestinians. With West Bank Palestinians being prevented from entering Jerusalem (mainly East Jerusalem), employment among East Jerusalem Palestinians who are still able to cross through the Wall will increase, and this will discourage uprisings among East Jerusalem Palestinians (Kimhi, 2006: 27–8). Yet if Israeli authorities are concerned with improving the standard of living of Palestinians in East Jerusalem, they have failed to invest in the East Jerusalem economy. They rely mainly on negative incentives – blocking West Bank workers and violating the rights of the unemployed – to encourage employment. Thus, the main achievement of such manipulation is to increase poverty in the West Bank, and drive a wedge between different Palestinian groups.

Unemployment among East Jerusalem Palestinians is lower than in the rest of the West Bank, but Palestinians left on the eastern side of the Wall suffer from an even higher unemployment rate than the rest of the West Bank. In 2005, unemployment in the West Bank was 20.3 percent, compared with 15.5 percent in the IWA and 21.9 percent in the OWA (PCBS, 2005a).

Unemployment among East Jerusalem Palestinians is under the OPT average, though still quite a lot higher than the Israeli rate. In the IWA unemployment in 2005 stood at 15.5 percent. In the OWA it was 21.9 percent – a clear indication that being cut off from the Israeli market is a cause of unemployment. By comparison, Israeli unemployment in 2005 was 9 percent (PCBS, 2005a; ICBS, 2008a).

BINATIONAL REALITY

Jerusalem has officially been unified according to Israeli law, but discrimination and prejudice still differentiate the West from the East of the city. Nevertheless, after over 42 years of occupation, the separation project seems more futile than ever. Kimhi argues that even a withdrawal to the 1967 border would leave many social problems unsolved, because of the connections and dependencies that have formed during the occupation. The healthcare, education, water, sewage, and electricity systems have been enmeshed, and the Jewish settlements have been constructed in a way that makes it impossible to draw a line between the two populations (Kimhi, 2006).

The extent of the damage caused by the Wall in Jerusalem demonstrates that people's lives have irreversibly adapted to a unified urban space, and that artificially separating that space has far-reaching economic and social implications. The city has already in effect become a binational city, where constant discrimination, favoritism, and unequal distribution of resources reproduce the reality of a poorer eastern side and a wealthier western side. The oppressed Palestinian residents of the city harbor a growing resentment towards the Israeli government, which is giving preferential treatment to the Jewish population.

International law calls for the separation of Jerusalem's two parts and the complete Israeli withdrawal from the illegally annexed eastern side. Yet in the current reality, a blind implementation of the stipulations of international law would cause widespread suffering among both Jews and Palestinians. Palestinians would lose access to West Jerusalem and settlers would be either cut off from Israel or evacuated from their homes.

The legitimate demands to end the illegal occupation are sometimes at odds with the demands of East Jerusalem Palestinians to receive full Israeli citizenship and all the social rights that come with it. However, an increasing number of Palestinians and Israelis realize that the choice is not only between separation or continued occupation: a third solution is also possible. Instead of creating an artificial border, reinforced by a wall that dissects the city, a unified city with free movement can be established. Many possible solutions have already been proposed under this framework – a city that would be declared the capital of both Israel and a Palestinian state (with two municipalities), a confederation of two states which allows people to have either citizenship but to live in either part of the city, a city managed by an international agency, or a unified city which serves as the capital of a unified state for both Jews and Palestinians. These solutions all require a larger perspective than Jerusalem itself, and all of them involve a fundamental change in the relations between Israel and the OPT. See Chapter 8 for a further discussion on binationalism.

CONCLUSION: THE ECONOMIC DAMAGE OF THE WALL

After recounting the various forms of damage that the Wall of Separation has inflicted upon the Palestinian population in Jerusalem –

and the threats it poses to Israeli interests – Kimhi attempts to offer various solutions and alternatives to the Wall. However, he does not even consider the possibility of dividing Jerusalem and withdrawing to the 1967 international borders, as international law requires, arguing instead that in order to maintain its control over East Jerusalem, Israel must also maintain the free and steady connections between East Jerusalem and the neighboring Palestinian cities: Bethlehem, Beit-Jala, Beit-Sahour, Ramallah, Jericho, and various other small towns and villages (Kimhi, 2006). This argument effectively undermines the idea of a two-state solution. If Israel needs cities like Ramallah and Bethlehem in order to maintain its control over East Jerusalem, and if Israel has worked since 1967 to prevent any future division of Jerusalem, then it becomes increasingly apparent that drawing a border between Israel and the Palestinians is difficult, if not impossible (Kimli, 2006).

Taking into account the Wall's many detrimental effects on Jerusalemites, it is not surprising that the participants in the Jerusalem Institute for Israel Studies were adamantly against it. Many said that they believe the Wall must be stopped or destroyed; others said that nothing can alleviate its damage. Only 11 percent of the people surveyed said that there was any possibility of leading a normal life with the Wall, and then only if Israel provided services to replace the lost services, the Israeli courts took action to defend the public, and special support was given to the residents of Jerusalem (Kimli, 2006.).

Compared with the rest of the Wall of Separation in the non-Jerusalem area, the Jerusalem Wall is especially damaging because it cuts through an urban area and affects hundreds of thousands of people on a daily basis. Unlike the rest of the Wall, ad hoc solutions (such as special permits or adding a few gateways) cannot even begin to repair the long-term damage that the Wall has already created.

The damage caused by the Wall, estimated here (see pages 126–7) at nearly US$200 million annually, is a heavy burden on the city's economy. As a result of the Wall, not only are the economic gaps between Israelis and Palestinians widening, but the Israeli state is also accumulating an onerous economic debt. Since the International Court of Justice has ruled that the Wall is illegal, there is a legal possibility for Palestinians to demand compensation from Israel for the damages inflicted upon them. This accumulating debt could turn out to be one of the greatest threats to the integrity of the Israeli economy, and could be a crucial factor in determining the political solution to be negotiated between Israel and the Palestinians.

PART II

IMPLICATIONS OF THE ECONOMY OF THE OCCUPATION

The previous section was mostly descriptive in nature, detailing some of the facets of the economy of the occupation. This section deals with the conclusions that can be drawn from the facts that were presented, and how these facts can be organized into a theoretical understanding of the economy of the occupation. It begins by attempting to clarify the reason for the continuation of the occupation despite the heavy costs to the Israeli economy, and proceeds to a discussion in the possible ways in which the occupation can end and the conflict be resolved, in light of contemporary economic realities.

7

BEYOND EXPLOITATION

The occupation of the OPT has taken a heavy toll on the Israeli economy, as I have tried to show in Chapters 4 and 5. Many Israelis have paid a heavy personal price for Israel's policies. Yet Israeli voting patterns demonstrate that the lower classes in Israel, who suffer the brunt of the economic costs of the occupation, are not likely to vote for political parties that call for an end of the occupation and for a reallocation of public resources towards civilian projects. Amongst Israeli Jews, it is specifically the upper classes, the people who are materially more comfortable and need change less urgently, who exhibit a greater tendency to vote for parties that support withdrawal from the OPT (Hever, 2008b).

If the occupation is seen as a project undertaken by the state of Israel, then the project's heavy cost begs the question, "Why does the Israeli government persist in occupying the OPT?" The explanations are either apologetic or critical of the occupation. Apologetic explanations, which support the occupation or see it as a necessary evil (that is, Israel must maintain control of the OPT because all other options are worse for Israeli security), are not discussed here. There is sufficient bibliography available to prove that the occupation does not improve Israel's security situation (for example, see Swirski, 2008a: 30). Furthermore, arguments that advance the biblical rights of the Jewish people to the entire "Land of Israel" (the borders of the "Land of Israel" are controversial; some argue that they extend as far as the Nile River in Egypt and the Euphrates River in Iraq) are faith-based, and I can summon no arguments to counter a person's faith. As for nationalistic arguments contending that territorial expansion is required in order to create a place for Jews from all over the world to settle in, the occupation has only proved that the extra territory acquired by military conquest undermines the Jewish majority in Israel and thus the country's chances of survival as a Jewish state. Today even mainstream Israeli political discourse recognizes that fact.

The critical arguments that explain the occupation, however, have traditionally been based on the assumption that there is some sort of material gain to be won from Israel's occupation of the OPT. That is the incentive for Israel to keep the OPT under its control. Such material gains, which were discussed in Chapter 1, indeed provide a powerful explanation for Israel's occupation in the first two decades following the war of 1967. However, as the economic burdens of the occupation mounted, the Israeli authorities did not reconsider their strategy. Although they have presented the occupation as a temporary phenomenon, they have taken measures to entrench it more deeply with increasing regularity, even as the occupation has become less profitable for Israelis. This process was initiated in Jerusalem from the very first days of the occupation (Amirav, 2007: 55–64), but quickly spread to the rest of the OPT (Azoulay and Ophir, 2008: 12–13, 65–7, 149, 360–3).

In order to understand this seemingly irrational choice by Israelis, we must go beyond the traditional explanations and look at some social theories that can offer an insight into the nature of the occupation and its seeming contradictions. Towards that end, I will examine the theories of Thorstein Veblen, Pierre Bourdieu, and Amartya Sen.

Thorstein Veblen (1857–1929) was the founding father of the institutional school of political economy. His achievements and those of his followers in economic theory amounted to a full-fledged body of thought, offering a holistic vision of the economic workings of human societies throughout history (Hodgson, 2004: 3–11, 176–205, 248–82). Despite the fact that Veblen developed his theory many decades before Israel occupied the OPT, some of the theoretical insights may shed some light on the occupation and the reasons for it.

Although Veblen offers a comprehensive economic theory, only two specific concepts are relevant to the discussion at hand: "conspicuous consumption" and "sabotage." Both have to do with the waste of economic resources, and offer interesting applications for an economic examination of violent social situations in general, and the occupation of the Palestinian territories by Israel in particular.

"CONSPICUOUS CONSUMPTION"

In his book *Theory of the Leisure Class* (1899), Veblen articulates his theory of social hierarchy, dividing the roles of human beings into "production" and "predation." He claims that when a prehistoric society became able to produce a surplus beyond the minimum necessities, members of that society became "predators" – living off the surplus produced by others. Social institutions such as the military, religion, fashion, higher education, and governments are all institutions of "predation" – they serve to consume the production surplus by fortifying social status. Veblen argued that people who dedicate their time to the aforementioned institutions avoid using their time for the production of goods. By this means (and others), social institutions help to control and limit industrial production.

Veblen's main argument is that instead of pursuing material wealth as a goal in its own right, people tend to see themselves only in relation to others. What concerns them is not absolute wealth, but relative wealth. The struggle to increase relative wealth and social status is manifested both within the institutions that a person belongs to, and in the constant striving to belong to more prestigious institutions (Veblen, 1897: 43–62).

That is a far-reaching assumption with respect to human nature. And although human nature is a risky subject, in both philosophy and the social sciences, it may be best to temporarily suspend judgment in order to properly understand Veblen's position. In the contemporary scientific discourse of Veblen's time, such assumptions were not out of the ordinary; they can be seen, for example, in the writings of Herbert Spencer (1820–1903) (Young, 1990). It is crucial to keep this criticism of Veblen in mind when discussing his theory, and to take his conclusions with a pinch of salt. However, Veblen's analysis holds even if only a part of human society acts in keeping with his distinction between "production" and "predation."

The struggle for relative wealth and social standing, according to Veblen's analysis, is neither internal nor individualistic. People require affirmation of their success, recognition from society that they have indeed achieved relative wealth. This recognition can be seen as something akin to social status. People do not simply amass wealth, Veblen claims, but strive to publicly demonstrate more wealth than their colleagues, and thus to fortify their social position (Veblen, 1897: 43–62). The means for demonstrating wealth is "conspicuous consumption" – a purposeful waste of resources, which proves that the demonstrator can afford such waste. Luxury is therefore an exercise in self-limitation. For example, rich people tend to wear fashionable clothes that place appearance over function, and which make it difficult them to perform manual labor, as such clothes would then be ruined. Their clothes inhibit their actions, thus proving that they do not need to perform manual labor to survive (Veblen, 1897: 103–16).

Social institutions often determine patterns of conspicuous consumption. By setting standards for clothing, by expending time on rituals, ceremonies, and studies,[1] institutions limit the productive capacity of their members, and therefore belonging to them is a form of "conspicuous consumption" (Veblen, 1897: 203–22.). The standards are important – they prove to the onlooker that the person belonging to an institution does not have to devote all their time to earning a living from other sources, and thus reinforce the prestige of the individual as being well-off enough that they can afford to spend their time pursuing their interests, faith, or political beliefs.

The Israeli occupation of the OPT indeed seems to be such an exercise in expense, which can be seen as "conspicuous consumption" – a way of purchasing social status for Israelis, and not just material benefits (such as land and cheap labor). Although the public image of colonial occupiers may not be a positive one, this might not carry too much weight, for Veblen argues that the main function of prestige is to demonstrate one's wealth. Colonial occupiers do indeed enjoy and project an image of wealth, even if at a heavy cost to their standard of living.

"SABOTAGE"

The most important concept for our purposes is "sabotage," a concept developed by Veblen in several of his publications (the first was "The opportunity of Japan," Veblen, 1915). Veblen defines this term as a "willful retardation, interruption or obstruction of industry by peaceable, and ordinarily by legally defensible, measures" (Veblen, 1917: 167). In other words, he defines "sabotage" as an activity that destroys or hinders the production of wealth, using means that are not warlike or illegal (though they may be violent). The reason for such destruction is that it enables a reallocation of wealth, and it also has the capacity to boost the value of objects of wealth that have been spared from destruction.

Veblen sees "sabotage" as a prerequisite for profit. According to Veblen, industry is at odds with profit. Industry (meaning production in all forms, not necessarily industrial production) is indeed required for profit, yet too much industry is actually harmful to

1 Studying creates human capital and thus can be seen as productive investment. But many fields of study are not directly related to industry. Veblen notes that subjects like history, literature, and philosophy bestow prestige on experts in the field, but do not contribute to the production of goods.

profit because of the competition and the lowering of prices that it creates. This dialectical relation between industry and profit can best be understood by examining the two possible extremes: no industry and maximum industry. Without industry, there are no products or commodities. There can therefore be no value of any kind and profit cannot exist. At the other extreme, industry that operates at maximum capacity creates such a plethora of products and commodities that the exchange value of goods must drop to zero (even though they still have use value). Without exchange value, profit cannot exist.

Veblen assumes that at maximum industrial capacity, when the entire society is efficiently employed, profit cannot thrive. For Veblen, profit is understood in the classical economic sense – as revenue that accumulates from the possession of capital, rather than from labor or trade. If there is no scarcity of capital, production is not constrained by it and therefore profit cannot exist. With capital too abundant, revenue can only be generated from labor and trade. Profit, therefore, is only possible in the area between no production and maximum production.

There are similarities between Veblen's theory of a trade-off between profit and industry and the neoclassical theory of monopolies. Monopolies in neoclassical theory also limit production in order to get a better price for their goods, something that can be seen as a limited form of "sabotage." However, Veblen's theory is more overreaching and discusses the economy as a whole, while the neoclassical theory of monopolies focuses on individual companies.

Figure 7.1 is based on Bichler and Nitzan's analysis of the Veblenian concept of "sabotage," with minimal changes (Bichler and Nitzan, 2001: 72–81). It is wholly theoretical and not based on any

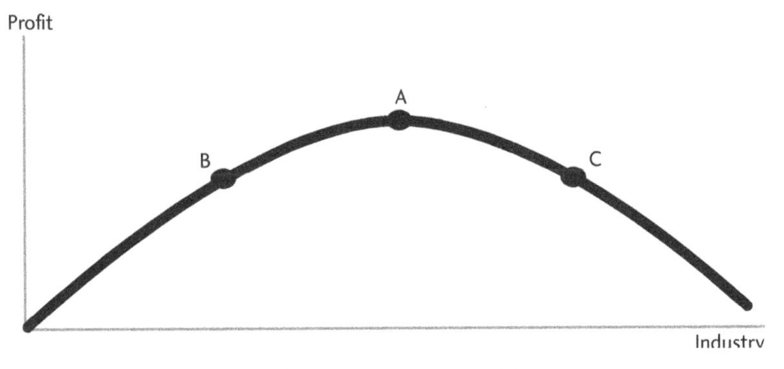

Figure 7.1 Sabotage: the relations between profit and industry

empirical data, although Bichler and Nitzan have found empirical reinforcements for the theory elsewhere (see below).

The concept of "sabotage" stipulates that when society is at around point A in Figure 7.1 (maximum profit), the situation is "business as usual." Although businesspeople still vie against each other, they make no attempts to transform the general economic system. When society is at around point B (meaning that industry is below the point that enables maximum profit), the method for increasing profit is industry. Here Veblen agrees with both conservative and Marxist economists that profit is proportional to production. Increasing profit through increasing production is a common notion of both conservative and Marxist thinkers (Marx, 1867). Veblen, however, argues that this only occurs when social production is below the optimal level for profit. When society is at around point C (meaning that industry is beyond the point of maximum profit), the relations between industry and profit are reversed. If industrial capacity expands beyond point A, more and more business owners are in a position to increase their profits if output is reduced. It is at this point that "sabotage" comes into play – the means by which the business community moves, or attempts to move, to the left side of the graph.

This, of course, is just a coarse generalization. Different sectors of the economy or different countries can be located at different points along the graph, with different ratios between industry and profit. However, globalization and the ability of investors to shift their capital quickly from one sector or country to another have created a tendency for a certain regime of production (a certain ratio between industry and profit) to spread geographically.

It is also important to stress that the graph does not imply that point A is an equilibrium point. Businesspeople may try to increase their profits by the best means available to them, and may either increase or decrease production, depending on the current regime of production. However, there are other players in the economic playing field who also affect the economic relations. Labor unions, governments, customs, and public opinion can prevent businesspeople from achieving optimal profit ratios.

"Sabotage" is effectively a series of actions that contribute to the destruction, delay, and inhibition of production. Without actually destroying the economic system itself, "sabotage" creates obstacles to free production. These obstacles are a source of profit to the people who control them and a means of increasing the exchange value of goods that cannot be produced or traded freely. One common example of "sabotage" is when a business intentionally lowers prices in an attempt to drive competitors out of the market, at the cost of lower profits in the short run (that is, dumping). The result is an overall drop in production, leaving the businesses with the greatest staying power (usually the businesses to initiate such a move) with a larger share of the market, and the ability to generate more profits as a result of their newly acquired monopolistic position. Another common example is when raw-material extraction companies intentionally leave mines, quarries, and wells idle to drive up the price of commodities.

It is important to note that Veblen did not think of "sabotage" as a tool that only businesspeople and capitalists could use to create value and increase profits. He claims that workers also use "sabotage" to increase the value of their labor. The paradigmatic example is the strike: by halting production, the workers increase the exchange value of their labor, which means their wage and/or social benefits. An important qualification must be made that this refers to a localized strike – one that attempts to force a redistribution of wealth in an existing economic arrangement, not to overthrow that arrangement altogether. Actions that seek to revolutionize society itself, such as a general strike, go beyond the definition of "sabotage."

In Veblen's theory of economic relations, "sabotage" is therefore an important tool used by economic agents. It is present, in varying degrees, in every aspect of economic activity. Economic agents, be they producers or consumers, employers or employees, use "sabotage" to increase the value of their assets. Although the extent of the "sabotage" is up to the wishes and the limitations of the individual user, it exists wherever there is profit (Veblen, 1921).

The extension of Israel's authority into the OPT and the establishment of an Israeli-controlled legal system there have enabled Israelis, business owners as well as workers, to sabotage Palestinian production and ensure their economic superiority. As mentioned in Chapter 1, the Israeli authorities have prevented economic development in the OPT and implemented severe limitations on the bargaining power of Palestinian workers. These limitations have increased the ability of Israelis to generate income in the combined economy of Israel and the OPT.

The Palestinian resistance, however, is not a form of "sabotage," since it rejects the Israeli occupation and seeks to reformulate the legal, political, and economic conditions in the OPT according to different principles. The Palestinian resistance is able to undermine Israel's reallocation efforts, and it has rendered Israeli "sabotage" ineffective as a means of increasing the income of Israelis. There are, however, exceptions to this. A few Israeli and international companies have positioned themselves in key industries that profit from the occupation. The fact that Israeli authorities continue to escalate the struggle despite the Palestinian resistance, and continue to perform "sabotage," demands further explanation, which will be offered below.

MARXIST DISCOURSE ON THE ISRAELI OCCUPATION OF THE OPT

Maxine Molyneux and Fred Halliday 1984) argue that the Marxist tradition has influenced many aspects of Middle Eastern liberation and resistance movements, and that its influence is apparent in all "anti-imperialist" movements. As a paradigm of political economy, Marxism is a holistic science which attempts to formulate broad explanations. Therefore, Marxists have frequently argued that the occupation can be explained by Marxist theory, meaning that it does not fall outside the scope of Marxist thought. Political sentiments cannot be externalized in Marxist theory, but must be an integral part of the understanding. The actual academic Marxist discourse on the Israeli occupation is, however, limited in scope.

Comparatively recent studies of the occupation that use Marxist arguments include those by Marwan Bishara, Jake Bower, Efraim Davidi, Jeff Halper, Amira Hass, Yagil Levy, and Sara Roy. Danny Gutwein's work is discussed in the next section.

Marwan Bishara, in his 2001 book *Palestine/Israel: Peace or apartheid?*, argued that the Oslo Process enabled Israel to exert control over the Palestinian economy and exploit it. During the 1990s the Palestinians suffered from an economic crisis, while at the same time Israel enjoyed years of economic prosperity, directly resulting from the exploitation of the Palestinians (Bishara, 2001: 43, 139).

Jake Bower, in his article "Why it rains: Hamas holding 'Israeli' gas reserves hostage" (2006), analyzed Israel's attack on the Gaza Strip in July 2006. Bower sees the attack as a military operation designed mainly to achieve control over the gas reserves in Gaza and the profits that could come from them. His article is one of many over the years describing the policies of the occupation as intended to appropriate Palestinian resources. Bower's analysis posits exploitation as the main and central reason for the attack, while all other explanations – cultural, political, military, and so on – are relegated to secondary importance (Bower, 2006).

Efraim Davidi, in his article "Who is a communist?" (2006), suggested that the Israeli occupation of the OPT plays a double role. First, it confers control of the Palestinian market, and second, it divides the Israeli and Palestinian working classes, thus facilitating the control of capitalists over both parts of the economy – the Israeli and the Palestinian. The economic burden of the occupation to Israel is, therefore, part of the cost of maintaining class differences and the hegemony of the capitalists. It is also part of the cost of production of a false consciousness. The occupation, according to Davidi, creates a state of struggle and insecurity which helps the Israeli elites distract the working class (in Israel and the OPT) from the way in which they are being exploited. This is another paradigmatic article, which clearly demonstrates the most common perception of the occupation by Marxist thinkers (Davidi, 2006).

Jeff Halper, an anthropologist and political activist, has formulated the concept of "the matrix of control" in order to explain Israel's occupation of the OPT. Halper argues that all of Israel's policies toward the Palestinians share one common trait – they all strive to deepen and fortify Israel's control over every aspect of life of the Palestinians. In Halper's writing, there is no distinction between the desire to control and the desire to own. The underlying explanation suggested by his description is that Israel is extending its control over water reservoirs, land, and other natural resources. In other words, the matrix of control allows Israel to exploit the Palestinians' natural resources (Halper, 2005: 3, 20, 23–4, 31, 73, 81, 87).

Amira Hass, one of the most prominent journalists covering the Israeli occupation, is known for her extensive writing on the damages and casualties to the Palestinians caused by Israel. Hass has described the occupation not only as a source of suffering for the Palestinians, but also as a source of profit for Israel, especially through the exploitation of cheap Palestinian labor (2002a, 2002b). Hass also sees international aid as part of the mechanism used by Israel to extract material profit from the occupation (2009). Additionally, Hass argues that class struggle among the Palestinians prevents the emergence of an effective resistance movement against the occupation. She hints that the exploitation which the occupation makes possible yields gains not only to Israelis, but also to certain upper-class Palestinians who turn into Israel's accomplices and assist the occupation (Hass, 2002b).

Yagil Levy has also echoed the exploitation argument. In his 2006 article "Materialistic militarism," Levy argued that the Israeli army serves as a tool for the forcible appropriation of capital from the

Palestinians. The Israeli bourgeoisie, says Levy, uses the army as it would any other means of production – only the army in turn has shaped Israeli society as well, and set it on a different path from most liberal democracies (Levy, 2006).

Levy also argues that when military service began to hinder the economic prosperity of middle-class and upper-class Jews, it brought them into conflict with the military tradition. This conflict revolves mainly around the public budget, with the military brass pushing for more military spending and the economic elites for tax cuts instead. This conflict has not yet been resolved. Levy adds that in this conflict, the army attempts to intensify the fighting with the Palestinians in order to increase the resources allocated to it. Levy thus maintains a materialistic view of the conflict, but shifts the focus away from the Palestinians as historical subjects. The conflict, according to him, is internal to Israeli society. It is a conflict between different kinds of capitalists, those that rely on the military as their source of income and those that see the military as an obstacle to their material prosperity. In this framework, the cost of the occupation is the cost of the internal conflict in Israeli society (Levy, 2006).

Sara Roy has written a great deal on the economic subjugation and exploitation of the Palestinians. She has coined the phrase "de-development," to accentuate the idiosyncratic nature of the Israeli occupation, which sets it apart from "under-development." Roy was inspired by the under-development arguments of the Marxist "dependency theory," which contends that poor countries are held back by rich countries as a result of unfair trade relations. But Roy goes beyond the under-development argument to claim that the Israeli occupation does not only delay Palestinian development, but actually forcefully prevents and even retards it. Roy claims that Israeli policies that arrest Palestinian development are put into place in order to favor Israeli over Palestinian businesses (Roy, 1999, 2000). Roy has also pointed out that Israel, especially since Oslo, has used the Palestinians as hostages, asking for aid and political concessions from the international community as the "price of peace." That is another way by which Israel profits from the occupation and exploits the Palestinians (Roy, 2001).

There are two challenges to Marxist reasoning regarding the occupation, however. First is the "Israeli anomaly," the tendency of lower-class Israelis to vote against their class interests; and second is the difficulty in demonstrating the prominence of exploitation in the economic relations between Israel and the Palestinians. The first challenge is discussed below. The second challenge – the difficulty in proving the centrality of exploitative relations between Israel and the OPT – is the bigger one, perhaps because exploitation is simply not as prominent as many Marxist thinkers would like to think.

THE ISRAELI ANOMALY

One specific aspect of the Marxist discourse on the occupation deserves special notice, and that is the "Israeli anomaly." The Marxist discourse seeks to analyze the occupation and the conflict between Israel and the Palestinians not merely as a national conflict, but as a manifestation of class struggle. That requires an analysis of the class divide within Israeli society, since Israel cannot be seen as a homogenous group. Before I offer an explanation for the phenomenon, it may be useful to show how this problem has created unease for Marxist thinkers.

That raises some difficulties. Analyzing the class interests of Israel's working class as opposed to the capitalist class seems to suggest, as most Israeli Marxists agree, that the working class in Israel suffers economically because of the occupation. While the Israeli capitalist class is flexible enough to shift its investments into areas that are less prone to be affected by the occupation, the working class suffers from government expenditure on the occupation. That is because government resources are directed toward military build-up and the control mechanisms in the OPT rather than toward public services and welfare, and because Israeli workers suffer lower wages and high unemployment rates because of the competition with Palestinian workers whose wages are much lower than those of Israelis (Swirski, 2005: 11–42).

Marxist theory, as a political economic theory, rejects the separation between economic and political struggles. Each and every struggle is at the same time both economic and political. Therefore, the Palestinian struggle against the occupation is part of a larger class struggle. The struggle can be seen either as a direct conflict between working-class Palestinians and oppressive Israeli forces in the service of capitalists, or as a struggle intended to sow discord among members of the working class by dividing them by national distinction between Israeli and Palestinian workers (Laclau and Moufe, 2004).

Therefore, a key problem in the attempts to explain the occupation lies in explaining the so-called "Israeli anomaly," namely the fact that working-class Jewish citizens of Israel would rather identify with a nationalist agenda than form a solidarity movement with the

Palestinian working class (in both Israel and the OPT). Furthermore, working-class Jews often support political parties that promote the use of resources to entrench military power and to take over Palestinian lands, rather than the parties that promote using the state's resources for welfare or social reform (Gutwein, 2004).

A study conducted in 2000 by Michael Shalev, Yoav Peled, and Oren Yiftachel, entitled *The Political Impact of Inequality: Social cleavages and voting in the 1999 elections*, has addressed this phenomenon, which the authors call "the Israeli paradox." The paradox is characterized by voting patterns that do not follow class interests, especially with poor Israelis tending to vote for nationalist parties. The authors stress that in other countries the connection between class differences and voting patterns is usually the opposite. To explain Israel's special case, they argue that the class struggle has been submerged beneath ethnic struggle and national strife. Though conceding that certain elements of class struggle have been incorporated into the ethnic struggle of the Mizrahim,[2] they maintain that the relation between Jews and Palestinians remains at the heart of the class paradox (Shalev et al., 2000).

In the study's conclusion, the authors reflect on the Israeli paradox of class voting without traditional class politics, speculating that it may be explained by the interplay between class, ethnicity, and culture under the specific conditions that pertain to the Israeli case. The class position of Ashkenazim versus Mizrahim and the surge of identity politics in Israeli politics in recent years have created a complex pattern of interests. The authors therefore argue that there are alternative foundations for the class voting among non-Arab Israelis, and downplay the importance of the occupation and national questions (Shalev et al., 2000). In short, their study attempts to explain how class politics in Israel are not represented in the voting patterns, even though the evidence clearly indicates that class is important in Israeli voting patterns.

The Israeli anomaly was addressed from a different angle by Danny Gutwein in his article "Comments on the class foundations of the occupation" (2004). Gutwein focuses his analysis on internal Israeli issues and questions regarding the distribution of national resources. He attempts to explain the anomaly from a materialistic aspect, arguing that the right-wing parties that abolished the Israeli welfare state also created an alternative welfare state in the amply

---

2 "Mizrahim" is the name of Jews originating from Arab countries, or descended from Jews who originated from Arab countries.

subsidized settlements in the OPT, thus providing the poor people of Israel with an escape from their deteriorating economic conditions (Gutwein, 2004).

That argument was severely criticized by Efraim Kleinman in his response to Gutwein's article. Kleinman argued that Gutwein's claim is not supported by the economic reality. In fact, Gutwein's insistence on making his argument, despite the lack of proper data to support his claim, only accentuates the problem that arises when the Marxist perspective is brought to bear on the "Israeli anomaly" (Kleinman, 2005). Nevertheless, Gutwein's article can be seen as an example of Marxist logic.

The Israeli anomaly in the political sphere is only one of many historical examples that challenge Marxist logic. The internal divisions among the working class and the political choices of laborers have sparked a century-old crisis in Marxist thought. Laclau and Moufe described this crisis and claimed that it was the reason for the emergence of orthodox Marxist thought and the development of strict determinism and scientific prediction among some Marxists. A second response to this crisis has been revisionism – the separation of the political from the economic sphere, and acknowledgment of autonomy for each (Laclau and Moufe, 2004).

One way that Marxists have tried to explain hierarchical structures based on ethnicity, nationality, or race, and which apparently break down the class model, is by advancing theories of middleman minorities. Edna Bonanich's articles "A theory of ethnic antagonism: the split labor market" (1972) and "A theory of middleman minorities" (1973) have described this phenomenon in great detail. Bonanich offers her own method of resolving the apparent contradiction between an ethnic or national understanding of conflict and the Marxist version of class conflict. Her theory suggests that the working class is split into a high-paid class and a low-paid class. Thus, Bonanich brings the class conflict back to the forefront, claiming that ethnic conflicts stem from class conflicts. The high-paid laborer class uses segregational practices and gives political and social meaning to ethnic, national, and religious differences in order to exclude certain groups from the well-paid positions and keep them in the low-paying jobs or unemployed (Bonanich, 1972, 1973).

The relevance of this argument to the case of the Israeli occupation of the OPT is clear – it offers a possible explanation of the Israeli anomaly. Working-class Jews have an economic incentive to marginalize non-Jews in order to protect their access to high-paying jobs. However, if such is the case, why do so many working-class Jews object to a two-state solution, which offers the potential of reducing the movement of Palestinian labour into Israel?

A possible partial reply to this question is that Israel's policies towards the occupied Palestinians prevent the Palestinians from performing productive work by limiting movement, confiscating land, and blocking raw materials. Therefore, as long as the occupation continues, Jewish and Palestinian citizens of Israel enjoy an advantage over Palestinians from the OPT in the competition over the limited supply of jobs available in Israel and the OPT (Arnon et al., 1997: 89). However, this reply becomes less convincing when we take into consideration the Palestinian citizens of Israel – who share similar economic interests with working-class Jews, but often have radically different political views (Faier, 2002). This phenomenon is one of the major thorns in the side of Marxist explanations of the occupation, because Palestinians with Israeli citizenship as well as Jewish Israelis tend to act on the basis of national or ethnic identity more often than on the basis of class interests.

The "Israeli anomaly" is not just a secondary issue that can be ignored. It is one of the reasons for the political paralysis in Israel, which has kept the Israeli negotiators in a state of continuous procrastination since negotiations between Israel and the Palestinians began in Madrid in 1991. Israeli leaders have been guided by the knowledge that compromise with the Palestinians will not win them any popularity with the Israeli public, their voters. Israeli governments have known that it would be political suicide for them to end the occupation, and have therefore used delaying tactics of various kinds to avoid making any progress in the peace process. Understanding the reasons for this procrastination, and for Israelis' insistent avoidance of political compromise, even at great cost, is a key to understanding the failure of the peace process to date.

EXPLOITATION

The exploitation of a subjugated group in order to generate profit for capitalists, which is manifested in the relations of production, is a central and indispensable part of Marx's economic theory of capitalism. The causal connection between this exploitation and the tendency of the working class to rebel is another central point Marx makes. In Marxist theory, therefore, the connection between exploitation and repression is based on the connection between the relations of production and the superstructure. Repression exists in order to enable exploitation (Boswell and Dixon, 1993; Marx and Engels, 1848).

Using capital and exploitation as a means of describing the control mechanisms imposed on the Palestinians creates a certain framework for understanding the occupation. This framework assumes that this structure of exploitation and repression is prominent in Israeli–Palestinian relations.

The methods used to exploit the Palestinian economy in the first two decades of occupation have been described in great detail, especially by Marxists, and a summary of these methods of exploitation was presented in Chapter 1. However, following the first intifada, the economic conditions have changed. Although certain Israeli companies continue to exploit the Palestinian economy, Marxists have failed to show how such companies are able to determine Israel's overall policy, or even to influence it.

If we assume that the Israeli government has the power and authority to continue the occupation, then we would need to find a control mechanism that connects the very specific capitalists who profit from the occupation and the policymakers who serve their interests. There are also many capitalists who suffer a loss of economic opportunities because of the occupation, but they have thus far failed to influence the Israeli government to withdraw. Therefore, that part of the Marxist argument that insists the occupation is a tool for exploiting the Palestinian economy to the benefit of Israeli capitalists is inadequate.

An answer to this problem can possibly be found in an article published by Terry Boswell and William J. Dixon in 1993, "Marx's theory of rebellion: a cross-national analysis of class exploitation, economic development and violent revolt." The article presents an empirical analysis of various cases of revolt in several countries, and finds that economic development has a positive effect on the chances of uprising, increasing the chances that exploited groups will rebel. The authors claim that this conforms with Marx's theory – that economic development leads to increased class tension and eventually to revolution – despite the apparent contradiction it poses to the famous quote from the *Communist Manifesto*, that revolution comes only when "The proletarians have nothing to lose but their chains" (Boswell and Dixon, 1993).

One of the article's weaknesses is that in order to support their arguments, the authors use econometric methods and statistical methodology. These instruments are based on a static, rather than dialectical, perspective, and are therefore counterintuitive to Marxist thought. The authors nevertheless use this approach in order to stress their point by means acceptable to mainstream economic research. The value of this argument to the authors stems from the difficulties that Marxists encounter when attempting to explain nationalist movements of revolt. It is difficult to demonstrate the connection between development, exploitation, and violent uprisings by empirical means, as is evident by the compromise that the authors make in order to advance their argument and yet still be able to promote their agenda of defending Marxist thought.

This claim of a positive correlation between development and uprising can be used by Marxists to explain Israeli policy against the Palestinians. Retarding the Palestinian economy, even at great cost to Israel, could be seen as a tool with which Israeli capitalists forestall the possibility of a Palestinian class-based revolt, and especially of such a revolt potentially spilling over into Israel (through first the Palestinian citizens of Israel, and later the rest of Israel's working class). However, this argument still fails to explain why Israel would maintain its control over the Palestinians in the first place. After all, without occupation, a rebellion against the occupation cannot occur.

Additionally, Israeli officials openly stated in the first years of the occupation already that the best way to keep the Palestinians from rebelling was to support a higher standard of living (Gordon, 2008b: 9–20, 44–7), and indeed there is a correlation – the two intifadas erupted following economic crises in the OPT (see Chapter 1).

FILLING THE GAPS

Notwithstanding the impressive descriptive power of Marxist theory, some aspects of the occupation – mainly the escalation of violence which damages both sides – continue to elude a Marxist explanation. Answers to these points may perhaps be found in other theories. This is therefore an opportune moment to return to Veblen. The aspects of the occupation that seem to defy Marxist explanations relate to an understanding of human behavior beyond the framework of class struggle. Interestingly, the reduction of human behavior to class struggle was one of the central points of Marxism criticized by Veblen:

> While the material interpretation of history points out how social development goes on – by a class struggle that proceeds from maladjustment between economic structure and economic function – it is nowhere pointed out what is the operative force at work in the process. It denies that human discretion and effort

> seeking a better adjustment can furnish such a force, since it makes man a creature of circumstances. This defect reduces itself ... to a misconception of human nature and of man as exclusively a social being, who counts in the process solely as a medium for the transmission and expression of social laws and changes; whereas he is, in fact, also an individual, acting out his own life as such. Hereby is indicated not only the weakness of the materialistic theory, but also the means of remedying the defect pointed out. With the amendment so indicated, it becomes not only a theory of the method of social and economic change, but a theory of social process considered as a substantial unfolding of life as well.
>
> (Veblen, 1897)[3]

The theory proposed by Veblen attempts to overcome this reductionism and to acknowledge the importance of understanding individual decisions.

OUTLINES OF BOURDIEU'S THEORY

The next theorist relevant to this discussion is Pierre Bourdieu (1930–2002). Bourdieu's theory, heavily influenced by Veblen, builds on the concepts of social status and hierarchy utilized by Veblen in order to describe economic realities. Its relevance to the issue of the Israeli occupation of the OPT stems from Bourdieu's attempt to create a framework of multi-causal understanding of economic and social practices. The argument developed in the previous chapters of this book suggests that the occupation is a complex phenomenon, which defies any explanation based on rational decision making by profit-seeking individuals. Therefore, a complex theory of social relations is required in order to form a clearer understanding of the occupation.

In his conceptualization of social hierarchies in modern society, Bourdieu rejects not only the neoliberal explanation, but also the Marxist explanations. Bourdieu's criticism of neoliberal thought, which is extensive and well-developed, is not detailed here, beyond noting that his theory attempts to address matters that he believes to be improperly addressed by neoliberal theory (Bourdieu, 1998a: 29–30).

In addition, Bourdieu rejects the main challenge that the left poses to neoliberalism by rejecting Marxist arguments as well. His criticism of Marxism has two layers. First, he claims that Marxism tends to

3 This text, originally appearing in Veblen (1897), was also quoted in Hodgson (2004).

overestimate the importance of classes. Second, Marxism is a form of "economism" – reducing every aspect of social existence to the level of relations of production, and ignoring cultural and social aspects of human life which are too complex to be understood as elements of production (Bourdieu, 1985: 723–7). Bourdieu even wrote that Marxism is the biggest obstacle to the development of contemporary social theory (1985: 742).

Bourdieu claims that Marxist thought fails to articulate the process by which a class forms "class consciousness" and becomes a class in its own right, acting according to its class interests. This failure, he suggests, is the result of the "economism" embedded in Marxist and neo-Marxist thought. The symbolic power relations and the "schemes of evaluation," which bestow value on objects through a cultural process, are overlooked by Marxists and neo-Marxists, because they are too complex to be understood solely within the framework of the class struggle (Bourdieu, 1985: 723–44).

This critique is not unlike the criticism voiced by Veblen, which was discussed above. Bourdieu thus attempted to fill the gaps that he perceived in Marxist thought, and to arrive at a more detailed understanding of key concepts in Marxist thinking, such as "class consciousness."

Bourdieu's second critique of Marxism is that Marxist theory tends to underestimate the power of theory. Bourdieu, like Marx, sees the ideology of the ruling class as a construct devised in order to justify its social privileges. He argues that neoliberalism is a weapon used by the upper classes to defend their position. However, unlike Marx he argues that the theory itself is a form of symbolic and cultural capital, and is therefore an essential part of the mechanism of repression, and not just the superstructure built upon the material relations of exploitation. In that light, the conservative shift that began in the 1970s and 1980s known as neoliberalism was not just a new economic order of dispossession and redistribution of wealth, but also a shift in what is considered to be a valuable theory, a valid argument in economics, and in the symbolic capital of competing ideologies (Bourdieu, 1998a: 29–30).

It is important here to note that Bourdieu does, in fact, offer an economic social theory. He does not downplay the importance of economic thought, but rather expands on what he means by "economy," namely a field where conflicting interests collide – be they material, symbolic, scientific, or religious (Bourdieu, 2006).

Bourdieu's innovative contribution to social theory is the rejection of the two-dimensional structure of the class system, according to which all the classes are arranged from top to bottom in strict order. Instead, Bourdieu suggests a three-dimensional "social space," where the economic issue or the class conflict is but one axis among several. Capital is therefore not only an economic asset; Bourdieu conceives also of cultural capital, social capital, and symbolic capital, or prestige. Although the material layer is not overlooked by Bourdieu, he argues that social power relations cannot be reduced to the material level alone (Bourdieu, 1985: 724).

This analysis, which replaces a two-dimensional with a three-dimensional space, is the way in which Bourdieu managed to combine Marxist insights with certain aspects of Veblen's theory. The economic struggle of the class conflict exists alongside the competition over prestige and domination which Veblen articulates. Social and economic behavior must be understood along both the material axis and the axis of social prestige.

Bourdieu continues the spatial analogy with the concept of distance, which is a measure of obstacles to mobilization or cooperation. A class, according to Bourdieu, is an economic group that faces fewer economic obstacles to its mobilization as a unit. Yet limitations may still be imposed along other axes – such as obstacles created by "distance" in prestige or cultural capital between members of the same class (Bourdieu, 1985: 724). Another advantage of the spatial analogy is that it allows a more complex understanding of social hierarchy. Instead of a linear hierarchy based on a single scale, such as wealth, Bourdieu suggests that hierarchy is based on several scales. In this concept of multiple scales, Bourdieu is following in the footsteps of Max Weber (Bourdieu, 1985: 724).

For example, a schoolteacher might have less money than a professional electrician, but she has more social prestige. The hierarchy between them is therefore not clear-cut, and who comes out on top depends on the circumstances – which might be more conductive to symbolic capital, economic capital, or cultural capital, at any given moment. This might also make the two of them less likely to cooperate in a labour struggle (Bourdieu, 1985: 724).

The complexity of hierarchical relations between people only serves to intensify the social struggles for domination. People not only strive to increase their material wealth, but also attempt to achieve "distinction." The concept of distinction is central to Bourdieu's theory, and is one place where Veblen's influence on Bourdieu is most visible, and even acknowledged by Bourdieu.

Bourdieu also refers to Weber's work on deciphering the creation of differences and "classes" (*Stand* in the original German). Unlike

Marx, Weber posits a powerful connection between social distinction and ideological power. Weber's analysis, however, is less critical from a political aspect (Bourdieu, 1985). Also, according to Gil Eyal in his 2002 article "Dangerous liaisons between military intelligence and Middle Eastern studies in Israel," Bourdieu expanded on Weber's concept of "ideal types," and by unraveling their various components, manages to create an encompassing social theory of relations between consumers and producers.

Weber's important comments on the establishment of expertise and the co-dependency of producers and consumers have been adopted by Bourdieu in his argument that the economic sphere cannot be detached from the sphere of symbolic power. This argument is also a central tenet of Veblen's theory. Veblen claims that profit is the result of the combination of two forces – the forces of production, which produce goods, and the forces of "sabotage," which destroy these goods and give them their value at the same time (Eyal, 2002). Bourdieu therefore goes beyond both Veblen and Weber, and tries to explain distinction in a broader sense:

> Distinction does not necessarily imply the pursuit of distinction, as is often supposed, following Veblen and his theory of conspicuous consumption. All consumption and, more generally, all practice, is "conspicuous," visible. Whether or not it is performed in order to be seen; it is distinctive, whether or not it springs from the intention of being "conspicuous," standing out, of distinguishing oneself or behaving with distinction. As such, it inevitably functions as a *distinctive sign* and, when the difference is recognized, legitimate and approved, *as a sign of distinction* (in all senses of the phrase).
> (Bourdieu, 1985: 730)

Differences between groups do not sprout automatically from visible differences or differences in location. They are rooted in the social significance that is attached to these differences. Although the attachment of social significance to differences is a conscious act, according to Bourdieu, his main criticism of Veblen is that not all distinction is consciously sought after (Bourdieu, 1985: 730–2).

DISTINCTION, SYMBOLIC CAPITAL, AND HABITUS

Bourdieu's work has been especially important in deciphering and elaborating on the processes by which identity becomes a source of power or capital, the accumulation of prestige through the development of identity, and how this, in turn, contributes to the structuring of social hierarchies. Bourdieu focused mainly on occupational status (occupation in the sense of a profession) – the creation of social hierarchies between the different levels of status awarded to different professions. Bourdieu notes that some professions, while providing a lower income, are still preferable due to the increased prestige that they carry. According to Bourdieu, the profession has its own value, which is a measurement not simply of income, but also of social status and symbolic power.

The steepness of the hierarchy depends to a large extent on the level of distinction that each profession or social group achieves. There can be certain overlaps between groups, since the lower-status groups usually choose to identify themselves in loose categories so that their members can be mistaken as belonging to a higher-status group. At the same time, the higher-status groups try to create exclusive identities for themselves to minimize overlap (Bourdieu, 1985).

Bourdieu uses politicians' anti-immigration policies to illustrate this process of attaining symbolic capital through the creation of categories. He argues that speaking against foreigners is a way to gather easy votes. Common citizens who suffer from inequality and acute economic problems are still xenophobic enough to make them susceptible to vote for anti-immigration candidates, because these candidates offer them an opportunity to increase the value of their symbolic capital. Even if anti-immigration laws have only a negligible effect on the economic standard of living of lower-class voters, their symbolic capital can nevertheless be boosted by creating a category of people who are immune to anti-immigration laws, and placing those voters in that category.

Bourdieu uses the concept of "shibboleth"[4] – a test given to foreigners to separate them from the "locals." The signifier works both ways: it imprints its mark on the foreigners as unwanted, and at the same time it marks the locals as having a certain form of significance. The relevance of this argument will become clearer when we discuss mechanisms of identification and classification in Israel below (Bourdieu, 1998a: 15–18).

4 The term originates from a biblical story (Judges, chapter 12), in which the pronunciation of a word ("shibboleth" – meaning grain spike) was used to distinguish between members of different groups, for the purpose of identifying one group and killing its members.

BOURDIEU'S THEORY AND THE OCCUPATION

Although Bourdieu did not discuss the Israeli occupation of the OPT directly while formulating the principles of his theory, it lends itself with ease to the occupation. This is partially because Bourdieu's theory deals with a situation of struggle and conflict on both a material and a social and cultural level. Bourdieu views hierarchy as a transient object, which is constantly being challenged within the framework of a power struggle (Bourdieu, 1985: 734).

One of Bourdieu's most valuable contributions to the understanding of the occupation is his rejection of the view, often adopted by mainstream economists, of the nature of society as static and uniform, as well as the view of uniform and consolidated classes that Marxists use in their theory. Instead, he offers a view of a complex and layered society in which individual agents belong to many overlapping groups with conflicting and adjoining interests and goals. This stratified and fragmented view of society greatly resembles Veblen's view of society.

Bourdieu's theory can further augment our understanding of the Israeli occupation of the OPT, by providing insight into the invisible and mute forms of power accumulation and discrimination which underlie the occupation. One of the important aspects of Bourdieu's theory is the exploration of concealed methods of attaining symbolic power (Gebauer, 2000). When attempting to apply his theory to the Israeli occupation of the OPT, we must assign the different mechanisms of power and hierarchy to different axes.

Group identity in Israel/Palestine is often based on nationality and religion more strongly than on economic income, and individuals draw upon these different aspects in forming their individual identities as well. Bourdieu claims that the most powerful incentives to the creation of group identity are frustration, anger, and insult. Therefore, groups are formed, among other reasons, to protect themselves when they sense that they are being attacked by a common threat. The Zionist narrative clearly identifies anti-Semitic attacks as the main reason for the emergence of Zionism. The Palestinian national identity is also very much constructed from a feeling of persecution – by Zionists and by Arab countries.[5] These are two instances where

5 Palestinian nationalists are often critical of Arab countries, claiming that they neglected the Palestinians in 1948 and since then have mistreated Palestinian refugees, forgetting the Palestinians in peace negotiations with Israel. They have also accused Jordan of suppressing the Palestinian national identity.

a feeling of persecution has led to the creation of national identities (Bourdieu, 1985: 729).

Bourdieu says that groups are formed not only by identifying themselves as victims of persecution, but by identifying the groups they accuse of wrongdoing. He points out that the word "category" comes from the root *kategoresthai*, meaning to publicly accuse (1985: 729). This kind of identity-creation process is even more pronounced in the Israel/Palestine framework. In his 2004 article "How did the Mizrahim 'become' religious and Zionist?", Yehouda Shenhav presents a prime example of such identity development, demonstrating that Mizrahi Jews have adopted a religious discourse in order to arm themselves for two purposes: to fight the suppression imposed by Ashkenazi Jews, and as a means of distinguishing themselves from Arabs (Shenhav, 2004).

Without going into the details of the Mizrahi identity among Israelis, there is an important argument to be made here about the "Israeli anomaly" discussed above. There is a deep correlation between the Mizrahi population in Israel and the lower socioeconomic classes. Although Mizrahi people had deep roots in Arabic culture and language prior to coming to Israel, their arrival into a situation of conflict between Jews and Palestinians prompted them to quickly create their own group identity (Swirski and Konor-Attias, 2005).

Bourdieu also offers a theory connecting issues of identity and classification with political opinion and votes:

> The political stances taken at a given moment (e.g. those expressed in election results) are thus the product of an encounter between a political supply of objectified political opinions (programs, party platforms, declarations, etc.) which is linked to the whole previous history of the field of production, and a political demand, itself linked to the history of the relations between supply and demand. The correlation that can be observed at a given moment between stances on a particular political issue and positions in the social space cannot be fully understood unless it is seen that the classifications that the voters implement in making their choices (right–left, for example) are the product of all the previous struggles, and that the same is true of the classifications the analyst implements in order to classify not only opinions but also the agents who express them.
>
> (Bourdieu, 1985: 737–9)

Bourdieu's theory, then, stipulates that political opinions are part of the process by which people choose their own classification and establish their identity and their symbolic capital (1985).

According to Bourdieu, the lower classes are not only economically impoverished, but are deprived of their fair share of symbolic capital as well. Yet symbolic power is constantly being produced and redistributed, just like economic capital, and the struggle over its distribution never ceases. Bourdieu suggests that the redistribution of symbolic capital is accomplished faster than the redistribution of material wealth, and thus lower classes have a smaller disadvantage in the field of symbolic conflict than in the field of economic conflict. He goes on to say that relations of domination are stronger the closer they are to the economic axis, and weaker the more they rely on cultural and social domination (Bourdieu, 1985: 735–9).

With reference to the Israeli occupation of the OPT, what this latter argument means is that the religious, nationalist, and identity conflict takes a front seat for lower-class Jews and Palestinians, while the economic struggle seems to offer much less possibility of immediate improvement. Whereas the contours of the nationalist conflict are determined in armed clashes and by the score-sheets of casualties on both sides, the economic conflict is harder to follow because of its complexity. This argument can shed light on the shortcomings of both the neoliberal and Marxist thinkers discussed above, for it shows that human behavior cannot be predicted on the basis of only an economic analysis. The theoretical solution is still incomplete, however, and the theory remains embryonic, as it does not formulate an alternative mechanism for predicting human behavior.

Taxonomies and categorizations, according to Bourdieu, are methods for creating social hierarchies. They attach labels and values to various aspects of an individual's identity, thus making the individual easier to control. Hierarchy is established by assigning values between two extremes: insult and nomination. Certain identity factors can turn someone into a subject of sanctioned scorn and humiliation, while other identity factors entitle their bearer to honor and prestige (Bourdieu, 1985: 732). This may help us understand why Israeli–Palestinian politics is dominated to such a great degree by identities.

Under the Israeli regime, police officers, soldiers, and security guards may approach people on the street and ask for identification papers. Since profiling[6] is a practice that the Israeli authorities legitimize, the people asked to present their papers are often selected because of their physical appearance, clothing (especially religious

6 Racial profiling is defined as a form of racism, consisting of the (alleged) policy of police officers who stop and search vehicles driven by persons belonging to particular racial groups based on physical appearance. See WordNet, <http://wordnet.princeton.edu/perl/webwn?s=racial%20profiling>.

garb), or the vehicle they drive. Officially, presenting the adequate papers should let the person continue on their way, but not before they have been delayed, sometimes searched, and invariably humiliated by each incident (see for example, Arab Association for Human Rights and Center against Racism, 2007). However, the impact such encounters have on the creation of social hierarchy has not been fully understood by either neoliberal or Marxist thinkers. The authority of a civil servant to question the rights of a person just because of their appearance, even if their papers are found to be in order, casts a stigma on the social group that is placed under constant suspicion. In the case of Israel, this refers to the non-Jewish or non-Ashkenazi population (Bourdieu, 1998a: 78–9).

Bourdieu also coined the concept of "habitus," another valuable theoretical tool towards alleviating some of the difficulties in understanding the occupation. "Habitus," defined as the non-discursive aspects of culture that bind individuals to larger groups, was developed by Bourdieu to explain the underlying structure of cultural and social power relations. According to Lois McNay, in her 1999 article "Gender, habitus and the field: Pierre Bourdieu and the limits of reflexivity," habitus is a theoretical steppingstone which can explain large-scale group discrimination:

> Bourdieu claims that large-scale social inequalities are established not at the level of direct institutional discrimination but through the subtle inculcation of power relations upon the bodies and dispositions of individuals.
>
> (McNay, 1999)

McNay argues that "symbolic violence," another term coined by Bourdieu, is used to replicate discrimination on the individual level. "Symbolic violence" attacks the Palestinians' status and symbolic worth, thus making it easier for Israelis to look down at them. This process eventually creates "distinction" for the upper classes. Therefore, Jewish Israelis who employ "symbolic violence" against the Palestinians eventually benefit from the "distinction" (which is a form of symbolic capital) that they accumulate as a result, and the entire process can occur independently of institutionalized means of discrimination (McNay, 1999). The "distinction" that Jews accumulate is something that largely they alone appreciate, when they compare themselves with the less fortunate Palestinians. Denying the value of Palestinian rights increases the value of their own rights.

Gil Eyal, whose article was mentioned above, has incorporated Bourdieu into his analysis of the role that the Israeli intelligence forces play in the Middle East conflict. Eyal has found that Israeli scholars are often willing to forgo much of their academic autonomy in order to collaborate with the Israeli intelligence forces. He argues that their willingness to make this sacrifice does not stem simply from a desire to make money, but that they are attempting to establish homologies between their field of study and military intelligence, to blur the difference between an academic study and an intelligence report. The search for homologies, which Bourdieu would call "habitus," increases the prestige of the scholars (Eyal, 2002).

SHORTCOMINGS OF BOURDIEU'S THEORY

It has not been my aim to argue that Bourdieu's theory solves all of the theoretical questions arising from the study of the sociology of the occupation. For example, Bourdieu claims that the dominated tend to demonstrate "realism" or "pragmatism" on the cultural axis, out of their need to survive, while the dominating tend to be more spiritual or whimsical (Bourdieu, 1985: 728–9). Although this claim might sound reasonable when applied to people who are on the brink of starvation (see Sen's discussion below), in Israel/Palestine the dominated groups often demonstrate that they attach a higher symbolic value than the dominating groups to non-pragmatic issues. Surveys conducted among OPT Palestinians, who clearly are a dominated group, often show that nationalist interests are more important to them than economic prosperity. Palestinians have expressed reservations about international aid, and claimed that they feel that the aid undermines their prospects for independence (Palestinian Ministry of Planning, 2003).

Inside Israel, citizens from the lower classes most often support political agendas that place nationalist and religious identity above employment or welfare. In the aforementioned study by Michael Shalev and colleagues (2000), the authors, using surveys and voting data from the 1990s, argued that ethnic, national, and religious matters take precedence over economic considerations among lower-class Israelis.

Bourdieu's idea can perhaps be expanded to incorporate the concept of compensating for the lack of a certain type of capital by focussing on the accumulation of another. When economic capital is in short supply, certain groups might aspire to accumulate symbolic and cultural capital instead. For example, a group of people may pursue an ascetic religious lifestyle to prove their piety (a form of symbolic capital), instead of accumulating wealth and luxuries.

Bourdieu's hierarchy, despite his best efforts, is still relatively static. Although it may extend to three dimensions, it loses some descriptive power in relation to time, the fourth dimension. Bourdieu's description of the dominated portrays them as meek and accepting of their fate. His analysis of insult versus nomination is unidirectional, but insult is one of the methods by which the dominated can target the dominating groups. Insult can even work both ways – an Israeli soldier at the checkpoint who is humiliating a Palestinian is not only reinforcing their own hierarchical supremacy over the Palestinian, but, by exerting arbitrary force with disregard to their orders, is also rebelling against the state and its right to dictate that soldier's behavior. The soldier's actions simultaneously further two different forms of symbolic capital accumulation – in the context of Jews versus Palestinians, and in the context of the soldier versus their commanders (Bourdieu, 1985: 732).

In coming to analyze the Israeli occupation of the OPT, the major problem with Bourdieu's theory is that it is too general and focusses on conceptualization, instead of offering a research methodology to analyze specific issues. It should therefore be seen as a complementary theory. Institutional political economy, discussed below, can bolster that theory and help scholars in formulating methodologies appropriate to an analysis of the economic aspects of the occupation.

OUTLINES OF AMARTYA SEN'S THEORY

Amartya Sen is a Noble Prize laureate and far more widely known and accepted than Bourdieu or Veblen. Although he began his career as a mainstream economist, he developed a trenchant critique of the way neoclassical and neoliberal economics treat poverty and hunger. Sen's work is very relevant to the Palestinian situation, specifically to the issue of humanitarian aid.

One of the first important distinctions offered by Sen, and one of his greatest contributions to the study of poverty and famine, is that hunger is the outcome of a situation in which people *do not have* food rather than one in which food does not exist. Although per capita food production in the world rose steadily throughout the second half of the twentieth century, famine and death from starvation were on the rise as well. Food shortages can result not only from a lack of food, but also from difficulties in purchasing sufficient amounts of the food produced (Sen, 1981: 42, 103). Sen proposes the concept of "entitlement" – the legitimate ownership of goods, or the legitimate ability to exchange one's original endowment (of either goods or labour power) for necessities (1981: 1–3) – which allows him to incorporate the struggle against poverty and famine within the framework of liberal thought. He claims that famine should not be permissible in a liberal democracy, because entitlement and freedom from hunger are among the basic civil rights (de Waal, 1997: 2–3, 7–8).

Through "exchange entitlement," Sen is able to remain within the paradigm of mainstream economic theory, which speaks of poverty and wealth in terms of available consumption bundles. Neoclassical and neoliberal economists use the income approach to calculate options for diets. They calculate the possible nutritional mixtures available for every level of income, and analyze human behavior on the basis of people's choices of certain bundles of foodstuffs at various income levels. Economists have sought to identify the food bundles that can sustain human beings at minimum cost, and defined poverty as any level of income that is insufficient to purchase these bundles. However, as Sen points out, these diets are often boring or socially unacceptable in the societies to which poor people belong (Sen, 1981: 22–3).

Social security, according to Sen, is also a form of entitlement. Social security assistance is based on the concept of insurance, and a person owns such insurance prior to the actual deprivation, even if merely as a result of being a citizen of a certain country. Because social security potentially exists for people whether they are hungry or not, it should be considered as part of their original entitlement (Sen, 1981: 6–7). Sen describes charitable aid too as a form of entitlement, albeit at a lower level – something that emanates from compassion. His logic is that if people who draw the pity of others also draw support from others, so that being pitiful is a source of income or entitlement. The distinction between entitlement through earned income and through pity is discussed below (Sen, 1981: 9–11).

The cycle of deprivation–misery–compassion–aid is not deterministic, but only one of many possible outcomes. Another option, for example, is the abandonment of deprived people to their fate. However, the connection between misery and compassion is not an arbitrary one. Sen believes that poverty is detrimental to society as a whole, and goes on to quote M. Rein: "People must not be allowed to become so poor that they offend or are hurtful to society." Poverty, then, is offensive to the non-poor as well as to the poor (Rein, 1971). The upper classes also have an interest in combating poverty, as it threatens the social cohesion of the society that awards them their wealth and social status. Poverty is also a blemish on the image of society, and wealthy people in a society with sharp inequalities may be seen as ruthless.

SEN'S THEORY AND THE OCCUPATION

Another facet of hunger described by Sen, and one especially pertinent to the Palestinians, is its time-sensitivity. Whereas in most cases goods can be stored for long periods, or their consumption can be delayed until they are available, food consumption must be continuous and relatively uninterrupted. Sen criticizes conservative economic theory for neglecting this important factor when calculating food supply and hunger. Since economists tend to aggregate findings, their calculations may ignore short-term decreases in food supply (lasting a few weeks or months), which nevertheless can have devastating effects on society and cause illness and death, even when the economic data for the entire year show a food surplus (Sen, 1981: 40; 1995).

Sen's most important insight towards an understanding of the occupation is the application of the concept of entitlement to humanitarian assistance. One of the most distinctive features of the Israeli occupation of the OPT is the fact that while Israel maintains control over the Palestinian population and prevents the Palestinians from establishing a working economy, the international community is shipping large quantities of aid to the Palestinians to sustain them (see Chapter 1 and Hever, 2008c).

Sen, as we have seen, differentiates between two kinds of entitlement. There is entitlement through exchange, and entitlement through charity or aid. Exchange entitlement means that someone gives something in exchange for the goods that they are receiving. Most often, this is an exchange of labour power for goods (intermediated by currency). The other kind of entitlement is a one-way deal – aid is given with no expectation of return. Although Sen discusses these two kinds of entitlement, he does not examine the social and cultural consequences of the differences between them.

For the purpose of our discussion, it is crucial to understand that by forcing Palestinians to rely on one-sided aid that does not involve any exchange, Israel is effectively devaluing the exchange value of Palestinian labour in the eyes of the world and in the Palestinians' own eyes – perhaps not in monetary terms, but in social and cultural terms (Sen, 1995). Since many Palestinians are denied participation in the labor market, they are also prevented from accumulating job experience and business connections, as well as from keeping up to date with innovations in their occupations or crafts. In the current situation created by the occupation, Palestinians have lost so much of the value of their human capital that many Palestinians can no longer exchange their labor for food, simply because they are unable to reach their workplace. This does not just limit the Palestinians' ability to consume, but also strikes at their dignity and sense of self-value.

Although Sen does not incorporate any of Bourdieu's terminology into his theory, entitlement can certainly be seen as consisting of more than just access to material goods: it is also a form of symbolic capital. Herein, as I see it, lies the main difference between Sen's two forms of entitlement. Entitlement through production and exchange is suffused with a powerful aura of legitimacy over the goods produced or purchased. However, entitlement through charity awards symbolic capital to the donor, not the recipient. It even reduces the symbolic capital of the recipient.

Therefore, Palestinians who must rely on aid see their symbolic capital deteriorating as a result. This process was examined and analyzed by Nancy Fraser in her 2004 article "Dilemmas of justice in the 'post-socialist' era." Fraser argues that although welfare and aid partially alleviate the immediate symptoms of an unequal distribution of wealth, they erode the public image of the recipients, who come to be seen as "parasites." This eventually leads people to stop believing in the reasons for providing aid in the first place, and the basic rights of the disempowered groups deteriorate (Fraser, 2004). Fraser's claims with respect to welfare also apply, to some extent, to humanitarian aid, and indeed the image of "parasites" has begun to become associated with Palestinians. Aid workers and donors have said, in interviews, that they are displeased with Palestinians who express a sense of entitlement to aid. They expect Palestinians to be perpetually grateful and meek (Fast, 2006).

The conflict between Israel and the Palestinians can be seen in broader economic terms than solely in reference to money and material goods. As Bourdieu suggests, the bigger picture must include symbolic, cultural, and social perspectives as well, and thus enhance the economic understanding of the situation. Upon analysis, the case of humanitarian aid to the Palestinians vividly highlights the advantages of the larger perspective.

It is easy to understand why the Palestinians accept humanitarian aid when they have almost no other form of income. In fact, aid accounted for nearly 50 percent of Palestinian gross national income

(GNI) in 2002 (see Chapter 2), although its reception was occasionally accompanied by protest and resistance. However, the efforts that Israel has made to keep the aid flowing can only be understood in light of the advantages that accrue to Israel from this aid. The direct economic advantages to Israel, such as taxes and increased sales for Israeli companies, have already been analyzed by economists, as described in Chapter 2 (World Bank, 2004b; Arnon et al., 1997: 89). Aid also redistributes symbolic capital to the disadvantage of the Palestinians, because it leaves them in a state of dependency on the constant charity of the international community. This charity, in turn, depends on the continued goodwill of the donors, and on their continued ability to donate. The international economic crisis of 2008, for example, could result in cuts in aid shipments to the OPT.

Although reliance on charity erodes the symbolic capital of Palestinians and their entitlement, Palestinian agency has not been completely neutralized by the occupation and the aid. Sen's entitlement theory can also shed light on the reasons why the humanitarian catastrophe in the OPT is not as severe as might be expected. According to the World Bank, the Palestinians maintain levels of nutrition and mortality that are not normally observed under conditions of a rapidly deteriorating economy such as they are experiencing (World Bank, 2003: 49). This is an indication that Palestinian society has concealed forms of entitlement working within it as well, such as social solidarity and unofficial charity. Sen draws attention to the issues of acquirement and distribution as even more important aspects of combating famine than actual food availability. Therefore, the Palestinians' durability and resilience may attest to a system of social cohesion and egalitarian distribution (Sen, 1995).

This is an example of how Palestinian national and religious identities have contributed to empowering them in their conflict against the occupation, and supplies further evidence that the conflict is one not just of arms or of economic power, but also of cultural capital and of identities. It also shows the importance of examining economic mechanisms of entitlement beyond the transfer of money between people.

Israel's continuing siege of the Gaza Strip since 2006 has severely limited the amount of food that the United Nations and other agencies are allowed to send to Gaza. The siege, which culminated in the bombardment and assault on Gaza in December 2008, has created a new reality of aid in the OPT. For the first time, even though humanitarian aid had been paid for by international donors, it was denied to the Palestinians. Israeli authorities have thus began to change the Palestinians' status: that is, the latter are no longer a people receiving aid because of their entitlement, but a people whose right to live is completely at the mercy of Israel, and they receive aid only if Israel graciously allows it, not because they deserve it (Azoulay and Ophir, 2008: 276, 296).

The Israeli media have published hundreds of articles with titles such as "Israeli allows more trucks of humanitarian aid to enter the Gaza Strip." Such articles obfuscate the fact that Israel profits from aid and does not pay for it, and they create the image – especially for domestic purposes – that Israel is graciously sending aid to the Palestinians despite the "ungrateful" Palestinians' continued use of violence against Israel.

DRAWBACKS OF SEN'S THEORY

One of the (self-acknowledged) drawbacks of Sen's entitlement approach is that it deals only with legal entitlement. Sen points out that impoverished people can resort to looting or robbery in order to obtain sufficient food, circumventing the limits of their entitlements (Sen, 1981: 45–9). There are two other extralegal points that Sen does not address. One is that looting, robbery, and vandalism can also result in an entitlement failure and poverty for the victim, meaning that victims of such crimes will not receive what they are entitled to. The second issue, which is more relevant to this discussion, is that no legal obligation binds charity and gifts. That is, people are not entitled to gifts. Therefore, humanitarian aid can allow people to avoid starvation without actually improving their long-term entitlement. Long-term humanitarian assistance can actually erode the recipient's entitlement.

Sen's argument that a liberal democracy can prevent famine has been extensively criticized by de Waal. Two of his criticisms are especially relevant here. One is that political rights and liberalism cannot always fend off external forces that cause poverty or famine. The second is that the humanitarian organizations that distribute assistance gain power of their own, and ultimately have a large impact on the situation in which they are involved, beyond the simple distribution of aid (de Waal, 1997: 2–3). The first criticism is especially relevant to the occupation of the OPT. The main cause for the current poverty and malnourishment in the OPT, as identified by the World Bank, is the limitations on movement imposed by the Israeli army, rather than a lack of democracy in the Palestinian Authority (Bendel, 2005: 27). The second criticism raises a more interesting question, that of the complicity of humanitarian organizations with the Israeli occupation. This complicity, which has been discussed in Chapter 2, is of crucial importance to understanding the occupation.

SEN AND VEBLEN – ENTITLEMENT AND SABOTAGE

Sen's concept of entitlement is especially useful to expand on the points most neglected by Veblen. Veblen divides the economic process into production and sabotage. Production is a sort of "black box" in Veblen's theory – it has its own independent development and it occurs naturally and spontaneously. Sabotage is an act that creates a redistribution of the produced goods. Through destruction emerges value, and value determines the distribution of goods. However, Sen's concept of entitlement tackles distribution from another angle – by analyzing the social attributes that entitle people to wealth, such as gainful employment, inheritance, and social security (Sen, 1981: 22–3; Veblen, 1917: 167).

While sabotage can be used to describe how Israelis prevent Palestinians from accessing the fruits of their own production, the distribution of the fruits of labor is still not fully explained. It may be better understood by applying Sen's concept of entitlement. Sabotage denies wealth, and entitlement awards it. The two concepts together create a theoretical framework for understanding the forces that distribute wealth.

OUTLINES OF INSTITUTIONAL THEORY

Paul Homan, in his 1932 article "An appraisal of institutional economics," tried to define the institutional school of economic thought as economic theory that not only denies the "quasi-mechanic terminology of equilibrium which is embedded in systematic economic theory," but has very little in common with it even beyond this rejection. This definition of institutional economics through what it is not (that is, not an economic practice that uses equilibrium models based on mechanical analogies) demonstrates how wide and diverse, and thus hard to define, this school of thought actually is.

The variety of thought that exists among institutional economists is impressive. It is beyond the scope of this book to describe the development of institutional thought and the extensive scholarly debate over its borders and exact definitions. For the purposes of this book, I wish to focus mainly on Veblen's contribution, namely the notions of "conspicuous consumption" and "sabotage," which were described at the beginning of this chapter.

It is important, however, to clarify that the term "institutions" as used by institutional economists refers to something else than the term "institution" in everyday language. In everyday language, "institutions" are often perceived as government or corporate organizations. Institutional economists, though, do not limit themselves to studying these organizations, but also focus on large-scale social institutions such as marriage, money, wage labor, and absentee ownership. The field of study attempts to discuss these social constructs as developing and evolving objects, which have a profound effect on the lives of human beings (Commons, 1931).

Institutions are collectives, inasmuch as people "belong" to them. The decision-making process of an individual cannot be fully understood without recognizing the various institutions to which that person belongs: religious organizations, professional affiliations, families, and so on. However, since an individual can belong to many different institutions at the same time, the institutional explanation does not imply a deterministic or a mechanistic approach to individual choice (Commons, 1931).

Bourdieu, heavily influenced by institutional theory (a fact he readily acknowledged), defined the institution as a "magical construction, that doesn't exist physically but is no less real. It is a fetish, created through a mass of accumulated social labour. A 'mystical body'" (1985: 742). This insight is useful in conveying not only the fluidity of the category, but its significance as well.

In conclusion, a group of institutional economists wrote a joint paper in 1932 summing the basics of their theory:

> Yet, amid disagreement, institutionalists have this core of agreement: (1) group behavior, not price, should be central in economic thinking; (2) more attention should be given to uniformities of custom, habit, and law as modes of organizing economic life; (3) individuals are influenced by motives that cannot be quantitatively measured; (4) economic behavior is constantly changing; therefore, economic generalizations should specify limits of culture and time to which they apply; (5) it is the task of the economist to study the sources of the conflict of interests in the existing social structure as an integral factor in rather than a something diverging from a hypothetical norm.
>
> (Kiekhofer et al., 1932)

The relevance of the ideas expressed by the institutional economists above to the study of the Israeli occupation of the OPT should be clear: they offer a historic analysis of large-scale group agendas as well as of individual behavior through the understanding of conflicting interests.

VEBLEN AND INSTITUTIONAL THEORY

Although Veblen is generally considered to be the founder of the institutional school of economic thought, his own writing was quite distinct from that of most other institutional economists (Homan, 1932). Veblen was even classified as a Marxist (in an accusatory manner) by D. A. Routh, although the only Marxist trait ever attributed to him was economic determinism. The difference between Veblen and Marx, as noted by Routh, is that Veblen rejects the concept of the class struggle as the main historical driving force and focuses on sabotage instead (Routh, 1937).

The debate about the nature of institutional economics, which raged during the 1930s, was largely dedicated to discussions of how Veblen himself fits into the definition of institutional economics. At one extreme Veblen was declared to be the one and only institutional economist, while at the other extreme it was argued that he was not part of that school of thought at all. This wide range of opinion was due, in part, to Veblen's attempt to combine evolutionary science and biology with economic thought, which was a less prominent feature among other institutional economists. Veblen was also said to stand apart from other institutional economists for having made a sharp distinction between industry, which is powered by technology, and business, which is powered by sabotage, and for clearly favoring the former. Veblen's preference for industry over business was part of his worldview, which was far to the left of most of the other institutional economists (Scott, 1933).

Veblen's theory, though innovative, was not conceived in a vacuum. His writings were heavily influenced by the thinkers of his time, and prominent among them was Herbert Spencer, whom he met in person. The influence is especially obvious in the importance that Veblen attributes to biological analogies and to evolution, as a process that applies not only to organisms but also to social constructs. Borrowing from Spencer the idea that evolution can be used to describe the development of human societies and not only of organisms (Dorfman, 1932), Veblen criticized neoclassical economics as a "non-evolutionary" science. He argued that economics is a frozen way of thinking, whereas history is a changing process which it is difficult, if not impossible, to capture in a single moment, at the same time ignoring everything that has led to that moment (Homan, 1932).

Veblen did not continue Spencer's work, but set out on a different, even contrary path. While Spencer adored progress, Veblen saw the modern economy as the height of barbarism. Joseph Dorfman argued that Veblen's book *The Theory of the Leisure Class* (1899) was actually a satirical work, most of its barbs aimed against Spencer and against modern society (Dorfman, 1932). Veblen, then, sees violence, deprivation, and exploitation not as anomalies, but as hallmarks of modern economic structures.

CAPITAL BEYOND MEANS OF PRODUCTION

A crucial foundation of Marxist thought is the concept of capital. Marxists understand capital as a physical and tangible means of production which is owned by the capitalists. Anwar Shaikh attempted to expand the Marxist definition of capital, interpreting the concept as a social relation in capitalist society that allows one person to live off the fruit of another's labor. Thus, capital is essentially a means of exploitation. This expanded Marxist interpretation, when applied to Israel/Palestine, leads to the conclusion that Jewish identity itself (in the sense of being classified officially as Jewish by the Israeli state) is a form of capital – since it enables people to enjoy certain privileges of which Palestinians are deprived (Shaikh, 1990).

Taking this notion a step further, we find that another reason for Israel's occupation, beyond the acquisition of money or material goods, is that it provides a way of accumulating social capital. The very ability to control the Palestinians is a form of capital in and of itself, even if this control does not necessarily lead to material gains. This, however, is already stretching Marxism to the limit, and actually brings us closer to institutional economic thinking, and more specifically to Veblen's economic theory.

The concept of a Jewish state, which was discussed in Chapter 6, already allocates social capital to Jews and away from non-Jews within Israel. But the occupation of the OPT accentuates this allocation even further, as it adds complexity to the social hierarchy among non-Jewish subjects of Israel, and reinforces the centrality of the military and the police in Israel, organizations in which Jews enjoy a clear dominance.

VEBLEN AND THE OCCUPATION

The challenges that economists face in explaining the occupation lie in understanding the motivations and decision making of political actors, who often act in ways that appear contrary to their interests. One of Veblen's important contributions, which was later incorporated into the work of other institutional economists, was the rejection of the concept of rationality as the major force for explaining human behavior. Veblen argued that habit takes precedence over reason, and that people normally act according to traditions developed within the institutions to which they belong (Hodgson, 2004: 171–5): "History teaches that men, taken collectively, learn by habitation rather than precept and reflection; particularly as touches those underlying principles of truth and validity on which the effectual scheme of law and custom finally rests" (Veblen, 1917).

It can certainly be argued that Bourdieu's concept of "habitus" can be traced back to Veblen's (and to other institutionalists') habits, as well as to Weber's influence, as a network of forces that influence human decisions. Through this use of traditions, institutions, and habits, Veblen finds a middle ground between the methodological individualism that characterizes neoliberal thought and the methodological collectivism that characterizes Marxist thought. Instead of reducing his social explanations to the level of either the individual or the class, Veblen, like other institutional economists, strikes a careful balance between the two through the concepts of institutions and habits (Hodgson, 2004: 176–9).

Furthermore, part of the reason for the failure of many economists to understand the occupation lies in their focus on a single type of transaction – bargaining transactions between two parties. One of the most well-known followers of institutional economics after Veblen was John R. Commons. In his 1934 book *Myself*, Commons offered a wider approach to transactions, of which he described three types. In addition to bargaining transactions, he also included managerial decisions and distribution transactions. The main attribute of the first type of transaction, the bargain, is that it implies a certain equality between the bargaining sides. The other two types of transaction, however, have a strong element of unequal power relations. Therefore, they are much better suited to explaining the economic relations between Israelis and Palestinians. Commons argued that bargaining transactions transfer wealth, managerial decisions create wealth, and rationing transactions distribute it (Commons, 1934).

Rather than delve into an extensive discussion of the application of these forms of transaction to the Israeli occupation of the OPT, we would do better to showcase the checkpoints employed by the Israeli army as focal points where each type of transaction takes place, making them a paradigmatic example for the application of institutional theory in understanding the occupation. The establishment of the checkpoint creates a nexus for transactions involving the distribution of value, in the form of the right to pass. Each checkpoint thus extends the ability of Israeli authorities to redistribute value.

The managerial decision that establishes the checkpoint creates wealth by turning freedom of movement into a scarce commodity at the checkpoint. Although wealth in this example is not a true indication of affluence, freedom of movement has a socially recognizable value only when it is limited, and hence the checkpoint creates value for something that had none before. The managerial decision also creates wealth because the checkpoint itself becomes an asset, which can be privatized. Following the Israeli Ministry of Defense's decision to privatize all of the permanent checkpoints, private companies have begun to take them over, making a profit from managing the checkpoints on Israel's behalf (Levy, 2008a; Sadeh, 2008b).

The rationing transaction determines the eligibility to pass through the checkpoint: for example, which permits are necessary, and what lines and checks exist for different kinds of people who wish to pass. Israelis, most often settlers, may pass without delay into or out of the settlements in the West Bank, while Palestinians are often turned away even when traveling between two Palestinian cities. International observers, aid workers, and activists must comply with certain requirements in order to cross the checkpoints. These requirements often involve submission to Israeli surveillance and to invasion of their privacy, as well as avoiding activities of which Israel disapproves, such as participation in demonstrations and reporting on the occupation.

Finally, a multitude of bargaining transactions occur when individuals who fall between the cracks of the regulations attempt to gain entry through the checkpoints. Arguments with the soldiers, pleas for special consideration, appeals to organizations, lawyers, and even bribes are all methods by which a person denied passage may attempt to gain access to the "wealth" created by the checkpoint – the freedom to pass.

INSTITUTIONAL THEORY AND THE OCCUPATION

Marxist theory allocates only a secondary role to violence in the sphere of economic production and the creation of profit. In the words of Ernest Gellner, Marxists believe that "violence itself initiates or maintains nothing" (1990). However, in institutional theory, which emphasizes habit and tradition over rational behavior, violence plays a prominent role. It can serve as a powerful tool for explaining social and economic phenomena.

Amira Hass has contributed texts which are helpful towards an institutional understanding of the occupation. A careful reading of her descriptions of the violent aspects of the occupation reveals that sometimes prestige and sabotage are even more important than profit to the Israeli occupiers. This is evident from Hass's comments on Israel's system of passes and permits. Palestinians have to carry different documents which must be renewed frequently (a process that involves spending time and paying a fee) and do not guarantee actual passage through the checkpoint. The occupation is composed of acts of economic sabotage, which increase the cost of everyday activities:

> Since the outbreak of the al-Aqsa Intifada in October 2000, the theft of time and of any semblance of normal activity has reached undreamed of proportions: students do not reach universities, ailing people and pregnant women are held at checkpoints, and some even die or deliver on the road; municipality technicians cannot get an Israeli permit to repair a broken pipe at the outskirts of their own town; offices are half staffed; water tank trucks are not allowed into villages. Travel costs have tripled because one must change transport every 20 kilometers; people spend hours at a stretch waiting or detained at roadblocks. Raw materials travel faster between China and the Ashdod seaport than between Ashdod and Nablus.
>
> (Hass, 2002b)

The argument that sabotage itself is a form of profit to Israelis can be exemplified by Hass's argument about the permits: "The pass system turned a universal basic right into a coveted privilege – or portion of a privilege – allotted to a minority on a case-by-case basis. For the privilege was not whole: it had gradations" (Hass, 2002b).

Although Hass does not attempt to formulate a theory to explain the occupation, her descriptions help demonstrate the value of institutional theory to the study of the economy of the occupation. By constructing an elaborate array of obstacles, checkpoints, and walls, Israel has been able to turn the freedom of movement into a commodity which it can control. Israel can decide how many passes are issued and to whom, and since the passes clearly are of great value to their holders, Israel has created value through sabotage – an act of commodification of the freedom of movement. In order to understand this argument, it is necessary to put aside the neoclassical idea that value is measured in utility, and that the creation of value entails an increase in overall utility. Veblen's argument is that value is created through the limitation and destruction of utility (sabotage), and therefore the distributive transaction and the value-creating transaction cannot be separated from each other.

Although Hass recognizes that the passes have value, she fails to make the connection between this value and the reason for issuing the passes in the first place. In her eyes, the act of turning a basic right into a scarce and cherished possession is absurd, an "improvised policy," in her own words, and she makes no attempt to explain it as anything beyond a measure to take over land and water resources (Hass, 2002b).

The concept of "sabotage," which was described above, is therefore still very relevant to understanding the occupation. Mehrdad Vhabi, in his 2004 article "The political economy of destructive power," articulated some theoretical points for understanding "destructive power" in the economy – the role of destruction not only as part of production, but also as part of the allocation of wealth. Destruction is part of the production process because when an item is produced, the raw materials consumed in the process are effectively destroyed. More relevant to our case, though, is how destruction can also be used as a means to reallocate wealth.

Vhabi argues that destruction can have a "rule-producing" function, by means of which it becomes a repository of wealth in itself. Those with the power to destroy have the ability to control others and make rules. Destruction creates value by limiting free access to something that was formerly taken for granted. These last two ideas correspond closely to Veblen's use of sabotage, further reinforcing the connection between the destructive capacities of Israel's occupation forces and the economic structure of the occupation (Vhabi, 2004). In addition to sabotage, the concept of prestige, which Veblen associated closely with the concept of conspicuous consumption, should also play a central role in understanding the occupation.

One example of how prestige can be used to understand the occupation at the political and economic levels can be found in the argument by Yagil Levy, whose article "Materialistic militarism," was mentioned earlier. Levy argues that marginalized groups in Israeli society – Mizrahim, new immigrants, Druze, and Bedouins – have begun to play a bigger role in the army and to occupy more senior positions within it. For these minority groups, serving in the military is a way of increasing their social prestige in Israeli society. Levy showed that this has had two important effects. First, the casualty rate of minorities in the Israeli army far surpasses their actual share of the population. Second, the prestige that serving in the military awards to non-minority soldiers has declined since the minorities have become more prevalent in the army (Levy, 2006).

Applying the concept of prestige to understand the Israeli occupation of the OPT answers the dilemma raised by the "Israeli anomaly" discussed above. Jewish-Israelis from the lower classes may not enjoy material benefits from the occupation, but their prestige increases if they position themselves within the social hierarchy in a place that is based on their nationality (Jewish) rather than on their class (low). As long as the occupation continues and there is no separate economic system for the Palestinians, lower-class Jews are not at the bottom of the social hierarchy, but somewhere in the middle, above both non-Jewish citizens in Israel itself and Palestinians from the OPT, who together comprise about half of the population living under Israeli control (Hever, 2005b).

Having described the components of institutional thought that are relevant to enhancing our understanding of the occupation, we can go on to discuss the writing of two contemporary institutional economists who have written directly on the occupation: Shimshon Bichler and Jonathan Nitzan.

THE THEORY OF SHIMSHON BICHLER AND JONATHAN NITZAN

Although relatively few contemporary economists are followers of the institutional school, Shimshon Bichler and Jonathan Nitzan, deserve mention here. Their work, which has been inspired to a high degree by the institutional school of economic thought, has focussed on understanding the Middle East and the economic interests surrounding it in a global context. Categorizing Bichler and Nitzan as institutional economists is no simple matter, as they refuse to identify themselves as belonging to a certain genre of economic thought. However, both have studied institutional economy, refer to it in their work, and frequently use sabotage in the Veblenian sense in their writing (Nitzan, 1992; Bichler and Nitzan, 2001: 68–86).

Bichler and Nitzan adopt the conception of capital as a social relation, which had already been suggested by certain Marxists (Shaikh, 1990), but they take this understanding a step further. They see capital as the allocation of power and rights. Specifically, capital is the right of ownership over a portion of all socially produced goods and services. Finance and financial assets are the most common representation of this allocation in contemporary capitalist society (Nitzan and Bichler, 2002: 10, 26, 58–62).

Bichler and Nitzan argue that Marx saw the economic crisis as the source of the eventual downfall of capitalist society. They also point out that certain neo-Marxists have argued that capitalism has learned to overcome those economic crises. Bichler and Nitzan, on the other hand, see the economic crisis as an essential part of the capitalist accumulation process, a source of prosperity for certain capitalists. Not only is a crisis not a threat to capitalist accumulation, it is in fact an integral part of that accumulation. Crises redistribute wealth, help to roll back the achievements of workers, and create opportunities for profits (Nitzan and Bichler, 2002: 15, 24, 47–57, 183).

The main concept that lies at the center of Bichler and Nitzan's theory is "differential accumulation." They analyze the behavior of firms or individuals not on the basis of the "maximum profit" maxim of neoliberal economics, but according to the principle that each individual or firm seeks the maximum relative profit. Average profit becomes an institution in itself, affecting the expectations and desires of economic agents. Whereas the profit-maximizing individual compares their profit with their own experience (attempting to increase their future profit over past profit, and considering the alternative sources of profit they can draw upon), the differential accumulator compares themself with others, and attempts to earn no less, and preferably more, than they do (Nitzan and Bichler, 2002: 10–15, 37–40). Although these may seem to be equivalent propositions, the strategies of profit maximization are very different from those of differential accumulation. The main difference relates to how an individual chooses strategies that affect other people. The profit maximizer will work hard to boost their riches by 1 percent, even if everyone else achieves a gain of 5 percent, but the differential accumulator will sometimes agree to a 1 percent drop in their riches if everyone else suffers a 5 percent reduction.

The behavior of investors in the stock market seems to corroborate Bichler and Nitzan's view, as they have shown in their writings. When the stock market crashes, nobody feels any shame at having lost a little money, but if the stock market soars, people become uncomfortable even if they are making a steady profit, because they also want to be among the high profiteers and not be left behind. Bichler and Nitzan have therefore constructed a methodology for analyzing differential profit, rather than absolute profit, and applied this methodology in their analysis of contemporary events.

In his 2001 article "Regimes of differential accumulation: mergers, stagflation and the logic of globalization," Jonathan Nitzan developed the argument that there are four different regimes of differential accumulation:

- green-field[7]
- mergers and acquisitions, where companies swallow other companies in order to increase their share of the market without increasing production
- cost-cutting, where companies attempt to increase profits by cutting costs and decreasing production
- stagflation, where companies compete to reallocate profit among them by increasing prices while production slows (Nitzan, 2001).

This is a more complicated theoretical model than the understanding of the behavior of companies usually held by economists, according to which companies either increase production through green-field activities or decrease it through cost-cutting. Nitzan has demonstrated that mergers and acquisitions as well as stagflation are frequently occurring phenomena which economic theory fails to address properly (2001). By adding the element of competition between the capitalists, but without accepting the neoclassical and neoliberal argument that competition leads to low profits and low prices, Nitzan has been able to formulate a framework for understanding political-economic events based on an analysis of the distribution of economic interests among competing companies (from either the same or different fields).

Bichler and Nitzan claim that in Israel the ruling class has undergone a prolonged process of consolidation. This process has been fuelled by crisis – war and occupation have been used to garner the support of the population at large for policy moves that centralize the economy, and to divert the public's attention away from the efforts of the big capitalists to increase their dominance over the Israeli economy. By the end of the twentieth century, Bichler and Nitzan assert, the ruling class in Israel had become extremely centralized.

---

7 In a green-field economic regime, companies seek to increase profit by increasing production and expanding into new fields. It is the economic regime where new companies are formed fast, and older companies increase their volume.

A handful of families and individuals own almost the entirety of the Israeli economy (Nitzan and Bichler, 2002: 84–136).

In their 2002 book *The Global Political Economy of Israel*, Nitzan and Bichler summarized the important points of their accumulated research. The book describes the emergence of the Israeli ruling class and its development through a retelling of the history of Israel in the twentieth century. Instead of repeating the conventional historical narrative, though, Bichler and Nitzan examine the economic events that occurred behind the scenes, and describe the effects of those events on the more familiar historical episodes (for example, the wars, the occupation, and the settlements: see Nitzan and Bichler, 2002: 84–136). Furthermore, the book takes a very broad view of the economic events, attempting to analyze them in light of global interests. The most important argument that is relevant to the occupation is their description of the relations between the military industry and the oil industry, and their effects on the Middle East (Nitzan and Bichler, 2002: 198–273).

Although Bichler and Nitzan have in general adopted the Marxist explanation for the early years of the occupation – the exploitation of cheap Palestinian labor – they have argued that this exploitation was forsaken in favor of larger economic projects, such as real-estate speculation on Palestinian lands and the formation of Israel's military industry. Later even these projects lost much of their economic power. They also note that in the 1990s labor immigrants could be brought to work for even lower wages than those of the Palestinians, so the exploitation argument cannot be applied any more. Bichler and Nitzan have also argued that neoliberal economists objected to the occupation mainly because it required the expenditure of valuable resources on security, a topic that was discussed in Chapters 4 and 5 (Nitzan and Bichler, 2002: 120–1).

Bichler and Nitzan have found that the Israeli economy militarized at a rapid rate after the 1967 war and the beginning of the occupation, and that this militarization was marked by the emergence of several large weapons companies which grew in size at the expense of many smaller firms. Until the 1990s there was a rapid increase in military industries' share of the Israeli economy. In his 1996 article "Military spending and differential accumulation: a new approach to the political economy of armament – the case of Israel," Bichler described how the occupation of the OPT created new economic interests and new political power relations which would support continued Israeli aggression for years to come. These conditions were developed as prominent capitalists in Israel not only found ways to exploit the Palestinian economy, but also used their influence in the political sphere to ensure that nothing would interfere with their enterprises (Bichler, 1996).

During the early 1970s, according to Bichler's and Nitzan's narrative, companies in the developed world shifted to an economic regime of stagflation and used the Middle East as a focal point for that shift. Stagflation implies increased prices and lagging production. Both of these effects were achieved through the rise in the prices of oil and armaments following the 1973 crisis and the war in the Middle East between Egypt, Syria, and Israel, and the subsequent slowdown in the economies of the West (Nitzan and Bichler, 2002: 244–9).

Yet the two scholars dismiss the very question whether Israel or the Palestinians have benefited or suffered from the occupation. They argue that there is no point in aggregating the benefits or cost to an entire society, claiming instead that societies must be disaggregated into specific agents – only through an understanding of the actions of these agents is it possible to say whether they have benefited or suffered (Nitzan and Bichler, 2002: 158–60).

The central agents in Bichler's and Nitzan's narrative are the global economic sectors: the worldwide financial sector, the electric power and pharmaceutical sectors, the construction and industrial sectors, and most importantly, the military industry and petrol industry sectors. Through their careful analysis of the differential profits of these sectors and others, Bichler and Nitzan demonstrated that Israeli policy and events in the Middle East have often corresponded to shifts in the relative profits of oil companies and weapons manufacturers, compared to the profits of all other kinds of companies (Nitzan and Bichler, 2002: 228–66).

The close relations and overlapping ownership between oil companies and weapons manufacturers were demonstrated in a 1989 article (Bichler, Nitzan, and Rowley, 1989a). These themes were further developed in relation to Middle East politics in the article "The armadollar–petrodollar coalition and the Middle East" (Bichler, Nitzan, and Rowley, 1989b), which showed that companies from different sectors had conflicting interests in shaping Middle East politics.

Figure 7.2, which is taken from their recent article "Cheap wars" (Nitzan and Bichler, 2006), demonstrates that after each period where the average profits of oil companies fell below the average profits of other companies, a war was fought in the Middle East, and each of these wars caused an immediate increase in the comparative profits of oil companies.

The graph's horizontal axis is temporal, demarcated into yearly intervals, and its vertical axis represents the difference in the average profits of oil companies compared with the rest of the companies included in the Fortune 500 index. The "0" level represents an equal average profit. The graph also denotes the years where an energy conflict erupted in the Middle East (that is, a war in which at least one country participating in the conflict had oil wells). Israel also has

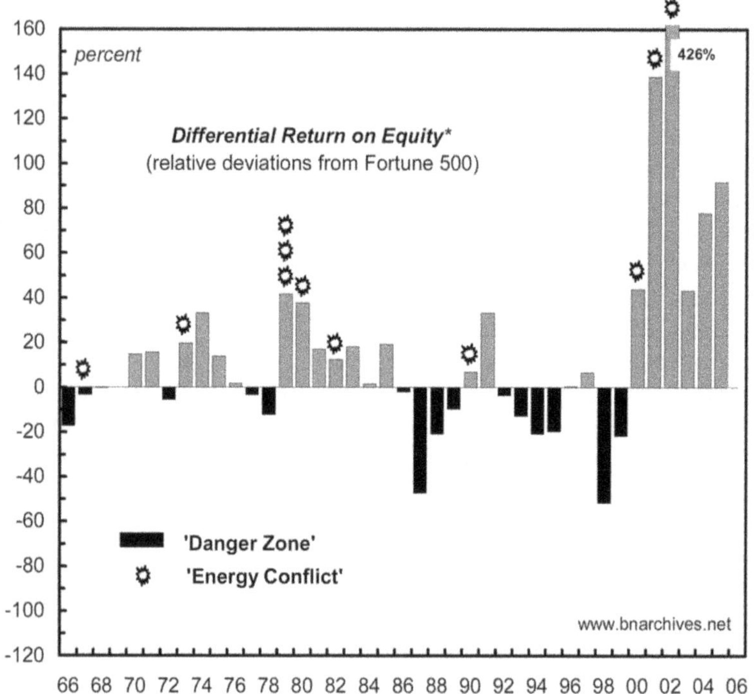

Figure 7.2 Leading oil companies: differential profits

* Difference between the return on equity of the oil companies and of the Fortune 500, expressed as a percentage of the return on equity of the Fortune 500. Note: The leading oil companies include British Petroleum (BP-Amoco since 1998), Chevron, Exxon (Exxon Mobil since 1999) Mobil (until 1998), Royal-Dutch/Shell and Texaco (until 2000). Company changes are due to merger. Until 1993, the Fortune 500 included only industrial corporations (firms deriving at least half their sales revenues from manufacturing or mining). From 1994 onward, the list includes all corporations. For 1992–3, the data for Fortune 500 companies are reported without SFAS 106 special charges.

Sources: Fortune and Compustat. Many thanks to Shimshon Bichler and Jonathan Nitzan for their permission to use this graph.

often participated in or started these conflicts, even though it does not have any oil wells of its own. The graph demonstrates that international oil companies are not always the big winners. Sometimes their profits fall below the average profits of other sectors. However, the Middle East wars have consistently coincided with above-average profits for oil companies.

Since many of the largest and most powerful oil companies and weapons manufacturers are situated in the United States and have a strong influence on US governments, Bichler and Nitzan argue that US involvement in the Middle East has not been intended to foster peace, but rather to instigate and perpetuate conflict. This has been accomplished by supporting Israel's belligerent policies, protecting Israel from the international community over violations of international law, and supplying armaments to the region. The United States has consistently supported Israel's settlement and occupation policies in order to sustain the potential for creating provocations, which may lead to violent outbreaks. These in turn lead to rises in the prices of oil and armaments, and hence in the profits of the oil companies and weapons manufacturers (Nitzan and Bichler, 2002: 198–273). Although the US economy as a whole is dependent on oil and would benefit from lower oil prices, it is necessary to distinguish between the interests of the population and the interests of key economic players.

Continuing Veblen's attempt to break out of the model of human behavior based on rationality, Bichler and Nitzan have directly confronted the question why Israel is pursuing policies that appear to be contrary to its interest, and formulated a theory to explain this without resorting to rationality. Why does Israel continue to launch adventurous attacks on neighboring countries or on the Palestinians, despite the fact that such attacks have so far failed to achieve the sought-after security which they have officially been claimed to achieve? Their answer is that these policies have been advanced by powerful interest groups. Using the Israeli Likud party as an example of Israeli policy towards the Palestinians, they say:

> There was of course no open conspiracy here. When preaching economic liberalization, Likud members usually meant exactly what they said .... they were merely removing the shackles of government from an otherwise competitive economy. What they did in practice, though, was deregulate an oligopolistic war economy, effectively inviting dominant capital to take the lead.
>
> Viewed from this perspective, their "political folly" no longer seems senseless. On the contrary, it looks as if their actions, unbe-

> known to them of course, were in fact serving a broader "latent function." For Israel's dominant capital, stagflation, rising military spending, growing dependency on the United States, and a ballooning debt were the basic ingredients for successful differential accumulation. These very policies were also consistent with the interests of dominant capital groups in the United States, particularly those related to armaments and oil, which benefited from the escalating regional conflict, and which played an important role in shaping US–Israeli relations. The most promising political platform for achieving these results was a combination of *laissez-faire* economics and racist militarism; and the party which believed in these principles, was ready to implement them, and, most importantly, *was to never fully understand their consequences*, was Likud.
> (Nitzan and Bichler, 2002: 135)[8]

It is not necessary to limit our scope to the policies adopted by the Likud politicians – the Likud party is merely a relatively outspoken example of how Israel has combined economic neoliberalism with the occupation and colonization of the OPT. Even before the emergence of the Kadima party in 2005, Avi Shlaim argued in his 1994 article "Prelude to the Accord: Likud, Labour, and the Palestinians," that only minute differences exist between the Likud party and the Labor party. The salient point here is that the occupation has shaped economic institutions in Israel, and in turn these institutions' struggle for survival has pushed Israeli policymakers to continue the occupation, even when overall economic indicators have suggested the opposite.

DRAWBACKS OF BICHLER'S AND NITZAN'S THEORY

Although I do contend that institutional political economy can resolve many of the problems that face neoliberal and Marxist thinkers when dealing with the occupation, this does not mean that the institutional explanation is bulletproof or that it can provide an adequate or complete account of the economy of the occupation.

First, like Veblen, Bichler and Nitzan have analyzed business as separate and even contrary to industry. Although their analysis of business is deep and incisive, industry and production remain a black box. The business aspect of oil and weapons may be analyzed and

8 Although Bichler and Nitzan analyze the interests of political and economic agents, their theory also allows for certain agents to be manipulated, remain oblivious to the results of their actions, or simply be mistaken.

understood, but the production process is completely neglected. Hence their theory is not a complete economic theory, but only a theory of businesses. Therefore, one of the main points of criticism against Veblen remains valid when applied to Bichler and Nitzan. Their theory does not incorporate any discussion of the elements of production itself.

Second, the relation between company interests and actual government policy is not fully articulated. Although Bichler and Nitzan delve into an extensive discussion on the relations between the capitalists and government policymakers, and on the network of bribes between them, they have not articulated a social theory to explain the actual mechanism by which capital interests affect government policy directly and indirectly. A reader of their books might certainly be convinced that government decisions have been influenced by the interests of oil companies and weapons manufacturers, but will still not know how the latter have achieved this influence (Nitzan and Bichler, 2002: 198–273).

Third, Bichler and Nitzan claim that finance is the best representation of the distribution of power. This statement demonstrates their emphasis on an analysis of capitalists and large companies. Although their argument sheds light on the Israeli occupation through a better understanding of the decisions of policymakers and of large businesses, their theory leaves the lower classes out of the equation (Nitzan and Bichler, 2002: 198–273). Although the lower classes play only a marginal role in the financial sector relative to their size within the population, their importance to the economic-political sphere cannot be discounted. As shapers of public opinion, as the groups that are called upon to do the actual fighting in the name of "national interests," and as people who can refuse or evade this call, the lower classes play an important role in shaping the reality of the Israeli–Palestinian conflict and of the occupation.

This is an appropriate place to draw on Bourdieu. Just as large corporations compete and vie with each other to accumulate a larger share of monetary capital, lower-class social groups vie for a larger share of social, cultural, and symbolic capital. Even at the cost of a huge economic burden, certain groups in Israel are committed to preserving the sharply etched hierarchy that distinguishes between dominators and dominated, between citizens and subjects, between occupiers and occupied. This hierarchy awards social capital to Jews over non-Jews, and is one explanation why the majority of the Israeli public supports the continuation of the occupation, even to the detriment of its standard of living.

8

THEORETICAL ANALYSIS AND BINATIONALISM

> By confiscating more and more land and transferring hundreds of thousands of Jews to the OT [Occupied Territories], the settlement project rendered the one-state solution, in which Jews do not have a majority between the Jordan Valley and the Mediterranean Sea, increasingly probable.
>
> Neve Gordon (2008b: 16)

INTERNATIONAL INVOLVEMENT AND ISRAELI MARKETING

Although Israel/Palestine is very small compared with most countries in the world, it lies at an important nexus of colliding international interests, where three continents meet, near the Suez Canal, and in a central location in the Middle East through which oil and natural gas flows to the Mediterranean area (Bahgat, 2005).

Beyond the country's geographic importance, Israel was of immense symbolic significance for post-Second World War politics, having been seen as an opportunity to simultaneously redeem Europe from the crimes of the Holocaust and serve as a vehicle for postcolonial projects in the Middle East. In trying to garner international support for the establishment of an ethnic state, the Zionist leadership was very successful in capitalizing on European anti-Semitism and the Holocaust, exploiting the politics of guilt that evolved following the Second World War to convince world leaders to support the creation of a Jewish state in 1948, at a time when Jews were a minority in the area. Israel thus served a dual purpose in Europe's efforts to recover from the Holocaust. First, it was seen as a way to compensate the Jews for the Holocaust and ensure their future safety in their own state, thus dealing with post-Holocaust guilt. Second, it was a way to avoid rehabilitating the Holocaust survivors in their home countries in Europe, by sending them off to Israel instead.

The Israeli leadership quickly learned how to harness international support in other ways. This was first accomplished by taking sides in the Cold War and presenting Israel as a fortress against the spread of communist influence in the world. This position enabled Israel to find a powerful ally in the United States, which armed and supported Israel in wars against countries that were supported by the Soviet Union (Safran, 1978).

The collapse of the Soviet Union in 1991 forced Israel to reinvent its political position. Israel agreed to begin peace negotiations with the Palestinian leadership, a policy which went well with the rapid economic reform that Israel underwent at the time in order to carve out a place for the Israeli economy in global markets (Selby, 2003: 124). However, the internal structure of Israel's political system made it impossible for the Israeli government to make any real concessions, and Israel has consistently violated its commitments under the Oslo agreements, citing security reasons or giving no reason at all. Although Israel has accused the Palestinians of violating the agreements as well, it has retained authority over the OPT and almost complete control of all sovereign privileges, leaving the Palestinians very little space in which to either observe or violate the agreements.

In the 1990s Israel continued expansion of the illegal settlements in the OPT and tightened the control mechanisms over the lives of Palestinians. Most notable were the blanket closures that prevented Palestinians from working in Israel, and also limited movement inside the OPT. The closures, in violation of the Paris Protocol, thus eliminated one of the most important sources of income to the Palestinian economy. These were inherent flaws in the peace process, which created a build-up of resentment and frustration, and could only have led to the eventual collapse of the negotiations.

When the negotiations failed and violence broke out again with the second intifada, the Israeli forces reacted with deadlier venom than ever before. In fact, during the second intifada Israeli forces killed more Palestinians than in the entire 33 years of occupation prior to the intifada (Gordon, 2008b: xvii). As word of the atrocities slowly spread in the world media, Israelis began to talk about the need to generate a better "explanation." In other words, Israel was failing to win international support for its actions. Israeli journalists argued that the reason for Israel's loss of face was mainly the Palestinian's adeptness at public relations, not the actual events, in which the number of Palestinians killed by Israeli troops was dozens of times higher than the number of Israelis killed by Palestinians. Israeli nationalists expressed the opinion that Israel had to reinvent itself once more, find new ways to market itself to the world so that it could continue to enjoy international support without making any political compromises on the Palestinian issue (Mor, 2001).

The solution for the lack of "explanatory power" was found on September 11, 2001. Israeli officials were quick to claim that the attacks on the United States proved that global terrorism was becoming a greater threat, and that Israel stood at the forefront of the "global war on terror." The government quickly implemented a series of new methods to "fight terrorism," which were presented as innovations based on Israeli expertise in doing just that, and thus were marketed to other countries as well. These methods included the Wall of Separation, extrajudicial assassinations of suspects, enhanced methods of surveillance and tracking of civilians, and many others (Klein, 2007a).

This new type of marketing created an image of Israel as a "fortress state," supposedly secure despite its numerous enemies, as opposed to the country's previous image as an underdog state fighting for survival, where life was in constant peril (Pappe, 2005). This new image has an economic significance: on the one hand, it may reduce the willingness of donors to donate money to Israel and Israeli institutions (since Israel is now "strong"), but on the other hand, it makes it easier for the Israeli security industry to find markets abroad and bring in money to the Israeli economy (Klein, 2007b). In 2008 former Israeli prime minister Ehud Olmert said that the Wall of Separation is not only a means to protect Israeli citizens, but also a model to be exported to other countries in the world (Sofer, 2008).

This long history of marketing of the Israeli state brings up the question: why does Israel need international justification? In Israel, unlike other countries, political discourse is constantly preoccupied with the chances and right of the state of Israel to exist. Israeli politicians often accuse critics of Israel of "denying Israel's right to exist," and contend that such criticism is anti-Semitic. They are often right about the first part, for many critics indeed challenge Israel's right to exist as a state based on an ethnic principle, which awards full rights only to Jews. However, to oppose discrimination is of course not in itself anti-Semitic, and many Jews share the opinion that a Jewish state is immoral.

That is because Israel is a country unlike any other. It is a project-state, where the project, Zionism,[1] takes precedence over the needs of

1 Zionism has many definitions, and many Zionists have their own definition for their political beliefs. When referring to Zionism in this book, I

the actual citizens of the state of Israel. If the legitimacy of the project should be undermined, Israel's very definition would be challenged (Azoulay and Ophir, 2008: 395–414).

Indeed, the famous quote attributed to Henry Kissinger, asserting that "Israel has no foreign policy but only domestic politics" (Vilan, 2006), seems to have been prompted by Israel's historical tendency to focus on marketing rather than on a coherent, interest-based foreign policy. Israeli politicians are engrossed in winning approval at home by pushing forward a pro-Jewish and pro-Zionist agenda, expanding the land area available for Jews to colonize, treating the non-Jewish population of Israel as inferior, and by all these means and others increasing the symbolic capital of Jews at the expense of non-Jews. Foreign policy appears to be no more than a tool designed to keep international criticism at bay, and to make it possible for the Israeli government to keep pushing forward with its policies.

David Ben-Gurion's famous quote, "it doesn't matter what the gentiles say, it matters what the Jews do" (Amirav, 2007: 51), still echoes in the background of Israel's diplomatic efforts. That is evident, for example, in the way Israel has used Iran as a scapegoat, rallying international pressure against Iran and calling for an economic boycott and military strike to prevent Iran from developing nuclear weapons, and thus distracting the international community from Israel's own violations of international law (Maddox, 2008).

The deepening contradictions in Israel's model of control, which were discussed in Chapter 5, constantly challenge the legitimacy of the Zionist project. Therefore, Israeli public opinion is constantly concerned with the prospects and risks to the state of Israel's very existence, something that is taken for granted in most countries. Although Zionists rarely question Israel's right to exist, they often express uncertainty whether Israel can exist for any long period of time.

The Israeli Ministry of Foreign Affairs often attacks critics of Israeli policies, saying they "wish to undermine the very existence of the state of Israel." This accusation is frequently leveled for the purpose of delegitimizing criticism of Israel, but the accusation itself is not completely unbiased. Indeed, if Israel is ever forced to deal with its internal contradictions, to dismantle its repressive apparatus of control, and recognize the rights of all people under its control, then the very definition of Israel as a Jewish state will have to change.

---

mean the desire to create and maintain a Jewish state, meaning a state that serves Jews and/or Judaism.

NEGOTIATIONS AT A STANDSTILL

The increasing economic burden that the occupation imposes on both Palestinians and Israelis should serve to hasten the search for a solution, yet the economic aspects of proposed solutions are not often considered in depth, and are granted only secondary importance, far below nationalist considerations. For Israelis and Palestinians alike, to acknowledge or voice a preference for economic over nationalist interests is an unpopular stance. It can be perceived as being motivated by greed, or as a position of weakness, selfishness, or the abandonment of higher "principles." In mainstream economics, this phenomenon has been studied within the field of game theory, as a case in which both sides of a conflict make sacrifices in the hopes of hurting the other side sufficiently to win the overall struggle (see, for example, Bhattacharya, 2006).

One example of this is the tendency of Israeli leaders to propose a "compromise" with the Palestinians based on offering economic incentives to the Palestinians to give up their political rights. This tendency was evident already from the very first days of the 1967 occupation (Gordon, 2008b: 23–48), and could still be discerned in the campaign of Binyamin Netanyahu's Likud party in the 2009 Israeli elections (Koren, 2008). By now, most Palestinians have become wary of such promises, and fiercely reject the concept of normalization of the existing relations with Israel. The experience of the peace process with Israel has taught them that the Israeli leadership is eager to find ways to get the Palestinians to accept the current power relations and end their struggle. The Paris Protocol, aid efforts in the 1990s, special industrial zones built in the OPT in the 1990s, and the withdrawal from the Gaza Strip have all been accompanied by promises to improve the Palestinians' material living conditions, and all of these promises were proven false.

During the negotiations, many intermediaries and negotiators expressed their frustration at having come very close to a solution, which yet somehow kept slipping away. Intermediaries have repeatedly stated that they believe that all the points of contention could be resolved in a matter of days, and yet negotiations have dragged on for years, with no sense of advancement or improvement (Le More, 2005). This impression that a solution is just around the corner seems to be confirmed by the political opinions of most Palestinians and Israelis. Polls taken in 2006, 2008, and 2009 have consistently demonstrated that there is a majority (not an overwhelming majority, and sometimes a very narrow one) within both Israel and the OPT that supports the two-state solution (Bocco et al., 2006; Ha'aretz, 2009; Ynet, 2008). These polls create the impression that both sides are willing finally to reach a compromise, but such hopes are dashed time and time again in the course of the actual negotiations.

For Palestinians, what the two-state solution means is that Israel will withdraw to the 1967 borders, and that they themselves will make a painful compromise, giving up any hope of reclaiming historical Palestine. The two-state solution also signifies the beginning of a long journey of recovery from the destruction that has been wrought over decades of occupation.

For Jewish Israelis, the two-state solution is a compromise that involves relinquishing the hope of possessing all of the land between the Jordan River and the Mediterranean Sea as a single unit under Jewish control, a notion that has gradually crept into the Israeli mainstream since 1967. For some, the reluctance to withdraw stems from their belief that the entire land was promised to them by God. For others, it is the fear that a Palestinian state will threaten Israel's security.

So if the majorities exist to make the compromise, how come a solution has not yet been reached? Negotiations have been taking place since 1993, often interrupted by bouts of violence. The violence has taken a toll on Palestinians and Israelis alike, although the Palestinians have certainly paid the heavier price, yet the negotiators do not seem to be in any hurry to resolve the situation.

There are many reasons for this delay. One is the inherent disagreement on key issues, such as Israel's unwillingness to accept the internationally recognized pre-1967 borders, or to allow Palestinian refugees to return to Israel in accordance with UN Resolution 194. On the Palestinian side, negotiators have been unwilling to make concessions on these points, and they demand that international law be respected. Meanwhile, Israeli negotiators feel that time is on their side, because as negotiations drag on, Israel continues to control the area and to create "facts on the ground" (see below).

THE TWO-STATE SOLUTION

Often overlooked as one of the reasons for the failure of the efforts to reach a compromise is the economic aspect. The Israeli authorities have invested tremendous efforts and resources in erasing the Green Line, in establishing "facts on the ground," and making future withdrawals difficult and costly. Such measures include settlement expansion, new settlement construction, and construction of Jewish residential communities on the Green Line itself in order to render it meaningless, and the building of the Wall of Separation east of the Green Line. After decades of occupation, these efforts have been successful in creating a nearly insurmountable economic obstacle to the implementation of a two-state solution.

On the Israeli side, a two-state solution would mean the evacuation of hundreds of thousands of settlers from the West Bank, even if some territorial swaps are agreed upon. Those settlers will certainly demand compensation for being evacuated, citing the precedent of the settlement evacuation from the Gaza Strip. In that evacuation, Israel spent over €200,000 per settler. That could add up to tens of billions of euros (Hever, 2005c). The Israeli government would then face a choice: either bankrupt itself by awarding compensation to settlers, or create a socioeconomic crisis by evacuating settlers without fully compensating them. It is also important to note that Israeli opposition to evacuation has the backing of a strong movement, which is willing to resort to violence and wields a powerful influence over the Israeli military and police. Any evacuation is thus likely to intensify internal conflicts within Israeli society and lead to large-scale violence (Zertal and Eldar, 2007: 71, 174).

In addition, parts of the Israeli industrial and commercial sector would have to be rebuilt inside Israel, and companies whose profits are based on the exploitation of cheap Palestinian labour, Palestinian natural resources, and the captive Palestinian market would be forced to reinvent themselves or else shut down (Swirski, 2008b). Although the occupation as a whole is a burden to Israeli society (see Chapters 4 and 5), Israeli capitalists who profit from the occupation have the economic and political clout to put obstacles in the way of withdrawal.

However, the biggest economic commitment that Israel would have to undertake under a two-state solution is to compensate the Palestinians for decades of oppression and for countless crimes committed against them. Today most Israelis do not even consider future compensation to the Palestinians as a realistic possibility, and international pressure on Israel to forward such compensation is still in its infancy, because more urgent matters take a prior position in the political discourse. Demands for compensation are sure to gain momentum when the immediate series of emergencies subsides and the Israeli government declares that the conflict is over, whether at that time the conflict is indeed over or not.

Such compensation is very difficult to estimate. It would have to consider the extent of the damage that Israeli authorities have inflicted on the Palestinian economy: they have demolished houses, confiscated lands, uprooted trees, prevented access to workplaces and agricultural lands, prevented imports and exports, exploited Palestinian labour and natural resources (especially water), and inflicted bodily injuries and permanent disabilities on tens of thousands of Palestinians. The damages add up to a figure in the dozens of billions of dollars at the very least. Compensation of this magnitude could bankrupt the Israeli economy, bringing on years of stagnation, and putting a strain on the standard of living of most Israelis.

Finally, even if Israel withdraws its troops, evacuates the settlements, and pays full compensation, the Israeli–Palestinian conflict cannot end as long as Israel does not recognize the right of return of the Palestinian refugees or implement a gradual program to absorb them as Israeli citizens. The conflict also cannot end as long as Israel relegates its non-Jewish citizens to second-class status, as part of its self-definition as a Jewish state.

On the Palestinian side, great efforts would be required to find employment quickly for tens of thousands of unemployed young Palestinians. The evacuated settlements would demand creative solutions of the Palestinians, because a large part of the settlements' built-up areas consist of upper-class residences. If distributed to Palestinian families, large apartments, low-density housing, gardens and even pools could severely accentuate inequality and feelings of unfairness. On the other hand, leveling the settlements and building high-density residences on the land would require massive investment of money, time, and materials, and would cause more environmental damage to an area that has already sustained a great deal of it.

Rebuilding the infrastructure on both sides of the border is also a project of immense proportions. The existing infrastructure of utilities (water, sewage, and electricity) is a tangled mess which criss-crosses the West Bank, granting preferential services to the settlements. An independent Palestinian state would be hopelessly dependent on Israeli companies to provide basic services, as these companies already own much of the infrastructure and possess the technology, know-how, training, and capital to dominate both the Israeli and Palestinian markets. Otherwise, the Palestinians would have to create most of their infrastructure from scratch (Wright, 2000).

The hypothetical Palestinian state would also have difficulty finding trade partners other than Israel. Palestinian businesspeople are already accustomed to importing from Israel, but if a border is erected, they would have to begin paying customs on Israeli goods, significantly increasing the cost of living for Palestinians. There is as yet no infrastructure for mass-scale trade with Jordan or Egypt, the only adjacent countries other than Israel. The Sinai Peninsula in Egypt is a sparsely populated area, which means that overland trade would mostly have to cross over 150 miles to and from the container terminal on the Suez Canal at Port Fouad. Furthermore, neither the Gaza Strip nor the West Bank currently has an airport or a seaport. Until such facilities are constructed, the Palestinian state would be completely dependent on Israel for its imports and exports.

The Palestinian state would also need to establish its own currency, or sign a joint-currency agreement with Israel or another country. The small size of the Palestinian economy would make a separate currency weak, unstable, and prone to influxes as a result of currency speculations. On the other hand, if the Palestinians sign a joint-currency agreement, they would have very limited influence over monetary policy and not be able to maintain and operate a full-fledged central bank.

Finally, the main source of income to the Palestinian economy in the first years of independence is likely to be compensation from Israel. Compensation to the refugees who choose to resettle in the West Bank and Gaza Strip alone has been estimated at US$80 billion. Yet such a sudden influx of money, without the economic infrastructure to absorb and incorporate it into existing industries, could easily lead to a high inflation rate and to rampant corruption, both of which could eliminate a large proportion of the compensation payments and leave the Palestinian economy largely unimproved by them (Schnell, 2008).

All of the above obstacles do not necessarily make the two-state solution impossible, but they certainly make it difficult, and the price will be paid in the form of lowered standards of living for both Palestinians and Israelis for decades.

THE ONE-STATE SOLUTION

All the disadvantageous aspects of the two-state solution described above bring up the other possibility for ending the Israeli–Palestinian conflict: the one-state solution. A single democratic state as a solution to the conflict enjoys only limited support among the population of the region. A 2006 poll found that 46.6 percent of Palestinians supported a two-state solution, compared with 41.1 percent who supported a one-state solution. Most of those who supported the one-state solution proposed a binational unified state for Palestinians and Jews (30.4 percent of the total). These results in themselves do not indicate an overwhelming support for either solution, with only a slight majority for the two-state solution, but they do indicate a strong shift towards the one-state solution compared with previous polls (JMCC, 2006: 3, 5). In Israel, only a small fraction of Jews support the one-state solution.

From an economic point of view, the one-state solution does not solve the core problems of either the Palestinian or Israeli economies, but it does create a framework and tools for solving them eventually. The infrastructure that already crosses the Green Line can be expanded and connected to Palestinian cities and villages, thus creating a single network to serve the entire area, preferably managed by publicly owned companies, companies that answer to the political leadership and thus must prioritize accessibility above profits. Upper-class Palestinians could move into the settlements, into large houses that already exist there. Some settlers would be likely to leave, for in the absence of government subsidies to settlers and in the absence of an ever-expanding frontier, they would no longer have either the economic or ideological incentives to keep choosing to live in those communities.

The two major economic concerns that would have to be addressed by the future state are compensation to the Palestinians for decades of occupation and oppression, and the resettlement of Palestinian refugees. In a joint Israeli–Palestinian state with a joint parliament, the balance between the political and social need to heal the wounds of the past and the economic need to spread these efforts over a long period could be resolved in a democratic process. The strain on the economy would be heavy, sustained over a long time. Nevertheless, a joint representative body would have the authority and legitimacy to ration the efforts over a long period of time. In order to minimize the problems of inflation and corruption, a long-term plan would be needed to sustain the recovery and compensation efforts.

SCENARIOS OF CONFLICT

Feeling isolated, oppressed, and betrayed, many Palestinians believe that their only course of action is violence. Although their military capabilities seem woefully insufficient compared with the strength of the Israeli army, if escalation continues the Palestinian resistance will eventually prevail and overwhelm the occupation, and maybe even achieve the downfall of the state of Israel. This is simply because Israelis have much more to lose in the struggle. Many Israelis would rather leave the country than face constantly escalating levels of violence and terrorism, and the accompanying economic hardships (described in Chapters 4 and 5). Furthermore, the escalation keeps dragging Israel into more conflicts, such as the wars with Lebanon and a potential confrontation with Iran, and it affects the image of Israelis traveling abroad.

Nevertheless, we cannot ignore the fact that a Palestinian victory would exact a terrible price. The death toll among Palestinians has always been much higher than among Israelis in any violent struggle, and the cumulative trauma, loss of life, and economic devastation would not only destroy the occupation, but also transform Palestinian society. In a struggle against a much stronger foe, Palestinians have found that religious fervor, militancy, and self-sacrifice are powerful weapons, capable of mobilizing people on behalf of a nearly hopeless cause. These same qualities could be very harmful to a post-war society trying to heal and recover.

This is the pessimistic scenario, because it is one that involves more bloodshed, the creation of another generation of refugees, and the birth of a Palestinian state in violence and turmoil. History has taught us – in Algeria, Yugoslavia, and Israel – that when it takes too much fighting and bloodshed to achieve national liberation, the non-democratic states that emerge as a result replicate the discriminating and oppressive practices against which they once rebelled, and eventually direct their residual aggressive energies against their own populations. Political activists in Israel/Palestine often call this phenomenon "the abused child syndrome," noting that many abused children grow up to become abusive parents themselves.

The more optimistic scenario is still far from a utopian solution. It involves a different kind of struggle against the occupation. A growing number of Palestinians say that they have lost faith in the Palestinian Authority, and feel it has become a tool that is being used by Israel to continue the occupation. Palestinians in the Gaza Strip, the West Bank, and even within Israel are looking for a different solution, and what many of them are proposing is to turn their liberation campaign into a non-violent struggle, demanding civil rights from Israel. Today, most Palestinians feel that their negotiators with Israel have failed to improve the lot of the general public, and are looking for new strategies. A document from 2008, *Regaining the Initiative: Palestinian strategic options to end Israeli occupation*, by the Palestine Strategy Study Group, is a good example of this shift. It shows that the idea of a one-state solution is gaining a foothold among a growing number of Palestinian thinkers (PSSG, 2008).

These initiatives are indeed very threatening to Israel's Zionist regime, as their goal is the establishment of an egalitarian liberal democracy in Palestine in which Jews and Palestinians would live as equals, hence undermining the idea of a Jewish state. For Israel's Jewish population, though, this solution offers a change, relief from a life of constant conflict, fear, and moral dilemma, and the hope of finally achieving the original purpose for which Zionism was founded – to allow Jews to lead normal lives as equal citizens in a democratic country.

Israel has no effective strategy for deflecting such a non-violent struggle. If it chooses to deny Palestinians their basic rights, that will expose Israel's non-democratic regime. In November 2007 former Israeli prime minister Ehud Olmert said that "The day will come when the two-state solution collapses, and we face a South African-style struggle for equal voting rights. As soon as that happens, the state of Israel is finished" (Mermelstein, 2007).

Such a scenario would need support from the international community. Indeed the movement calling for consumer boycotts and divestments from Israel is rapidly spreading across Europe and North America, demonstrating that non-violent resistance to Israel's occupation can be effective. Israel's business sector is highly dependent on international trade, and a blow to Israel's exports is a blow that the Israeli government as well as the general public cannot ignore. The South African example shows that even though the end of apartheid did not solve all the country's ills, it certainly created a framework for dealing with the other problems through non-violent means.

The choice between these two scenarios depends on many factors, not least of which is the position of the international community, as expressed by governments, the organizations of civil society, or social movements. Continued support for Israel's "right to defend itself," effectively a blank check that allows Israel to violate international law with impunity, strongly increases the probability of the first scenario. As long as Israel continues to rely on its military might to postpone dealing with the root causes of the conflict and with its own internal contradictions, a process of escalation and ever-increasing hatred is very likely. However, confronting Israel on non-military fronts with economic pressure such as boycott and sanctions, legal pressure such as prosecution of Israeli war criminals, and psychological pressure such as cultural boycott and demonstrations, would make the second scenario more likely. When the Israeli authorities are unable to respond to pressure with military violence, they can rely only on propaganda. In the propaganda war, Israel has the weaker hand, because every reporter on the ground can see with their own eyes the disparity between the picture painted by the Israeli Ministry of Foreign Affairs and the Israeli media, and what is actually happening every day in the OPT.

Most importantly, an international show of solidarity with the Palestinian struggle for freedom would influence the way in which the Palestinians choose to frame and express their struggle. Internationals who demonstrate in front of Israeli embassies, boycott Israeli goods, promote an academic and cultural boycott of Israel, and even come to the OPT to join the non-violent protests and show their solidarity, give hope to Palestinians. They strengthen the belief that a non-violent struggle can be effective, and that living in a joint political framework with Israelis does not necessarily mean that the rights of Palestinians will be violated.

CONCLUDING REMARKS

Although I work and live in Israel, during my work in studying the occupation, I traveled to a number of different countries, including Belgium, Canada, France, Germany, Greece, Italy, Jordan, Qatar, Spain, Sweden, Switzerland, Thailand, the United States, and Venezuela. What amazed me most when meeting activists, politicians, scholars, and even just open-minded people in all of these countries is how important they consider the Israeli–Palestinian conflict to be. In each of these places I saw groups of people who have dedicated their free time and a great deal of energy (and sometimes money) to show solidarity with the Palestinian struggle, who have been trying to learn all they can about the occupation and demand justice. These people were not just Palestinian refugees or their families, but people from every walk of life.

The International Solidarity Movement (ISM) – hundreds of young international activists who have been coming to Palestine to witness firsthand the horrors of the occupation and to try to stop them with their own bodies (and without violence) – are a constant reminder to Palestinians and Israelis that the occupation is not forgotten or ignored.

It never failed to amaze me that these people have found the troubles of a remote land more important than, or at least as important as, their own local troubles in their native countries. So it was until I had a conversation with a group of activists in Barcelona, Spain. I asked them why they had decided to put so much effort into the Palestinian issue, and one of them said:

> In the 1930s, people from all over the world came to volunteer in stopping fascism in the Spanish Civil War. They did it not out of sympathy to Spain, but because they correctly saw it as in their own interests to stop fascism as soon as possible, before it engulfs the whole world. Today once more we must gather to stop the forces of violence and repression, and the place to do so is Palestine.

Never before had it been so clear to me that the Israeli–Palestinian conflict is of crucial global importance. It is a laboratory where civil resistance is pitted against the sophisticated machines of control, and where masses of people are pitted against towering concrete walls. The outcome of this conflict will determine not merely the future of the region, but the shape of future conflicts and occupations throughout the world.

This book was written with the clear aim of dispelling some of the propaganda disseminated by the Israeli and pro-Israeli authorities and media. I will have been successful if it makes a small contribution towards promoting the second scenario described above: an end of the occupation, the Jewish state and the violence, and the replacement of the existing system of repression through the creation of a democratic state to represent everyone who lives in the area currently controlled by Israel.

BIBLIOGRAPHY

All URLs were accessed in August, 2009, unless otherwise noted.

Abu-Bader, Suleiman, and Abu-Qarn, Aamer S., 2003, "Government expenditures, military spending and economic growth: causality evidence from Egypt, Israel and Syria," *Journal of Policy Modeling,* Vol. 25, No. 6–7, pp. 567–83.

Abu-Qarn, Aamer S., and Abu-Bader, Suleiman, 2008, "Structural breaks in military expenditures: evidence for Egypt, Israel, Jordan and Syria," *Public Policy,* Vol. 14, No. 1.

Adalah, 2007, *The Democratic Constitution,* Shafa'amr: Adalah, March.

Adut, Rami, and Hever, Shir, 2006, "Breaking the labour market – the welfare to work plan in Israel, focus on East Jerusalem," *Economy of the Occupation*, Parts 7–8, Jerusalem: Alternative Information Center (AIC), April–May.

Alexander, Esther, 1992, "Immigration economy in the first decade of the state of Israel," *Discussions in the Foundation of Israel [Iunim Bitkumat Israel],* Vol. 2.

Alternative Information Center, The (AIC), 2008, "'They fight it best themselves': AIC position paper on corruption in the Palestinian Authority," <http://*www.alternativenews.org/*>, April 3.

Amirav, Moshe, 2007, *The Jerusalem Syndrome [Syndrome Yerushala'im],* Jerusalem: Carmel.

Angrist, Joshu D., 1996, "Short-run demand for Palestinian labour," *Journal of Labour Economics*, Vol. 14, No. 3 (July), pp. 425–53.

Applied Research Institute of Jerusalem (ARIJ) and Land Research Center (LRC), 1999, <http://www.poica.org/index.htm>.

ARIJ and LRC, 2006, "The enclavement of Al Walajeh village," *Monitoring Israeli Colonization Activities in the Palestinian Territories,* April 8, <http://www.poica.org/editor/case_studies/view.php?recordID=806>.

Arab Association for Human Rights and Center Against Racism, 2007, "Suspected citizens: racial profiling against Arab passengers by Israeli airports and airlines," *Electronic Intifada,* January 12.

Arnon, Arie, 2007, "Israeli policy towards the Occupied Palestinian Territories: the economic dimension, 1967–2007," *Middle East Journal,* Vol. 61, No. 4, pp. 573–95.

Arnon, Arie, Luski, Israel, Spivak, Avia, and Weinblatt, Jimmy, 1997, *The Palestinian Economy, Between imposed integration and voluntary separation,* New York and Cologne, Germany: Brill.

Arnon, Arie, and Weinblatt, Jimmy, 2001, "Sovereignty and economic development: the case of Israel and Palestine," *Economic Journal*, Vol. 111, June, pp. F291–1F308.

Aronson, Geoffrey, 2006, "Barrier facts," *Report on Israeli Settlements in the Occupied Territories*, Summer.

Association for Civil Rights in Israel (ACRI), 2005, "Authorities must provide information on jurisdiction areas and settlement outline," <http://www.acri.org.il/eng/>, March 29.

Avigad, Doron, and Kol, Gil, 2008, "*Economist:* the growth and prosperity in Israel are based on the start-up industry and can evaporate any minute," *Globes Magazine,* April 25.

Awartani, Hisham, 1988, "Agricultural development and policies in the West Bank and Gaza," pp. 139–64 in Abed, George, T. (ed.), *The Palestinian Economy: Studies in development under prolonged occupation,* London and New York: Routledge.

Azoulay, Ariella, and Ophir, Adi, 2008, *This Regime Which is Not One: Occupation and democracy between the sea and the river (1967–) [Mishtar Ze She'eino Ehad]*, Tel-Aviv: Resling.

Badil, 2005, "Palestinian civil society calls for boycott, divestment and sanctions against Israel until it complies with international law and universal principles of human rights," Badil, July 9 <http://www.badil.org/Publications/Press/2005/press390-05.htm>.

Badil, 2008, *Al Majdal*, Vol. 38, Summer.

Bahgat, Gawdat, 2005, "Energy partnership: Israel and the Persian Gulf," *Energy Policy,* Vol. 33, No. 5, March, pp. 671–7.

Bahmad, Layla, 2007, *Palestinian Non-Governmental Organizations Caught Between Reality and Challenges,* dissertation, Kassel University, May.

Ben, Aluf, 2004 "Sharon: I hope a day will come when we won't be in the Strip," *Ha'aretz*, January 14.

Ben-David, Dan, 2002, "The central socio-economic problems and central policy foci," working paper, Department for Public Policy, Tel-Aviv University, July.

Ben-David, Dan, 2003, "Inequality and growth in Israel," *Economic Quarterly [Rivon Lekalkala],* Vol. 50, No. 1, March, pp. 27–104.

Ben-David, Dan, 2005, "The values of the settlers," *Ha'aretz*, June 9.

Ben-David, Dan, 2008, "Brain drained," working paper, Department of Public Policy, Tel-Aviv University, January.

Ben-Shakhar, Arik, Schuldineger, Zvi, and Toker-Maimon, Oshrat, 2006, *Unemployment Report 2006 [Dokh Avtala 2006],* Commitment to Peace and Social Justice.

Bendel, Maskit, 2005, *The Disengagement Plan and its Repercussions on the Right to Health in the Gaza Strip,* Tel-Aviv: Physicians for Human Rights, January.

Bengal, Maya, 2007, "'Olmert lost his mind,'" *NRG,* March 4, <http://www.nrg.co.il/>.

Benvenisti, Meron, 1988, *The Sling and the Club: Territories, Jews and Arabs [Hakela Veha'ala],* Jerusalem: Keter.

Berglas, Eitan, 1989, "The Israeli economy and the held territories: war and peace," *Economic Quarterly [Rivon Lekalkala]*, Vol. 139, pp. 599–600.

Bergman, Arie, 1974, *Economic Growth in the Administered Areas 1968–1973 [Tsmikha Kalkalit Bashtakhim Hamukhzakim 1968–1973]*, Jerusalem: Bank of Israel Research Department.

Bhattacharya, Sukanto, 2006, "The Israel–Palestine Question – a case for application of neutrosophic game theory," pp. 51–60 in Bhattacharya, Sukanto, Khoshnevisan, Mohammad, and Smarandache, Florentin (eds), *Computational Modeling in Applied Problems*, Phoenix, Ariz.: Hexis.

Bichler, Shimshon, 1996, "Military spending and differential accumulation: a new approach to the political economy of armament – the case of Israel," *Review of Radical Political Economics,* No. 28, pp. 51–95.

Bichler, Shimshon, and Nitzan, Jonathan, 1995, "The great U-turn: restructuring in Israel and South Africa," *News from Within*, Vol. 11, No. 9, pp. 29–32.

Bichler, Shimshon, and Nitzan, Jonathan, 2001, *From War Profits to Peace Dividend: The global political economy of Israel [Merivkhei Milkhama Ledividendim Shel Shalom]*, Jerusalem: Carmel.

Bichler, Shimshon, and Nitzan, Jonathan, 2006, "Cheap wars," *Economy of the Occupation*, Vol. 10, Jerusalem: Alternative Informtion Center.

Bichler, Shimshon, and Nitzan, Jonathan, 2007, "Israel roaring economy," *Bnarchies*, Jerusalem and Montreal, June, <http://www.bnarchives.net>.

Bichler, Shimshon, Nitzan, Jonathan, and Rowley, Robin, 1989a, "The political economy of armaments," working paper 7/89, Department of Economics, McGill University, Montreal.

Bichler, Shimshon, Nitzan, Jonathan, and Rowley, Robin, 1989b, "The armadollar–petrodollar coalition and the Middle East," working paper 10/89, Department of Economics, McGill University, Montreal.

Bimkom, 2006, "The village enclaves south of Jerusalem (the Nahalin Enclave), expert opinion," [Muvla'at Hakfarim Midarom Leyerushalaim (Muvla'at Nakhalin), Khavat Da'at Mumkhim, February.

Bishara, Marwan, 2001, *Palestine/Israel: Peace or apartheid*, London and New York: Zed.

Blau, Uri, 2009, "Secret Israeli database reveals full extent of illegal settlement," *Ha'aretz,* February 1.

Bocco, Riccardo, De Martino, Luigi, Friedrich, Roland, Al Husseini, Jalal, and Luethold, Arnold, 2006, *Politics Security and the Barrier: Palestinian public perceptions*, Centre for Democratic Control of the Armed Forces and Swiss Ministry of Foreign Affairs Centre for Analysis and Perspectives, November.

Bonanich, Edna, 1972, "A theory of ethnic antagonism: the split labor market," *American Sociological Review,* Vol. 37, No. 5, October, pp. 547–59.

Bonanich, Edna, 1973, "A theory of middleman minorities," *American Sociological Review*, Vol. 38, No. 5, October.

Boswell, Terry, and Dixon, William J., 1993, "Marx's theory of rebellion: a cross-national analysis of class exploitation, economic development and violent revolt," *American Sociological Review,* Vol. 58, No. 5, October, pp. 681–702.

Bourdieu, Pierre, 1985, "Social space and the genesis of groups," *Theory and Society*, Vol. 14, No. 6, November, pp. 723–44.

Bourdieu, Pierre, 1989, "Social space and symbolic power," *Sociological Theory*, Vol. 7, No. 1, Spring, pp. 14–25.

Bourdieu, Pierre, 1998a, *Acts of Resistance Against the Tyranny of the Market*, New York: New Press.

Bourdieu, Pierre, 1998b, "The essence of neoliberalism," *Le Monde Diplomatique*, December 8, <http://mondediplo.com/1998/12/08bourdieu>.

Bourdieu, Pierre, 2006, "Critique of the scholarly discourse," *Theory and Criticism [Teoria Ubikoret]*, No. 28, Spring, pp. 70–4.

Bower, Jake, 2006, "Why it rains: Hamas holding 'Israeli' gas reserves hostage," *The Electronic Intifada*, July 5, <http://electronicintifada.net/v2/article4909.shtml?url>.

Bowles, William, 2003, "Israel's proxy war?," CounterCurrents.org, October 8, <http://www.countercurrents.org/us-bowles081003.htm>.

Brauman, Rony, Hilal, Jamil, and Ophir, Adi, 2005, "Assistance or resistance: a false diemma? Humanitarian action in the Occupied Palestinian Territories and in other states of occupation," seminar proceedings, Van Leer Jerusalem Institute, November 18.

British Broadcasting Corporation (BBC), 2006, "Israel to impose Hamas sanctions," February 19, <http://*www.bbcworldnews.com/*>.

BBC, 2008, "Gazans flood through Egypt border," *BBC News*, January 23, <http://*www.bbcworldnews.com/*>.

B'tselem, 2002, *Land Grab: Israel's settlement policy in the West Bank*, Jerusalem: B'tselem, May.

B'tselem, 2005, *Under the Guise of Security, Routing the separation barrier to enable the expansion of Israeli settlements in the West Bank*, Jerusalem: B'tselem, December.

B'tselem, 2007a, *Crossing the Line: Violation of the rights of Palestinians in Israel without a permit*, Jerusalem: B'tselem, March.

B'tselem, 2007b, "The siege on the Gaza Strip," *B'tselem*, July 24.

Buhbut, Amir, 2008, "The big crossings are released from the IDF," *NRG*, March 18, <http://www.nrg.co.il/>.

Burne, P., 1949, "Bentham and the utilitarian principle," *Mind*, New Series, Vol. 58, No. 231, July, pp. 367–8.

Central Bank of Israel (CBI), 2008a, "Daily exchange rates" <http://www.bankisrael.gov.il/heb.shearim/index.php>.

CBI, 2008b, "Table B1: Gross domestic product and its components," in *Main Indicators on the Israeli Market*, <http://www.bankisrael.gov.il/deptdata/mehkar/indic/heb_b01.htm>.

Clawson, Patrick, 2002, "Aid to Palestinians exceeds Marshall Plan aid to Europe," *Jerusalem Post*, August 9.

Clyde, R. Mark, 2002, "Israel: U.S. foreign assistance," *Issue Brief for Congress;* received through the CRS Web, October 17, Foreign Affairs, Defence and Trade Division.

Cohen, Amit, 2005a, "Separation fence in the middle of school," *Ma'ariv*, November 25.

Cohen, Hillel, 2006, *Good Arabs: The Israeli security services and the Israeli Arabs [Aravim Tovim; Hamodi'in Haysraeli Veha'aravim Beysrael]*, Jerusalem: Ivrit.

Cohen, Shimon, 2008, "Security of settlements goes to private hands," *Arutz 7*, April 30.

Cohen, Yanai, 2005b, "Sitting on the fence," interview with Brigadier General Eran Ofir, Head of IDF Logistics, *Kol Ha'ir*, January 21.

Commons, John R., 1931, "Institutional economics," *American Economic Review*, Vol. 21, No. 4, December, pp. 648–57.

Commons, John R., 1934. *Myself: The autobiography of John R. Commons*, New York: Macmillan.

Dagoni, Ran, 2005, "The World Bank might help buy the homes of evacuees," *Globes*, May 13–14.

Davidi, Efraim, 2006, "Who is a communist?," *Mitsad Sheni*, Vol. 14–15, pp. 68–71.

Dayan, Arie, 2008, "Conflict of interests approved by law," *Eretz Aheret*, Vol. 43, January–February, pp. 34–41.

De Waal, Alex, 1997, *Famine Crimes, Politics and the Disaster Relief Industry in Africa*, London: African Rights and International African Institute.

Dickey, Christopher, and Dennis, Mark, 1995, "A fence across the sand," *Newsweek*. Vol. 125, Issue 6, February 6.

Dorfman, Joseph, 1932, "The 'satire' of Thorstein Veblen's theory of the leisure class," *Political Science Quarterly*, Vol. 47, No. 3, September, pp. 363–409.

Economist, 2008, "The next generation," *Economist*, Vol. 387, No. 8574, April 5.

Elgazi, Gadi, 2005, "Matrix in Bil'in – capital, settlement and civil resistance around the separation fences, or a story of colonial capitalism in Israel," *Ha'oketz*, <http://www.haokets.org/default.asp?PageID=10&ItemID=2917>.

Erlanger, Steven, 2007, "Embargo didn't stop Palestinian aid flow," *International Herald Tribune*, March 20.

Eyal, Gil, 2002, "Dangerous liaisons between military intelligence and Middle Eastern studies in Israel," *Theory and Society*, Vol. 31, pp. 653–93.

Faier, Elizabeth, 2002, "Domestic matters: feminism and activism among Palestinian women in Israel," pp. 178–209 in *Ethnography in Unstable Places, Everyday lives in contexts of dramatic political change*, Durham, N.C. and London: Duke University Press.

Falah, Ghazi-Walid, 2003, "Dynamics and patterns of the shrinking of Arab lands in Palestine," *Political Geography*, Vol. 22, No. 2, February, pp. 179–209.

Farah, Jafar, 2006, "Human rights status of Palestinian Arab citizens in Israel," *Mossawa Center*, June 19.

Farouz, Anat, 2006, "The residents of Ramot are against the separation barrier," *Kol Ha'ir*, June 1.

Farsakh, Leila, 2002, "Palestinian labour flows to the Israeli economy: a finished story?" *Journal of Palestine Studies*, 125, Vol. 32, No. 1, Autumn, pp. 13–27.

Fast, Larissa, 2006, "'Aid in the pressure cooker:' humanitarian action in the Occupied Palestinian Territory," *Humanitarian Agenda 2015*, case study no. 7, Feinstein International Center, November.

Feldman, Yotam, 2007, "I'm to blame, we are to blame," *Ha'aretz*, December 21.

Fischbach, Michael R., 2003, *Records of Dispossession: Palestinian refugee property and the Arab–Israeli Conflict,* New York: Columbia University Press.

Fischer, Stanley, 2007, "Chairman lecture in the Israel Jewish-Arab Business Conference," *Lectures and Articles of the Chairman*, Central Bank of Israel, Jerusalem, November 13, <http://www.bankisrael.gov.il/deptdata/neumim/neum250h.htm>.

Fraser, Nancy, 2004, "From distribution to recognition? Dilemmas of justice in a 'post-socialist' era," pp. 270–97 in Ram, Uri and Filc, Dani (eds), *The Power of Property: Israeli society in the global age [Shilton Hahon: Hakhevra Haysraelit Baidan Haglobali]*, Tel-Aviv: Hakibutz Hameukhad, Van Leer Institute.

Frenkel, Ami, 2001, *Unemployment Benefits in Israel: Trends and legislation changes: 1985–2000 [Dmei Avtala Beyisrael, Megamot Veshinuim Bekhakika 1985 Ad 2000],* Tel-Aviv: Adva Center, February.

Gamliel, Naor, 2005, "The cost of the settlements, how much do we pay?" unpublished.

Garb, Yaakov, 2005, *The Separation Fence and Arab Neighbourhoods in Jerusalem: Integration or separation – just not postponing the decision [Gader Hahafrada Vehashkhunot Ha'araviot Beyrushalaim: Shiluv o Hafrada Rak Lo Dkhyat Hakhra'a]*, Floersheimer Institute for Policy Studies, March.

Gazit, Shlomo, 1985, *The Carrot and the Stick: Israel's policy in Judea and Samaria, 1967–1968* [*Hamakel Vehagezer: Hamimshal Byhuda Veshomron 1967–1968*], Tel-Aviv: Zmora Bitan.

Gazit, Shlomo, 2003, *Trapped Fools: Thirty years of Israeli policy in the territories,* London: Frank Cass.

Gebauer, Gunter, 2000, "Habitus, intentionality, and social rules: a controversy between Searle and Bourdieu," *SubStance*, No. 93, pp. 68–83.

Gellner, Ernest, 1990, "Economic interpretation of history," pp. 148–58 in Eatwell, John, Migate, Murray, and Newman, Peter (eds), *Marxian Economics*, New York and London: Palgrave.

Gordon, Neve, 2008a, "The land, not the people," *The Alternative Information Center*, June 8, <http://www.alternativenews.org/english/1214-the-land-not-the-people-.html>.

Gordon, Neve, 2008b, *Israel's Occupation*, Berkeley, Calif. and London: University of California Press.

Gordon, Neve, and Filc, Dani, 2005, "Hamas and the destruction of risk society," *Constellations,* Vol. 12, No. 4, pp. 542–60.

Gray, Alice, 2007, "The water crisis in Gaza," *International Viewpoint,* Vol. 386, February.

Greenbaum, Lior, 2005, "Because of the Jerusalem envelope fence: 'house prices in the Eastern City jumped by 30%–40% in two years,'" *Globes,* September 14–15.

Gross, Oren, 2000, "Mending walls: the economic aspects of Israeli–Palestinian peace," *American International University International Law Review,* Vol. 1539, No. 16.

Gutwein, Danny, 2004, "Comments on the class foundations of the occupation," *Theory and Criticism [Teoria Ubikoret]*, Vol. 24, pp. 203–11.

Ha'aretz, 2003, "The price of the settlements," New Year supplement, *Ha'aretz,* September 26.

Ha'aretz, 2008, "The Israeli high-tech conceals a stumbling market," *Ha'aretz,* April 4.

Ha'aretz, 2009, "Poll: most of the Israeli and Palestinian publics support a two-state solution," *Ha'aretz,* April 22.

Ha'aretz and Reuters, 2008, "Report: Netanyahu says 9/11 terror attacks good for Israel," *Ha'aretz,* April 16.

Halper, Jeff, 2005, *Obstacles to Peace: A critical re-framing of the Israeli–Palestinian conflict*, Jerusalem: Israeli Committee Against House Demolitions, April.

Hamed, Osama A., and Shaban, Radwan A., 1993, "One-sided customs and monetary union: the case of the West Bank and Gaza Strip under Israeli occupation," pp. 117–48 in Fischer, Stanley, Rodrik, Dani, and Tuma, Elias (eds), *The Economics of Middle East Peace: Views from the region,* Cambridge, Mass.: MIT Press.

Hanafi, Sari and Tabar, Linda, 2004, "Donor assistance, rent-seeking and elite formation," pp. 250–83 in Amundsen, Inge, Husain Mushtaq, Giacaman, Khan, and Giacaman, George (eds), *State Formation in Palestine: Viability and governance during a social transformation*, London/New York: Routledge Curzon.

Hanafi, Sari, and Tabar, Linda, 2005, *The Emergence of a Palestinian Globalized Elite; Donors, international organizations and local NGOs*, Jerusalem: Institute of Jerusalem Studies.

Handels, Shuki, 2003, *Guards and Security Guards in Israel 1995–2003 [Meavtekhim Veshomrim Beyisrael 1995–2003],* Jerusalem: Ministry of Industry, Trade and Labour: Planning, Research and Economics Administration.

Hanieh, Adam, 1997, "Palestine: wealth gap widens after Oslo," *Green Left,* August 20, <http://www.greenleft.org.au/1997/286/16227>.

Harel, Amos, 2006a, "Mofaz instructed that the fence construction be resumed in areas frozen by the High Court," *Ha'aretz*, January 11.

Harel, Amos, 2006b, "IDF: at least a year until the separation fence is complete," *Ha'aretz*, May 17.

Hass, Amira, 2002a, "Are the occupied protecting the occupier?" pp. 162–4 in Carey, Roane, and Shainin, Jonathan (eds), *The Other Israel; Voices of refusal and dissent*, New York: New Press.

Hass, Amira, 2002b, "Israel's closure policy: an ineffective strategy of containment and repression," *Journal of Palestinian Studies*, Vol. 31, No. 3, Spring, pp. 5–20.

Hass, Amira, 2006, "Abu-Dis residents: replace the planner of the separation fence, because he lives in a settlement that is included in the Israeli side," *Ha'aretz*, March 3.

Hass, Amira, 2008, "The tunnel owners in the Gaza Strip became the new merchants generation that Hamas nurtures," *Ha'aretz,* January 26.

Hass, Amira, 2009, "The committee of donors to Israel," *Ha'aretz,* March 4.

Hever, Shir, 2005a, "The settlements – economic cost to Israel," *Economy of the Occupation*, Part 2, Jerusalem: AIC, July.

Hever, Shir, 2005b, "Divide and conquer – inequality and discrimination," *Economy of the Occupation*, Part 3, Jerusalem: AIC, September.

Hever, Shir, 2005c, "The Gaza withdrawal – winners and losers," *Economy of the Occupation*, Parts 4–5, Jerusalem: AIC, October/November.

Hever, Shir, 2006a, "Foreign aid to Palestine/Israel, 2nd edn," *Economy of the Occupation*, Part 1, Jerusalem: AIC, February.

Hever, Shir, 2006b, "The question of sanctions and a boycott against Israel," *Economy of the Occupation*, Part 6, Jerusalem: AIC, March.

Hever, Shir, 2006c, "The occupation through the eyes of Israeli economists," *Economy of the Occupation*, Part 9, Jerusalem: AIC, June.

Hever, Shir, 2007a, "The Separation Wall in East Jerusalem: economic consequences," *Economy of the Occupation*, Parts 11–12, Jerusalem: AIC, January-February.

Hever, Shir, 2007b, "Education in East Jerusalem: report on the educational system in East Jerusalem," *Economy of the Occupation*, Parts 13–15, Jerusalem: AIC, July-September.

Hever, Shir, 2008a, "Privatization of Israel's refineries," *Economy of the Occupation*, Part 16, Jerusalem: AIC, January.

Hever, Shir, 2008b, "On economic class and political choice in Israel," *Alternative Information Center*, April 14, <http://www.alternativenews.org>.

Hever, Shir, 2008c, "Political economy of aid to Palestinians under occupation," *Economy of the Occupation*, Parts 17–18, Jerusalem: AIC, November.

Hodgson, Geoffrey M., 2004, *The Evolution of Institutional Economics: Agency, structure and Darwinism in American institutionalism*, London and New York: Routledge.

Homan, Paul T., 1932, "An appraisal of institutional economics," *American Economic Review*, Vol. 22, No. 1, March, pp. 10–17.

Honig-Parnass, Tikva, 2001, "The Al-Aqsa intifada: taking off the masks," *New Politics*, Vol. 8, No. 2, whole no. 30, Winter.

Hoseini, Nasrin, 2006, *Co-opting Resistance*, Master's thesis, University of Stockholm, March.

Hoshen, Maya (ed), 2005, *Statistical Yearbook, 2004 [Al Netunaykh Yerushalaim 2004]*, Jerusalem: Jerusalem Institute for Israel Studies.

Human Rights Watch, 2001, "Second class – discrimination against Palestinian Arab children in Israel's schools," September, <http://www.hrw.org/en/reports/2001/09/30/second-class-0>.

Integrated Regional Information Networks (IRIN), 2008, "Movement restrictions limiting benefits of aid – World Bank," IRIN, UN Office of Coordination of Humanitarian Affairs, May 3.

International Court, 2004, press release, July, <http://www.icj-cij.org/presscom/index.php?pr=71&pt=1&p1=6&p2=1>.

International Monetary Fund (IMF), 2003, *West Bank and Gaza: Economic performance and reform under conflict conditions*, September 15.

IMF and World Bank, 2007, *West Bank and Gaza: Economic Development 2006 – A First Assessment*, March.

Israeli Central Bureau of Statistics (ICBS), 1966, *Annual Statistics Reader 1965*, Jerusalem: ICBS.

ICBS, 2006a, "Table 1.1. Employee jobs, total wages and average monthly wages per employee job," Jerusalem: ICBS, <http://www1.cbs.gov.il/reader/cw_usr_view_SHTML?ID=329>.

ICBS, 2006b, "Selected price indices," *Statistical Abstract of Israel*, Jerusalem: ICBS, <http://www1.cbs.gov.il/reader/?MIval=cw_usr_view_SHTML&ID=345>.

ICBS, 2007, "National spending on education 2003–2006," press release, Jerusalem: ICBS, <http://www1.cbs.gov.il/reader/newhodaot/hodaa_template.html?hodaa=200708138>.

ICBS, 2008a, *Statistical Yearbook 2007*, Jerusalem: ICBS.

ICBS, 2008b, *Statistical Monthly Abstract, no. 3, 2008*, Jerusalem: ICBS.

ICBS, 2009, *Statistical Yearbook 2008*, Jerusalem: ICBS.

Israeli Ministry of Foreign Affairs (IMFA), 2004, "Facts about Israel," <http://www.mfa.gov.il/MFA/Facts+About+Israel/Israel+in+Maps/Literacy+rate.htm>.

IMFA, 2002, <http://www.mfa.gov.il/MFA/MFAArchive/2000_2009/2002/5/The%20Involvement%20of%20Arafat-%20PA%20Senior%20Officials%20and>.

Israeli Revenue Authority, 2007, *Annual Report 2006, No. 55*, Jerusalem: Israeli Ministry of Finance.

Jerusalem Centre for Israel Studies, 2003, *On Your Stats, Jerusalem, 2002–2003, Current situation and trends of change [Al Netunaikh Yerushalalim, 2002–2003, Matsav Nokhekhi Vemegamot Leshinui]*, Jerusalem: Jerusalem Centre for Israeli Studies.

Jerusalem Centre for Israel Studies, 2006, *Statistical Digest of Jerusalem, 2005–2006 [Shnaton Statisti Leyerushalaim 2005–2006]*, No. 22, Jerusalem: Jerusalem Centre for Israeli Studies.

Jerusalem Media and Communications Centre (JMCC), 2001, *International and Local Aid During the Second Intifada: An analysis of Palestinian public opinion in the West Bank and the Gaza Strip (October 2000–February 2001)*, East Jerusalem: JMCC.

JMCC, 2006, *Poll No. 60, Sep. 2006, 6 Months on the Formation of the 10th Palestinian Government*, East Jerusalem: JMCC.

Kanovski, Eliyahu, 1970, *The Economic Impact of the Six-Day War: Israel, the Occupied Territories, Egypt, Jordan*, New York, Washington and London: Praeger Special Studies in International Economics and Development.

Karmi, Ghada, 2005, "With no Palestinian state in sight, aid becomes an adjunct of the occupation," *Guardian*, December 31, <http://www.guardian.co.uk/world/2005/dec/31/comment.israelandthepalestinians>.

Keinon, Herb, 2006, "US keen on giving Israel time in Lebanon," *Jerusalem Post*, July 25.

Khaider, Ali (ed.), 2005, *Government Policy Towards Arab Citizens 2004–2005 [Mediniut Hamemshala Klapei Haezrakhim Ha'aravim]*, Jerusalem and Haifa: Sikkuy, December.

Khouri, Rami G., 1980, "Israel's imperial economics," *Journal of Palestine Studies*, Vol. 9, No. 2, Winter, pp. 71–8.

Kiekhofer, W. H., Clark, John, Maurice, Homan, Fletcher, Paul T., Wasserman, Hugh M., Atkins, Max J., Tyson, Willard E., Hewett, Francis D., William W., and Ely, R. T., 1932, "Institutional economics," *American Economic Review*, Vol. 22, No. 1, supplement, papers and proceedings of the Forty-fourth Annual Meeting of the American Economic Association, March, pp. 105–16.

Kimhi, Israel (ed.), 2006, *The Security Fence in Jerusalem: Its impact on the city residents [Gader Habitakhon Beyerushalaim: Hashlakhot Al Ha'ir Vetoshaveya]*, Jerusalem: Jerusalem Institute for Israel Studies.

Klein, Naomi, 2007a, "Laboratory for a fortress world," *The Nation*, July 2.

Klein, Naomi, 2007b, *The Shock Doctrine: The rise of disaster capitalism*, New York: Metropolitan Books.

Kleinman, Efraim, 2005, "Theory without criticism," *Theory and Criticism [Teoria Ubikoret]*, Vol. 26, Spring, pp. 275–85.

Koren, Ora, 2007, "The sum of orders from the security industry for 2006 reached an all-time peak at US $4.4 billion," *Ha'aretz*, October 10.

Koren, Ora, 2008, "Netanyahu: 'economic peace' before negotiations," *Ha'aretz*, January 21.

Kraus, Vered, and Yuval, Yonay. 2000. "The power and limits of ethnonationalism: Palestinians and Eastern Jews in Israel, 1974–1991," *British Journal of Sociology*, Vol. 51, no. 3, pp. 525–51.

Laclau, Ernesto, and Moufe, Chantal, 2004, *Hegemony and Socialist Strategy*, pp. 54–9, Tel-Aviv: Resling.

Lan, Shlomit, 2005, "Check, please!," *Globes*, May 2–3.

Landau, Pinhas, 2008, "Dealing with the wealth," *Eretz Aheret*, Vol. 43, January–February, pp. 42–6.

Laviv, Igal, 2003, "A dead-end roadmap," *The Left Bank [Hagada Hasmalit]*, April 20, <http://hagada.org.il/hagada/html/modules.php?name=News&file=article&sid=840>.

Le More, Anne, 2005, "Killing with kindness: funding the demise of a Palestinian state," *International Affairs*, Vol. 81, no. 5, pp. 983–1001.

Le More, Anne, 2008, *International Assistance to the Palestinians After Oslo: Political guilt, wasted money*, New York: Routledge.

Lein, Yehezkel, 2000, *Thirsty for a Solution: The water crisis in the Occupied Territories and its resolution in the final-status agreement*, Jerusalem: B'tselem, July.

Levitin, Assaf, and Horenstein, Gal, 1993, "What do we need them for?" *Bamahane*, March 23.

Levy, Daniel, 2008a, "A more private occupation," *Ha'aretz*, April 13.

Levy, Gideon, 2005, "Hillary Clinton wasn't here," *Ha'aretz*, November 18.

Levy, Tal, 2007, "Stanley Fischer calms the fears: the crisis will not have a large effect on the world market; Israel's situation is good and even very good," *Ha'aretz*, August 2.

Levy, Tal, 2008b, "Optimism at the Central Bank: the global crisis finds the Israeli market at its best since the foundation of the state," *TheMarker*, November 3.

Levy, Yagil, 2006, "Materialistic militarism," *Mitsad Sheni*, Vol. 14–15, pp. 42–7.

MachsomWatch, 2008, "Sheikh Sa'ad," <http://www.machsomwatch.org/en/checkpoint/373>.

Mada Al-Carmel, 2007, *The Haifa Declaration*, Haifa, May.

Maddox, Bronwen, 2008, "Iran is an inevitable distraction but a Palestinian pact is vital," *TimesOnline*, September 19, <http://www.timesonline.co.uk/tol/comment/columnists/bronwen_maddox/article4783403.ece>.

Magnier, Mark, 2002, "Israel impedes relief efforts, aid groups say Israel impedes relief work," *Los Angeles Times*, June 11.

Malihi, Assaf, and Sikolar, Na'ama, 2008, "'The crisis in the American market will have a limited effect on Israel," *Ynet*, January 11, <http://www.ynet.co.il>.

Maor, Ziv, 2006, "Democracy in a state of emergency," *OMedia*, October 4.

Maoz, Shlomo, 2008, "Intentional policy to hurt the weak," *Eretz Aheret*, Vol. 43, January–February, pp. 72–5.

Margalit, Meir, 2005, "Distribution of the municipal budget between the East and West Jerusalem," *Occupation Magazine [Magazin Kibbush]*, <http://www.kibush.co.il/datapage.asp?lang=0§ion=2&yr=2005&mn=5>.

Marx, Karl, 1938 [1867], *Das Kapital*, ed. F. Engels, vol. I; English trans. by S. Moore and E. Aveling (1887), as *Capital: A critical analysis of capitalist production*, vol. I, London: Sonnenschein; republished Allen & Unwin.

Marx, Karl, and Engels, Frederick, 1969 [1848], "Manifesto of the Communist Party," in Marx, Karl, and Engels, Friedrich, *Selected Works in Three Volumes*, vol. 1, Moscow, Progress.

Massar Associates, 2003, A *Strategy for Private Sector Development in the West Bank and Gaza: From crisis to sustainable growth*, World Bank, March.

McNay, Lois, 1999, "Gender, habitus and the field, Pierre Bourdieu and the limits of reflexivity," *Theory, Culture and Society*, Vol. 16, No. 1, pp. 95–117.

Mermelstein, Hannah, 2007, "The end of Israel?," *The Electronic Intifada*, December 19, <http://electronicintifada.net/v2/article9169.shtml>.

Mitnick, Jushua, 2004, "Israel selling its warfare expertise," *Jewish Week*, March 26.

Molyneux, Maxine, and Halliday, Fred, 1984, "Marxism, the Third World and the Middle-East," *MERIP Reports, No. 120, The Middle East after OPEC*, January, pp. 18–21.

Mor, Gal, 2001, "The wars of Israel and the Palestinians," *Ynet*, June 26, <http://www.ynet.co.il>.

Morav, Levy, 2008, "A moment before we sell the land too," *Eretz Aheret*, Vol. 43, January–February, pp. 60–4.

Morli, Andrea, 2004, *Palestine: Economy, development aid and higher education in international cooperation*, International University Masters in Cooperation and Development, 7th edn.

Müller, Andreas, 2004, *A Wall on the Green Line?* Jerusalem: AIC.

Myre, Greg, 2006, "Israel economy hums despite annual tumult," *New York Times*, December 31.

Nashashibi, Karim, 2007, "Palestinian finance under siege: economic decline and institutional degradation," paper commissioned by UN OCHA, April.

National Committee for the Heads of the Arab Local Authorities in Israel, 2006, *The Future Vision of the Palestinian Arabs in Israel*, Nazareth.

National Insurance Institute (NII), 2005, *Statistical Yearbook [Shnaton Statisti]*, third quarter.

NII, 2008, *Poverty Rate and Income Gaps 2006/7, Main Findings [Meymadei Ha'oni Vehapa'arim Bahakhnasot 2006/7, Mimtsa'im Ikariyim]*, NII Department of Research and Planning, February.

Newman, David, and Biger, Gideon (eds), 2006, *Geographical Theoretical Framework for Geographic Planning of a State Border Between Israel and a Palestinian State [Misgeret Giografit Ra'ayonit Lehatvaya Giografit Shel Gvul Medini Bein Medinat Ysrael Lemedina Falestinit]*, Herzliya, Israel: Interdisciplinary Center.

Nitzan, Jonathan, 1992, "From Olson to Veblen: the stagflationary rise of distributional coalitions," paper presented at the annual meeting of the History of Economics Society, Fairfax, May 30–June 2.

Nitzan, Jonathan, 2001, "Regimes of differential accumulation: mergers, stagflation and the logic of globalization," *Review of International Political Economy,* Vol. 8, No. 2, Summer, pp. 226–74.

Nitzan, Jonathan, and Bichler, Shimshon, 2002, *The Global Political Economy of Israel*, London: Pluto Press.

Nitzan, Jonathan, and Bichler, Shimshon, 2006, "Cheap wars," *The Economy of the Occupation,* No. 10, Jerusalem: AIC, July.

Organization for Economic Cooperation and Development (OECD), 2008, *OECD Factbook 2008: Economic, Environmental and Social Statistics,* Paris: OECD, <http://lysander.sourceoecd.org/vl=10021914/cl=23/nw=1/rpsv/fact2008/>.

Oxfam, 2007, "Continued commercial closure of Gaza will cause complete humanitarian dependency, groups warn in advance of Middle East Quartet meeting," *Oxfam International*, July 15.

Palestine Strategy Study Group (PSSG), 2008, *Regaining the Initiative: Palestinian strategic options to end Israeli occupation,* London: PSSG, August.

Palestinian Central Bureau of Statistics (PCBS), 2005a, *Social Survey of Jerusalem 2005,* November, Ramallah: PCBS.

PCBS, 2005b, *Jerusalem Statistical Yearbook* No. 7, June, Ramallah: PCBS.

PCBS, 2009a, <http://www.pcbs.gov.ps/>.

PCBS, 2009b, "Press release on labour force survey results (October–December, 2008) round," <http://www.ldf.ps/documentsShow.aspx?ATT_ID=1409>.

PCBS, Palestinian Monetary Authority (PMA), and Palestinian Economic Policy Research Institute (MAS), 2006, *Quarterly Economic and Social Monitor*, Vol. 5, May, Ramallah: PCBS.

PCBS, PMA, and MAS, 2007, *Quarterly Economic and Social Monitor, Vol. 9*, July, Ramallah: PCBS.

Palestinian Ministry of Planning (PMoP), 2003, <http://www.mop.gov.ps/>.

Pappe, Ilan, 2005, "Fortress Israel," *London Review of Books,* May 19.

Peace Now, 2007, *Settlement Construction Continues – Periodical report, Summer 2007 [Habnyia Bahitnakhluiot Nimshekhet – Dokh Tkuvati, Kaitz 2007]*, Peace Now – Settlement Watch Team, May–October.

Persico, Oren, 2008, "Barak strikes three times," *The Seventh Eye [Ha'ain Hashvi'it],* April 8.

Pfeffer, Anshil, 2008, "Dorner Committee report: 'the damage for every Holocaust survivor reaches NIS2.2 million,'" *Ha'aretz,* June 22.

Pfeffer, Anshil, 2009, "Head of the IDF's Manpower Department, Major General Zvi Zamir: the number of non-enlisted has grown, obligatory service will not be shortened," *Ha'aretz,* March 1.

Philo, Greg, and Berry, Mike, 2004, *Bad News from Israel*, London and Ann Arbor, Mich.: Pluto Press.

Physicians for Human Rights, 2005, *A Wall in its Midst [Beliba Khoma]*, Tel-Aviv: Physicians for Human Rights, December.

Plotsker, Sever, 2008, "There is an *Economist* that has roared! who will not be afraid?" *Ynet,* April 7, <http://www.ynet.co.il>.

Rabinovitch, Danny, and Abu-Baker, Khaula, 2002, *The Upright Generation [Hador Hazakuf],* Jerusalem: Keter.

Ram, Uri, 2004, "The new gaps: global capitalism, post-Fordism and inequality," pp. 16–33 in Ram, Uri, and Filc, Dani (eds), *The Power of Property: Israeli society in the global age [Shilton Hahon: Hakhevra Haysraelit Baidan Haglobali]*, Tel-Aviv: Hakibutz Hameukhad, Van Leer Institute.

Rapoport, Meron, 2007, "Outsourcing the checkpoints," *Ha'aretz,* November 27.

Rein, M., 1971, "Problems in the definition and measurement of poverty," in Townsend, Peter, *The Concept of Poverty*, London: Heinemann.

Resnik, Julia, 1999, "Particularistic vs. universalistic content in the Israeli education system," *Curriculum Inquiry,* Vol. 29, No. 4, Winter, pp. 485–511.

Reuters, 2008, "Hundreds of Palestinian policemen deployed in Hebron," *Walla,* October 25, <http://www.walla.co.il>.

Rimon, Ran, 2008, "The vice chairman: 'the crisis found the Israeli market in the best condition since the state was founded,'" *Globes Magazine,* November 3.

Rinat, Tzafrir, 2008, "'Yesh Din': Israel uses occupied land's natural treasures for its own purposes," *Ha'aretz,* December 15t.

Rollnick, Guy, 2008, "It's no longer a start-up," *TheMarker,* May 9.

Rose, Jacqueline, 2005, *The Question of Zion,* Princeton, N.J.: Princeton University Press.

Routh, D. A., 1937, "Veblen," *International Affairs*, Vol. 16, No. 2 (March–April).

Roy, Sara, 1999, "De-development revisited: Palestinian economy and society since Oslo," *Journal of Palestine Studies,* Vol. 28, No. 3, Spring, pp. 64–82.

Roy, Sara, 2000, "Palestinian de-development," *Journal of Palestine Studies*, Vol. 29, No. 3, Spring, pp. 98–100.
Roy, Sara, 2001, "Palestinian society and economy: the continued denial of possibility," *Journal of Palestine Studies*, Vol. 30, No. 4, Summer, pp. 5–20.
Rubinstein, Ariel, 2005, "The command of the market," *Ha'aretz*, May 15.
Rubinstein, Danny, 2004, "When it comes to electricity, Israelis and Palestinians stay connected," *Ha'aretz,* April 8.
Rubinstein, Danny, 2006, "What about the good of the settlements, for instance?," *Ha'aretz*, June 19.
Sadan, Ezra, 2004, "How is Israel's economy affected by the security situation?," *Jerusalem Issue Brief,* Vol. 4, No. 11, December 19.
Sadeh, Shuki, 2008a, "Shaul Arieli: 'The state built kilometers of fences only to destroy them,'" *TheMarker,* May 22.
Sadeh, Shuki, 2008b, "Broken wings," *TheMarker,* October 5.
Safran, Nadav, 1978, *Israel, the Embattled Ally,* Michigan: Belknap Press.
Saporta, Itzhak, 2001, "How the economists got it wrong 2," *Theory and Criticism [Teoria Ubikoret]*, Vol. 19, Autumn, pp. 223–30.
Sasson, Talya, 2005, *Illegal Outposts [Ma'akhazim Bilti Murshim]*, special report to the Prime Minister's Office, February.
Schiff, Benjamin N., 1989, "Between occupier and occupied: UNRWA in the West Bank and the Gaza Strip," *Journal of Palestine Studies*, Vol. 18, No. 3, Spring, pp. 60–75.
Schiff, Zeev, Yaari, Ehud, and Friedman, Ina (eds), 1990, *Intifada: The Palestinian uprising – Israel's third front,* New York: Simon & Schuster.
Schnell, Izhak, 2008, "The hidden treasure of the Palestinian economy: the economic implications of refugee compensation," *Palestine–Israel Journal,* Vol. 15, Nos. 1–2, pp. 195–202.
Scott, D. R., 1933, "Veblen not an institutional economist," *American Economic Review,* Vol. 23, No. 2, June, pp. 274–7.
Segev, Tom, 2005, *Israel in 1967 [1967 – Veha'aretz Shinta Et Paneha]*, Jerusalem: Keter.
Selby, Jan, 2003, *Water, Power and Politics in the Middle East,* London: I. B. Tauris.
Selby, Jan, 2005, "The political economy of the Israeli-Palestinian peace process: an introduction," paper for Panel on the Political Economy of Conflict Transformation, International Studies Association, Hawaii, March 1–5.
Sen, Amartya, 1981, *Poverty and Famines: An essay on entitlement and deprivation*, Oxford: Clarendon Press.
Sen, Amartya, 1995, "Food, economics, and entitlements," in Dreze, Jean, Sen, Amartya, and Hussain, Athar (eds), *The Political Economy of Hunge*, Oxford: Clarendon Press.
Sewell, David, 2001, *Governance and the Business Environment in West Bank/Gaza*, World Bank, April.
Shafir, Gershon, and Peled, Yoav, 2002, *Being Israeli: The Dynamics of Multiple Citizenship*, Cambridge: Cambridge University Press.
Shaikh, Anwar, 1990, "Capital as social relation," pp. 72–8 in Eatwell, John,

Migate, Murray, and Newman, Peter (eds), *Marxian Economics*, New York and London: Palgrave.

Shalev, Michael, 2004, "Did globalization and liberalization 'normalize' Israel's economic policies?" pp. 84–115 in Ram, Uri, and Filc, Dani, *The Power of Property: Israeli society in the global age [Shilton Hahon: Hakhevra Haysraelit Baidan Haglobali]*, Tel-Aviv: Hakibutz Hameukhad, Van Leer Institute.

Shalev, Michael, Peled, Yoav, and Yiftachel, Oren, 2000, *The Political Impact of Inequality: Social cleavages and voting in the 1999 elections*, Sapir College, January.

Sharabi, Linda, 2002, "Israel's economic growth: success without security," *Merida,* Vol. 6, No. 3, September.

Shearer, David, 2004, "The humanitarian crisis in the Occupied Palestinian Territory: an overview," *NPN Humanitarian Practice Network,* Issue 28, November.

Shenfeld, Yoni, 2007, "25% of 18 year-olds don't conscript to the IDF," *MSN,* July 17, <http://news.il.msn.com/>.

Shenhav, Yehouda, 2004, "How did the Mizrahim 'become' religious and Zionist? Zionism, colonialism and the religionization of the Arab Jew," *News from Within*, Vol. 20, No. 1, January/February, pp. 18–24.

Shlaim, Avi, 1994, "Prelude to the Accord: Likud, Labor, and the Palestinians," *Journal of Palestine Studies*, Vol. 23, No. 2, Winter, pp. 5–19.

Shlaim, Avi, 2000, *The Iron Wall [Kir Habarzel],* Tel-Aviv: Books in the Attic.

Shnell, Izhak, 2008, "The hidden treasure of the Palestinian Economy: the economic implications of refugee compensation," *Palestine–Israel Journal*, Vol. 15, No. 1 & 2, pp. 195–202.

Sikkui, 2007, *Sikkui Report 2006: The equality index between Jewish and Arab citizens of Israel,* ed. Ali Khaider, Jerusalem and Haifa: Sikkui, March.

Sofer, Roni, 2008, "Olmert: the Wall of Separation has become an example," *Ynet,* December 23, <http://www.ynet.co.il>.

Spiegel, Udi, 2001, *Youth Motivation for Service in the IDF [Motivatsia Shel Bnei Noar Leshirut Betsahal],* Israeli Knesset: Research and Information Center, June.

Spivak, Avia, 2008a, "1985," *Eretz Aheret,* Vol. 43, January–February, pp. 10–15.

Spivak, Avia, 2008b, "The shaky foundations of the Israeli economy," *Ynet,* April 15, <http://www.ynet.co.il>.

Stahl, Julie, 2008, "Investigation of Olmert casts shadow over peace making," *CNSNews.com,* May 5.

Strasser, Johano, 2003, *Wenn der Arbeitsgessellschaft die Arbeit ausgeht* [When labour runs out in the labour society,] Tel-Aviv: Hakibutz Hameukhad.

Strassler, Nehemia, 2004, "The domino theory," *Ha'aretz*, November 18.

Strassler, Nehemia, 2005, "Sharon's speech eeds reading too," *Ha'aretz*, August 18.

Strassler, Nehemia, 2008, "Where have capitalist pigs led?" *Ha'aretz*, June 4.
Svetlova, Ksenia, 2006, "A basic right," *Jerusalem Post*, September 14.
Swirski, Shlomo, 2005, *The Price of Occupation [Mekhir Hayohara]*, Tel-Aviv: Adva Center, MAPA.
Swirski, Shlomo, 2008a, *The Cost of Occupation: The burden of the Israeli–Palestinian conflict, 2008 Report,* Tel-Aviv: Adva Center, June.
Swirski, Shlomo, 2008b, *Is There an Israeli Business Peace Disincentive?* Tel-Aviv: Adva Center, August.
Swirski, Shlomo, and Konor-Attias, Etty, 2005, *Israel: A Social Report 2004,* Tel-Aviv: Adva Center.
Swirski, Shlomo, Konor-Attias, Etty, and Abu-Khala, Halla, 2008, *Israel: A Social Report 1998–2007,* Tel-Aviv: Adva Center, December.
Swirski, Shlomo, Konor-Attias, Etty, and Etkin, Alon, 2002, *Government Funding of the Israeli Settlement in Judea and Sumeria and in the Golan Heights in the 90s: Municipalities, housing construction and paving roads*, Tel-Aviv: Adva Center.
Taig, Amir, 2008, "*The Economist:* the Israeli economy staggers," *Kalkalist,* April 6.
Tel-Aviv Stock Exchange, 2008, <http://www.tase.co.il/TASEEng/Homepage.htm> (accessed June 2008).
Tobias, Yael, 2008, "Merrill Lynch: Israel is losing its place as a safe haven," *NRG*, April 8, <http://www.nrg.co.il/>.
TheMarker, 2008, "*Economist*: Israel has a strong economy with weak foundations," *TheMarker,* April 4.
Transparency International, 2006, "Corruption Perception Index, 2005," <http://www.transparency.org/policy_research/surveys_indices/cpi/2005>.
Tsaban, Dror, 2003, *Partial Estimate of Government Budgets Directed to the Settlements in the West Bank and the Gaza Strip and of the Over-Funding in 2001* [*Taktsivei Hamemshala Hamufnim Lahitnakhluyot Bagada Hama'aravit Ubirtsuat Aza Veomdan Hahashka'a Haodefet Bashanim 2001–2002*], Tel-Aviv: Peace Now, November.
United Nations, 1948, *United Nations Universal Declaration of Human Rights*, <http://www.un.org/Overview/rights.html>.
United Nations, 1967, "Security Council Resolution No. 242," Official Document System of the United Nations, <http://daccessdds.un.org/doc/RESOLUTION/GEN/NR0/240/94/IMG/NR024094.pdf?OpenElement>.
United Nations, 2003, *Executive Report of the Food Security Assessment,* West Bank and Gaza Strip Food and Agriculture Organization of the United Nations, in collaboration with World Food Programme, Rome.
United Nations, 2004, *The Impact of the Barrier on West Bank Communities*, March 7 to April 23.
United Nations, 2007, *Consolidated Appeals Process (CAP) Summary: Occupied Palestinian Territories, Summer 2007,* Summer.
UN General Assembly, 2006, "General Assembly establishes register of damage arising from construction of wall by Israel in Occupied Palestinian Territory," *General Assembly Plenary,* Tenth Emergency Special Session, 30th and 31st meetings, December 16.

UN Office of Coordination of Humanitarian Affairs (OCHA), 2005, <http://www.reliefweb.int/fts>.

UN OCHA, 2006, *Preliminary Analysis of the Humanitarian Implications of the Fence in the West Bank Based on the Planned Route in April 2006,* Update no. 5, Jerusalem: United Nations.

UN OCHA, 2007, *The Humanitarian Impact of the West Bank Barrier on Palestinian Communities: East Jerusalem*, Update no. 7, June.

UN OCHA, 2008a, "The Humanitarian Monitor: Occupied Palestinian Territory, no. 23," March.

UN OCHA, 2008b, "Gaza Strip inter-agency humanitarian fact sheet, March 2008," April.

UN OCHA, 2008c, "The Humanitarian Monitor: Occupied Palestinian Territory, no. 24," April.

UN OCHA, 2008d, *OCHA-oPt Socio-Economic Fact Sheet*, April.

UN OCHA, 2009, "Field update on Gaza from the Humanitarian Coordinator: 30 January–2 February 2009, 1700 hours," Jerusalem: United Nations, February.

UN Office of the United Nations Special Co-ordinator (UNSCO), 2002, *The Impact of Closure and Other Mobility Restrictions on Palestinian Productive Activities,* October.

US Department of Energy, 2008, "State and US historical data," Energy Information Administration, <http://www.eia.doe.gov/overview_hd.html>.

US Information Agency (USIA), 1996, "U.S. foreign assistance," *Economic Perspectives: USIA Electronic Journals,* Vol. 1, No. 11, August.

USA Today, 2007, "Palestinians report progress from secret talks between Hamas, Fatah," *USA Today,* January 13.

Veblen, Thorstein, 1897, "Review of Max Lorenz, *Die Marxistische Socialdemokratie*," *Journal of Political Economy*, Vol. 6, No. 1, December, pp. 136–7.

Veblen, Thorstein, 1994 [1899], *The Theory of the Leisure Class: An economic study of institutions,* New York: Dover.

Veblen, Thorstein, 1915, 'The opportunity of Japan,' *Journal of Race Development*, Vol. 6, July, pp. 3–38.

Veblen, Thorstein, 1917, *An Inquiry into the Nature of Peace and the Terms of its Perpetuation*, New York: Macmillan.

Veblen, Thorstein, 1921, *The Engineers and the Price System*, New York: B. W. Huebsch.

Vhabi, Mehrdad, 2004, "The political economy of destructive power," *Post-Autistic Economics Review*, Vol. 29, No. 6, December, <http://www.paecon.net>.

Vilan, Avshalom, 2006, "Populism instead of foreign policy," *Ha'aretz,* December 3.

Warschawski, Michael, 2008a, "Why should we support the Palestinian Authority?" *The Alternative Information Center,* January 20, <http://www.alternativenews.org>.

Warschawski, Michael, 2008b, "Sixteen anti-democratic laws submitted to the Israeli Knesset," *The Alternative Information Center,* September 4, <http://www.alternativenews.org>.

Weill, Sharon, and Azarov, Valentina, 2009, "Israel's authoritarian transformation," *The Electronic Intifada,* February 25.

Wold, Oz, 2008, "The professors strike ended," *MSN News,* January 18, <http://news.il.msn.com/>.

World Bank, 2003, *Twenty-Seven Months – Intifada, Closures and Palestinian Economic Crisis, An Assessment*, Jerusalem: World Bank, May.

World Bank, 2004a, *Disengagement, the Palestinian Economy and the Settlements*, June.

World Bank, 2004b, *West Bank and Gaza Update,* March.

World Bank, 2008, *World Economic and Financial Surveys*, April, <http://www.imf.org/external/pubs/ft/weo/2008/01/weodata/index.aspx>.

Wright, J.W., 2000, "Introduction: economic and political impediments to Middle East peace," pp. 1–9 in Wright, J.W., and Drake, Laura (eds), 2000, *Economic and Political Impediments to Middle East Peace,* London: Palgrave Macmillan.

Yahav, Dan, 2004, *The Origins of the Zionist-Palestinian Conflict [Mekorot Lasikhsukh Hatsioni-Falestini]*, Tel-Aviv: Sifrei Iton77.

Yftacheel, Oren, 2000, "'Ethnocracy' and its discontents: minorities, protests and the Israeli polity," *Critical Inquiry,* Vol. 26, No. 4, Summer, pp. 725–56.

Yftachel, Oren, 2002, "Territory as the kernel of the nation: space, time and nationalism in Israel/Palestine," *Geopolitics,* Vol. 7, No. 2, pp. 215–48.

Ynet, 2004, "The cost of the Separation Fence is double than a fence on the 1967 lines," *Ynet,* February 3, <http://www.ynet.co.il>.

Ynet, 2005, "Israel reached the 8th place in the global per-capita export rate," *Ynet,* November 8, <http://www.ynet.co.il>.

Ynet, 2006, "The lowest voter turnout in the history of the state: 63.2%," *Ynet,* March 28, <http://www.ynet.co.il>.

Ynet, 2008, "Poll: Netanyahu will advance peace and security more than Livni," *Ynet,* December 7, <http://www.ynet.co.il>.

Yoaz, Yuval, 2005a, "Cleaning house in the West Bank Municipalities Council," *Ha'aretz,* April 19.

Yoaz, Yuval, 2005b, "Palestinians that were hurt by the wall will be compensated with state lands," *Walla,* May 6, <http://www.walla.co.il>.

Yom, Sean L., 2008, "Washington's new arms bazaar," *Middle East Report,* No. 246, Vol. 38, Spring, pp. 22–31.

Young, Robert M., 1990, "Herbert Spencer and inevitable progress," in Marsden, G. (ed.), *Victorian Values*, London and New York: Longman.

Zelinger, Assaf, 2007, "Back to school: the teacher's strike has ended," *NRG,* December 14, <http://www.nrg.co.il/>.

Zertal, Idith, and Eldar, Akiva, 2007, *Lords of the Land: The war over Israel's settlements in the Occupied Territories 1967–2007,* New York: Nation Books.

Zino, Aviram, 2006, "The High Court rejected an appeal to change the barrier's route in the Abu-Dis area," *Ynet,* August 6, <http://www.ynet.co.il>.

Zino, Aviram, 2007, "Chief comptroller: stop perceiving exposers of corruption as 'squealers,'" *Ynet,* December 18, <http://www.ynet.co.il>.

Zuriel-Harari, Keren, 2005, "Mofaz: my help? uniting all of Israel's military industries into one big company," *Globes*, May 18–19.

FILMOGRAPHY

Azoulay, Ariella (director), 2004, *The Food Chain [Sharsheret Hamazon]*, Israel.

Sadaa Media, 2006, "Yatta," *Hole in the Wall*, Alternative Information Center, Israel.

INDEX

Milton Keynes UK
Ingram Content Group UK Ltd.
UKHW032102081124
450761UK00003B/54